Sport,

Sport, Rules and Values presents a philosophical perspective on some issues concerning the character of sport. Central questions for the text are motivated from 'real life' sporting examples, as described in newspaper reports. For instance, the (supposed) subjectivity of umpiring decisions is explored via an examination of the judging of ice-skating at the Salt Lake City Olympic Games of 2002. Throughout, the presentation is rich in concrete cases from sporting situations, including cricket, baseball, American football, and soccer.

While granting the constitutive nature of the rules of sport, discussion focuses on three broad uses commonly urged for rules: in defining sport; in judging or assessing sport (as deployed by judges or umpires); and in characterizing the value of sport – especially if that value is regarded as moral value. In general, *Sport, Rules and Values* rejects a conception of the determinacy of rules as possible within sport (and a parallel picture of the determinacy assumed to be required by philosophy).

Detailed consideration of some ideas from classics in the philosophy of sport, especially writings by Bernard Suits and William Morgan contextualize this discussion. Overall, this work exemplifies the dependence of philosophical considerations of sport on ideas from philosophy more generally. Thus it sketches, for example, the contrast between rules and principles, an account of the occasion-sensitivity of understanding, and the place of normative and motivating reasons within practical reasoning.

The book's argumentative structures originate in the writings of Ludwig Wittgenstein without explicitly being an exposition of those ideas. It views philosophy as addressing the specific issues of particular persons, rather than approaching perennial problems. In this way, the view of sport, and of sporting practices, that it supports has the flexibility to approach new issues. The result is a distinctive and appealing conception both of sport and of its philosophical investigation.

Graham McFee is Professor of Philosophy at the University of Brighton; and Vice President of the British Society of Aesthetics. He has written and presented extensively, both nationally and internationally, on the philosophy of Wittgenstein and on aesthetics, especially the aesthetics of dance.

Sport, Rules and Values

Philosophical investigations into
the nature of sport

Graham McFee

 Routledge
Taylor & Francis Group

LONDON AND NEW YORK

First published 2004
by Routledge
11 New Fetter Lane, London EC4P 4EE

Simultaneously published in the USA and Canada
by Routledge
29 West 35th Street, New York, NY 10001

Routledge is an imprint of the Taylor & Francis Group

Typeset in 10/12pt Times NR by Graphicraft Limited, Hong Kong
Printed and bound by The Cromwell Press, Trowbridge, Wiltshire

British Library Cataloguing in Publication Data
A catalogue record for this book is available from
the British Library

Library of Congress Cataloging in Publication Data
A catalog record for this book has been requested

ISBN 0-415-32208-1 (hbk)
ISBN 0-415-32964-7 (pbk)

Contents

Acknowledgements

Ancestors of parts of this work have been previously published (although all sections are extensively revised here). So my thanks for permission to recycle material to: Greenwood/Praeger for McFee (forthcoming) in Introduction; Leisure Studies Association for McFee (2000c) in Chapter 8; Meyer & Meyer for McFee (2000d) in Chapter 9, and sections of which I was the primary author from Keech and McFee (2000) in Chapter 10; Routledge for McFee (2000b) in Chapter 7, McFee (1998b) in Chapter 10.

This work has debts to many people: I hereby thank them all. Some of my key ideas have been presented to national and international conferences, or to other interested parties. But, in roughly its present form, this text grows primarily from teaching the Philosophy of Sport to students in the Chelsea School at the University of Brighton, to whom my thanks are due.

I single out for special thanks: Myrene, my wife, for all her help, both material and intellectual, as well as her aid in preparing the text; Katherine Morris for support, for discussion of some key themes here, and for giving me sight (again) of some unpublished work of Gordon Baker's; Mike McNamee as series editor, and especially for encouraging me to cast the text in terms of what I had to say about the study of sport; Paul McNaught-Davis for financial support (as Head of the Chelsea School) and moral support; Alan Tomlinson for discussion of many topics, and especially for encouragement with study of Olympism (and joint work on it).

Finally, my gratitude is due to the late Gordon Baker who contributed immeasurably to my understanding of philosophy in general and Wittgenstein in particular, through conversation and through commentary on things I had written. When I envisaged completing this book, I saw myself acknowledging specifically Gordon's contribution to (not to say, complete reshaping of) my view of rule-following. His death in 2002 raised a question about whether this was an appropriate way to recognize his massive contribution to my thinking on this issue alone – putting aside others – a huge debt going far beyond those places where I draw explicitly on some of his writings.

Although we discussed some of these issues (to my benefit), Gordon did not see this text – it would have been better if he had! I would not seek to saddle him, much less his memory, with any of my 'readings'. But, equally,

I do not want to imply that I would be presenting even any version of this view of the philosophical project without his friendship for roughly the past twenty-five years. I would certainly have dedicated the book to Gordon, had I thought it worthy. Were it not hubristic (and gross inflation of my powers), I would imagine his response to my efforts as John Wisdom expected Wittgenstein to view his: that giving a whole book to a small issue in philosophy was still '... not sufficiently hard working – a bit cheap and flash' (Wisdom 1952: 1 note). But, of course, I would have willingly accepted the censure, since it would have been discussed point by point, with unfailing good humour.

Introduction

Sport, rules and values

A common-sense idea – also propounded by some sociologists of sport – connects the idea of sport to systems of rules; and (ideally) to formalized and codified rules. For example, Eric Dunning and Ken Sheard (1979) argued that one feature of modern sports, marking them out from folk games, was the use (or presence) of a codified system of rules. Whatever one makes of the detail here, the initial intuition – connecting sport and rules – seems sound: on the face of it, we cannot have sports untrammelled by rules nor can there be sporting actions (such as the scoring of tries or touchdowns) without such rules. And this intuition has been explored and exploited by many writers on sport.[1]

The central ideas in this text, though, are first that misconceptions concerning the nature and operations of rules distort accounts of sports while, second, a clearer conception of rules can clarify some of the issues concerning both the nature and value of sport – and even solve (or resolve) some of them. Moreover, the misconception and the clarification both turn on views of determinacy, and especially on the nature of the requirement (if any) for determinacy within philosophy.

As those who know my other writings might expect, I find the appropriate discussion of rules and rule-following in the writings of Ludwig Wittgenstein. But this text is not an exposition of Wittgenstein, nor does it argue explicitly that this conception of rules *should* be ascribed to him, although I have included quotations from Wittgenstein to emphasize key points, sometimes giving references to places in his work where exemplification (and additional argument) might be sought. Rather, Wittgenstein's insights into the nature of rules and of rule-following are deployed to help understand the nature of sport, with explanation of those insights (to the degree needed) as we go along.

Organization of the text

This text is in three main parts. The first considers the role of rules in *defining* sport; the second looks to rules used in *judging* sport – hence, to the role of judges or umpires; the third considers how the *value* of sport might be explained in terms of rules, especially moral rules.

The first part primarily concerns ideals of definiteness: it is often assumed that rules *do*, or *should*, completely circumscribe a particular sport, such that we can exhaustively characterize or define that sport in terms of those rules. This assumption imports three kinds of mistakes: a mistake about the possibility of definition; a mistake about the need for definition; and a mistake about the connection of rules to definiteness.

These mistakes follow from a conception of rules whereby, if faced with some case the rules do not presently fit, one can always modify the rules – with the implication that, in principle, a *perfect* set of rules (one that deals with *all* possible situations) might be achieved. We see this conception, for instance, in attempts to modify definitions in the light of counter-examples, or in the attempt to rule out inappropriate behaviour on the sports field (or avoid refereeing judgement or discretion) by modifying the rules of sports – say, by changing the offside rule in soccer or the leg before wicket (lbw) rule in cricket. [For those unfamiliar with cricket, the batsman is out if the bowled ball hits the wicket; and the batsman will also be out if (roughly) his/her legs prevent the bowled ball from striking the wicket: leg before wicket or lbw. This is to prevent him/her avoiding the bowled ball striking the wicket by standing in front of it. (The rule itself is complex.)]

Of course, I may be puzzled about what a particular rule prohibits. (Can I wear nose-expanding strips when playing rugby? Well, if they are not specifically mentioned as permissible, and if the guiding idea is the enumeration of what *is* permissible, then. . . .) So this idea reflects the importance – and the difficulty – of determining what *exactly* follows from the application of a particular rule in a particular context. It highlights a central difficulty, confronted throughout this work, from occasion-sensitivity (see Chapter 2 pp. 49–51): that the application of a rule is less straightforward than is often assumed, as new circumstances of *this* context may leave that application unclear or problematic.

The examples reflect the fact that this text was written by a UK citizen. Yet the distinction among sports is tendentious; and the examples are not only from typical 'British' sports like soccer (football) and cricket but include both general sports such as tennis and figure-skating and US sports such as baseball and (American) football. Further, the examples are just that – if they help the reader to see the point, they have been successful: but readers should supply their own examples if those make the points more crisply for them than do mine.

Another word may be needed, not about the examples as such, but about their relative absence in some places. Perhaps the remarks could be more *generally* tied into particular sporting cases. But, as hinted at earlier, the general philosophical point can become lost or obscured, with the attention focused entirely, or largely, on the example – as Wittgenstein's discussion of the term 'game' (PI §§66–7[2]) is (sometimes) thought to be about *games*! Moreover, one can forget how *general* (and even *abstract*) much of the required discussion necessarily is: that this follows from its being discussion in philosophy. Many chapters contain an excursus into pure philosophy – on definiteness (Chapter 1 pp. 28–31); on occasion-sensitivity and understanding (Chapter 2 pp. 47–52); on *principles*, in Dworkin's sense (Chapter 6 p. 105); on value-particularism (Chapter 8 pp. 141–4); on the nature of reasons (Chapter 9 pp. 151–5); and on truth (Chapter 10 pp. 142–3). Even when philosophy is treated in a particularist and concrete fashion (see below; especially Chapter 8 p. 00), it will never be *wholly* particular or *wholly* concrete – and nor should it be: that would undermine its character as philosophy. For example, Arthur Danto (1993: 206) urges that his remarks on the nature of *art*, if philosophy, *must* apply to *all* art, rather than just to *some* artworks: 'Philosophy's task is to say what is essentially true of artworks as a class. . . .' So the idea is that – being philosophy – the position must apply to *all* genuine examples;[3] that the choice is between those where it is transparent or revealing and the rest.

But, to repeat, readers are encouraged at every stage to supplement my examples with their own (or to add their own where appropriate); or, where my *examples* fail to carry conviction, to replace them with their own.

The emphasis in Part I on the definition of *sport* might strike some readers as old-fashioned, especially since my chief example (Bernard Suits's linked definitions of *games* and *sport*) has been widely discussed. But the problems raised here for this example are problems for all possible attempts at definition; this example has the linked benefits (in a diffuse context) of familiarity, brevity, clarity, and a critical literature. Of course, were my point simply to ask whether or not *Suits* had defined the term 'sport', the accusation of old-fashionedness might be warranted. But my claim, argued in the text, is that the *project* of such a definition is flawed. Once this point is granted, all putative definitions have the same misguided status; one looks for collateral reasons to discuss this one rather than that.

Part II considers the role of judges or umpires. The ideal here might *seem* to be rules whose application was so transparent that umpires need do nothing more than *apply* the rule to this situation – conceived primarily as a species of 'reading the rule aloud'. But this conception is flawed in at least three ways. First, and following from our view of rules, rules cannot *in principle* deal with all situations (and cannot be modified so to do). Second, for some sports (roughly those David Best [1978: 104] calls 'aesthetic sports'), human judgement is necessarily integral to the scoring: what is important is the *manner* in which, say, the pairs skating or the gymnastic vault is achieved. Third, even for other kinds of sport, the application of the rules could never be as unproblematic as has been assumed – partly because what is being considered is *human action* (see pp. 5–6). So the question of what *action* was performed by such-and-such a sportsperson can rebound on a judge or referee – for example, as the question for American football: did he have *control* of the ball when he landed? That is, as a question where the rules have a bearing on the matter, or where the referee must decide if such-and-such did or did not occur.

For Part III, the connection to rules is, at first glance, less direct. The issue concerns what intrinsic value might be ascribed to sport: or, more perspicuously, whether or not that value can be thought a moral value (as, say, De Coubertin thought). The negative reply often given[4] is motivated, in part, by a view of morality as a system of rules, and partly by the way the application of rules is understood. For clearly some sport, sometimes, does not promote morality. Were this not so, we would know automatically that the accusations of domestic violence against former basketball star Dennis Rodman (McKibben 2003: B3) were unjustified – how could someone with such exposure to sport behave badly? For the same reason, we would know beforehand that basketball star Shaquille O'Neal (*Los Angeles Times*, Sports 2003d: D1) was not a racist, despite some badly chosen jokes – we would not need to judge his explanation. In fact, sports players and teams can behave badly: moreover, discipline on the field of play does not preclude indiscipline off it. But none of that disputes that sometimes consideration of what is appropriate in sport turns on notions of justice, exemplified through ideas such as *fair play* or a *level playing field*.

On the contrary, once we understand morality aright – which means in a *particularist* way, in contrast to the mainstream sports ethics literature – we are well-positioned to see that at least *some* sport *sometimes* has just that possibility. Perhaps this will not explain *the* value of *all* sport: but the idea will have earned its keep if it explains some value of some sport. A guiding thought here recapitulates, in a different context, an earlier point: that motivating forces for rule-changes in sport are regularly *moral*; in particular, the appeal to *fairness*. But, more concessively, the obligations to rule-following in sport already provide a (weaker) *moral imperative*.

Some central ideas for this text

Three further considerations help explain the distinctiveness of this text, considerations each shared with only *some* other texts in this area. First, when thinking or writing about sport, we must remember that sport is played in many contexts – in the park with one's friends as well as on the professional stage, and so on. Hence, while many of the real examples come from high-level or elite sport, the intention is that *most* remarks apply to sport at all levels. Sometimes a conception of the kind of definiteness it is assumed *philosophy* requires makes us doubt that, say, the game of soccer (football) in the park is *really* soccer. After all, it has – let us suppose – a heavily modified 'handball' rule (compared to professional soccer) to stop the ball disappearing into the distance; the goalposts are piles of coats; there are not exactly eleven players on each side; and so on. On the other hand, it is not obviously some *other* game; it is still recognizably football.

As often, considering a yet simpler case helps: I give my grandson a Queen's 'start' in a chess match – are we playing chess? Clearly, no simple answer is satisfactory. If my grandson wins, he will certainly claim a victory at chess: and, equally, we are not playing draughts, or solitaire, or bridge. . . . Still, if I play against the best player in the world, Garry Kasparov, in a simultaneous display where he gives me a Queen advantage, and (*per impossibile*) I win, I will not be claiming to have beaten the world's best at chess – or, at least, I will do so only in a highly qualified way.

My point, of course, is to move away from *some* idealizations of what sport *essentially* is: no set of activities is *really* chess or *really* soccer. On many occasions, an idealization of elite sport provides an image of sport 'played to the full' to which other occasions offer a tacit nod – as when children play-act the conflict between elite teams, taking the names of major players: as parodied in a school football lesson in the film *Kes* (1969: director Ken Loach), where the teacher designates his side as Manchester United, and himself their most famous player of the time. The importance of such cases can be overstressed. Yet sometimes, in order to consider sport at its zenith of performance, with all its (codified) rules in play, examples are best taken from elite or professional sport. Since a methodological commitment here is that *my* accounts of sporting events have no special weight or authority, I typically draw on others' descriptions of sporting events, where possible, so that nothing of substance relies on *my* view of events.

The second, complex consideration recognizes sport as the province of *persons*: that people (and only people) watch sport, participate in sport, referee sport, and enjoy sport. That may seem a trivial concession until it is recognized that the study of *persons* is not straightforwardly equivalent to the study of persons' bodies: that is, to the study area of the sports sciences. For the doings of persons are not simply equivalent to what happens to those bodies. To illustrate, imagine an English-speaking Martian arrives at a church on a Saturday afternoon (McFee 1992: 53; McFee 2000a: 85): he or she will understand what is said, of course, but not what is happening – he or she will not understand that these people talking together constitutes two of them *getting married*, which (in turn) has implications for, say, inheritance. And his or her perplexity will increase when, traveling backwards in time to the previous Thursday, he/she finds the same key players saying the same words, but with nothing following – for this is the rehearsal! So, to understand what happens here requires understanding it as a collection of human actions. Further, such actions require agents capable of intending, choosing or deciding: that is, these are agents, not robots (McFee 1992: 55–6).

Moreover, persons essentially act in contexts (McFee 2000a: 88–9): what distinguishes the person *able* to name a ship from the person *not able* will not, typically, be some capacity of either person's anatomy or physiology. I can *say* 'I name this ship *Morning Cloud*' as well as the present Queen; I am capable of breaking a champagne bottle across its bow. But her doing these things might name the ship while (at least typically) my doing them would not.

In these ways, we learn *not* to treat explanation of action in sport as essentially a matter of the causal, psychological story. For persons must be seen and treated as unities, rather than as minds (or souls!) attached in some mysterious way to bodies. In this guise, it is a familiar rejection of, say, dualistic assumptions about minds and meanings. For, as David Best (1999: 103–8) has repeatedly illustrated, there is still a lot of such dualism about! Moreover, the dualism of mind and body should not be replaced with some *other* account: instead, explanation of action is needed only when it *is* needed, for some particular purpose – persons should be regarded as autonomous agents living in social situations (which grants, of course, both that such situations *constrain* what actions can be performed and that characterizing actions makes ineliminable reference to the normativity of a network of social practices). In particular, persons should be taken as centrally able to follow rules, so that the question, '*How* do we follow this rule?', taken generally, is silly. For granting the kind of agents characterized above is recognizing (potential) rule-followers – or rule breakers! Then *obeying* the rule is just a matter of determining what it precludes or permits: simply *following* it is then not especially problematic – if one wants to, if the situations arise, and so on, and so on. (Wittgenstein captured this idea eloquently with a quotation from Goethe: 'In the beginning was the deed' [CV p. 31; OC §402; PO p. 395].)

This discussion becomes integrated with others since a typical way of putting this point speaks of human action as *rule-governed* or *rule-related* behaviour: the rules create contexts in which such actions are possible. Hence the actions cannot logically be separated from the rules thereby embodied. In this vein, we recognize the formal rules that turn the exchange and distribution of pieces of paper into cashing a cheque (McFee 1992: 53) – or the redistribution of pieces of wood on a chequered surface into playing chess – as well as the informal 'rules' that turn a wooden post by the side of a road into a signpost (PI §85, §87).

The crucial point here is sometimes made by saying that these activities are *institutional*.[5] Although not wrong, this formulation can mislead, because central cases, such as *promising*, are institutional in one sense but not in another. Certainly, the institution of promising holds in place my obligation to you, once I have promised you that I will do such-and-such; and therefore my having promised is an *institutional fact* (Searle 1969: 50–3; Anscombe 1981: 22–5). But no particular set of persons constitutes this institution – there is no authoritative body here (Baker and Hacker 1984: 272–3), which makes up the 'promising police'. And many important human activities – sometimes rightly called *institutions* – are of this sort: (human) language is perhaps the most important. The forces behind these institutions 'come to us from a distance' (Cavell 1981: 64): we do not sign-up to them, nor can we specify how they were started, or by whom. In contrast, some human institutions are regulated by a fairly specific authoritative body: for example, that such-and-such is money or currency is a human institution, but one with specific authoritative structures – a person cannot just *choose* such-and-such and proclaim it money. Further, whether or not something is a machine is not in the gift of just any Tom, Dick or Harriett, but one where those knowledgeable can have a 'say' in ways most of us cannot. Thus there are two kinds of institutional structures. So, for example, promising is not institutional in one sense (there is no authoritative body), but is institutional in the other sense. When, as for many sports, we have a body which regulates the competitions and the rules – as FIDE does for chess – it is tempting to study the institutional structure; but our concern with the nature of the sport renders many features of the institutional structures beside our (philosophical) point. Indeed, for most purposes, sport is better regarded – like promising – as institutional in the first of my two senses only: it features the product of human contrivance, without ascribing that contrivance to any particular group of humans. (This will be one way to avoid dealing with the sociology of sports consumption.)

The third consideration noted above has already been sketched: that nothing here depends on my view of sport. Indeed, given that this is a work of philosophy, it would be inappropriate if it did. (Discussion here takes us towards the fundamental insight of this work.) As discussed earlier (pp. 4–5), this idea provided a constraint on the examples used. That is, of course, correct. But it also points *across* to the outcome of this work: that, in most places, the arguments of this text will not change what we *say* about a particular sporting event. For, if what we say *might* be changed, we might need to look for the *best* (or even the *correct*) account of a particular event for our examples. Of course, there may be exceptions here: how we think of certain events *may* be inflected by how fair we take their judging to be – and justifiable *when* we take an official to be suspect. But, as we will see (Chapter 5 pp. 98–9), the mere fact that an official was pressured to act in a certain way does not mean he or she would not have acted in just that way without the pressure: the *outcome* might still be the right (or fair) one.

Of course, a big danger here concerns the *myths* sport attracts – it may be difficult to cut through the myth to what actually occurred. For instance, it has often been asserted (especially in the USA) that the outcome of the basketball final at the 1972 Olympics was unjust; that the US team was 'robbed'. But if an account recently given in the *Los Angeles Times* (Wharton 2002: D3) is correct, the two major incidents – that is, the fight between two players that got them both ejected from the game, but with the US player (arguably) the more valuable, and the two (or three) attempts at the end to correct problems in the timekeeping – were simply not as claimed. In the first, the player from the USSR was a 'starter' (that is, one of the major team members) and the one first fouled by his American opponent; the second resulted from confused signalling from the scorer's table, but was an outcome typical of games at the time. So the outcome of the final *was* fair: or, at least, was marred only by error. As one commentator reports it, 'It was obviously a poorly supervised game . . . but I don't think it happened the way many people remember it' (Wharton 2002: D3). Yet the event has acquired a mythic status, no doubt fuelled by Cold War jingoism: the story (that is, what happened) has become myth-eaten. As a result, any account of it – especially in the USA – is likely to be distorted, if not plainly mistaken. Even the *Los Angeles Times* forgot its own account when a later article concluded: 'Still waiting for their ... Gold medals: the 1972 US men's Olympic basketball team' (*Los Angeles Times, Sports* 2002b: D12). So determining in practice what occurred can be hard. For that reason, I simply accept the events as described – if it seems clearer, readers should treat them hypothetically: suppose such-and-such occurred, then. ... In this way, the *accuracy* of the examples should not become an issue here.

Hope for a philosophy of sport?

The above is partly an attempt to diffuse the criticism that nothing here *need* change how one views sports events. Actually, though, I doubt that my view will leave one's conception of sports events unchanged: seeing the rules of sport *my* way at least transforms how you *explain* appeals to rules, perhaps which rules you appeal to.

What is being advocated here might seem to amount to a contribution to the *philosophy of sport*. Certainly, philosophy provides the disciplinary tools and sport provides the subject matter. Is this going back on my commitment (McFee 1998a: 16–17) that – once moral questions are set aside[6] – discussion of sport can add nothing (except examples) to a quite general discussion from philosophy? Not really, for three reasons. First, the pedigree in (general) philosophy is quite apparent in the discussion of most topics: as noted above, many chapters contain explicit discussions of these general issues. So this connection to the *body* of mainstream philosophy is essential.

Second, the *appearance* of a change of heart reflects a change in the scale of my interest in the moral dimensions of sport. Arguments in Parts II and III suggest that perhaps the influence of the moral is more pervasive than previously thought. I always recognized (McFee 1998a: 5) that sport was not *just* one such human practice among many, since ethical questions arise naturally from the inherent characteristics of typical sports: for example, sports are typically culturally-valued[7] and viewed as united (as one thing, Sport); they typically have explicit rules (whose contravention is therefore possible); the possibility of harm to participants (especially if rules are not followed) does not prevent participation; and the rhetoric of sport is replete with metaphors employed in general ethical discussion – in particular, the idea of *fair play* or of a *level playing field*. In this way, ethical issues are ineliminably linked with the existence and practice of sport: a concern with such issues would be both a centrally philosophical concern *and* a concern with sport. I have added a stronger sense both of how fundamental for sport ethical principles are; and how the acquisition and mastery of such principles might explain (some of?) the value of sport. So sport has more to tell us about the moral – and vice versa – than I had thought.

But, third, even granting the rule-governed (or rule-related) character of sport, my thesis is *still* that the points are found in *other* activities where rules are important. So the issues here are mostly genuine but their employment in philosophical enquiries consists in applying conclusions from elsewhere *to* sport, or taking sporting cases as examples. Even questions about the concept *sport* – insofar as they are general, abstract questions – already have a home within philosophy.

A traditional account of philosophy as *reasoning about reasoning* fits with some of these considerations: that philosophical attention is turned onto the sayings (and doings) of those who discuss sport. But this can make philosophy seem second order, its rationale resting in tidying-up the first order practice. Yet philosophy is not, in this sense, second order. (As Wittgenstein might have pointed out [see PI §121], the situation is a bit like etymology, which itself studies the origins of the term 'etymology'.) To put the point concessively, one undervalues the scope and power of philosophy in taking it *purely* as second order.

A view of philosophy?

At a more profound level, the target in philosophy is less the misconceptions of detached practitioners, viewed with detachment, than powerful tendencies one recognizes in oneself. This picture of philosophy has been called a *therapeutic conception*, since it is directed at the specific puzzlement of some particular person. The aim is not to produce answers to perennial problems, nor to analyse concepts in ways that preclude future misunderstanding: indeed, both these targets are illusory since sources of misunderstanding appear and disappear – for example, from the activities of scientists (see below). And the question addressed is always contextual: the form of words in which you articulate your precise problems might ask something different in someone else's mouth. Further, drawing on some of the points about rules, one cannot preclude *all possible misunderstanding*, since there is no finite totality of possible misunderstandings, no sense to the word 'all' here. Instead, as Wittgenstein urges: 'Work in philosophy is . . . actually more a kind of work on oneself' (PO: 161). So philosophy typically consists in identifying how puzzlements arise either because some peculiar (and unwarranted) inference is being drawn – you hear me talk about sunrise, and infer that I have a pre-Copernican cosmology – or some piece of jargon has been misunderstood. For instance, talk of chaos theory leads someone to think that scientists now regard the world as chaotic: but, of course, chaos theory is fully deterministic (McFee 2000a: 155–8), as is demonstrated by the fact that the preferred research tool of chaos theorists is the computer! Rather, a clear view of one's (mis)understanding is needed here. But we regularly acquire misleading ideas. As Wittgenstein put it:

Teaching philosophy involves the same immense difficulty as instruction in geography would if a pupil brought with him a mass of false and falsely simplified ideas about the course of rivers and mountain chains.

(PO: 185)

One has to try to get a clear view of what is misleading one since, if it is a philosophical problem (and not one in, say, natural science, where empirical investigation might help), this is the only way to move forward. And one might be aided here. For example, in the best moment in the Derek Jarman film *Wittgenstein* (1993), two students assert that the reason 'people' typically believed that the sun went round the earth was that it *looked* as though it did – then Wittgenstein asks how it would *look* if the earth went round the sun. It takes a moment for the students to realize that, since that *is* what happens, it must look like this! The scales fall from their eyes.

But Wittgenstein also rightly insisted upon a *slow* cure: how is that compatible with the *revelatory aspect* I have been emphasizing? The answer lies in the following key passage: 'In philosophizing we may not *terminate* a disease of thought. It must run its natural course, and *slow* cure is all important' (Z §382). In this context, *slow* is contrasted with *hasty*: a *slow* cure here is one that takes its time, that is not hurried. Hence it must be suitably slow, for the 'working through' of the particular confusion. Of course, such a slow cure *might* be achieved in a flash (perhaps with a 'liberating word' [PO: 165]) were that the appropriate timing for *this* cure: what Wittgenstein speaks of as the cure running 'its natural course'. Relatedly, the danger here (as Wittgenstein identifies it) lies in trying to 'terminate' the condition – to bring it to a slick resolution. A kind of *briskness* would be a major vice: not genuinely addressing the problem. Thus philosophy can be done trivially, by (say) paying mere lip-service to alternatives, rather than investigating them.

The *therapeutic* conception of philosophy has a direct bearing on the structure of this text. For instance, how could we describe the *thesis* of this text? At one level, our reply is clear: it highlights misconceptions within the study of sport concerning rules and rule-following – in particular, concerning the determinacy of rules, and the degree to which an understanding of the (intrinsic) value of sport is concealed if one misunderstands rules. Yet such a concern with misconceptions and misunderstanding might *seem* puzzling: why do we not just say what is correct here, and be done with it? Whatever is urged must be both explained and proved: that alone must count against simple presentations. Further, in line with the *therapeutic* view, there are no abstract, general problems here, but only the perplexities of specific individuals, which must be *worked through* as best we can. So the text functions (at best) as a handbook for the self-treatment of some of those perplexities. We cannot expect that treatment to be achieved simply by being *told*!

Indeed, although much of the discussion might be phrased in terms of what to *say* in certain situations, our topic cannot be what *words* to choose.

First, that cannot bring about the insight, revelation or enlightenment required by philosophy; second, the *words* used are typically only important when they reflect some more profound contrast – say, in calling an action 'murder' as opposed to 'manslaughter': the different word here, if justified, amounts to something different having happened.

So philosophical problems are emphatically *not* problems with language.[8] Rather, one could *say* what one liked (see PI §79): the importance rests in what connections, distinctions and contrasts one is thereby drawing. What matters is not the *words* but, as Wittgenstein insisted, the *uses* to which those words were put on this or that occasion. Since typically these uses differ with the occasion or with speaker's interests or purposes (PI §132), assuming in advance of investigation that each term had just *one* use, or a fixed number of them, would be a potential source of confusion about what others were asserting, what questions they were addressing, and so on.

Of course, language matters to philosophy just because some of our philosophical problems arise when an *apparent* similarity (say, the same word being used or the same grammatical structure) conceals an important *difference*; or vice versa. We get inappropriate *'objects of comparison'* (PI §130). Failing to pay attention here can lead to 'the bewitchment of our intelligence' (PI §109). Yet the remedy is not found in language, but through careful attention to where we might be misled. And it is a central claim of Wittgenstein's that such 'misleading' occurs during schooling (hence besetting us all), and particularly when learning philosophy. So we must be especially on guard against the urgings both of 'experts' and of 'the philosopher in us' (Ms 219: 11).

The audience for this work

Describing the projected audience of this work says, roughly, what might be expected of 'the philosopher in us'. Although not conceived as a text primarily for students, this work is 'student-friendly' in not assuming too much of the *philosophical* literature, and so on. This also acknowledges the variety of backgrounds with which people come to the philosophy of sport. Hence, *some* things said at length may be self-evident, or very familiar, to some readers. As noted above, many of the chapters contain material in general philosophy, to provide additional background; and especially where my views diverge fairly widely from what is commonly assumed within philosophy. But these interventions are typically flagged clearly, so that anyone who is master of the material can see what to skip – and similarly for those not wishing to go deeper into the philosophical underpinnings. And I have regularly provided further references for those who wish to pursue them.

The material is not all equally transparent; and in places it may be compressed in a way that greater space would have prevented. I can only plead for clemency here, and ask (again: McFee 2000a: 36) for a reader 'ready to meet [the author] halfway . . . [and] . . . not begrudge a pinch of salt' (Frege 1960: 54). Further, my enthusiasm for pursuing philosophical issues, or their intrinsic interest (for me), sometimes leads me farther into philosophical thickets than the minimum this text requires – especially true of some passages in Chapter 2 (pp. 47–52), Chapter 4 (pp. 77–82) and Chapter 9 (pp. 151–60).

This text is continuous with my other writing on sport, and on persons; in particular as beginning to discharge some of the obligations of an earlier research agenda (from McFee 2000c) – repeated here, in modified form, in Chapter 8 – and partially discharged there, and in Chapters 9 and 10. But it remains a research agenda, partly because – consonant with my general view – much of the work lies in the consideration of general philosophical issues, not sporting cases.

This work aims to begin from fundamental concerns or first principles. For that reason, there is no detailed discussion of the vast literature growing up in philosophy of sport. Still, my perplexities sometimes arise from, or are fuelled by, what others have written. One strategy would have been to consider only those texts which lead *me* towards my perplexities. Yet my reading might be too eclectic to make that a profitable way forward. Moreover, the intentions here were never scholarly (in the sense of discussing the minutiae of other texts). Instead, 'classic' texts are used to elaborate and explore my issues. The texts chosen for discussion were selected partly as typical of important positions, partly for the clarity of the exposition of those positions, and partly for their wide use by others, especially students. But the discussion has always gone only as far as is necessary to explore my points. I hope those whose work is briefly discussed – with the discussion truncated by my purposes – will understand this.

The concerns with definiteness and rule-following that ground this work are not thought fundamental in much contemporary writing in the philosophy of sport.[9] (That is part of the 'old-fashioned' objection mentioned above.) But these *are* fundamental issues; moreover, ones which reveal the potential contribution of philosophy, partly through showing how conflicting insights can sometimes both be acknowledged. Were I right, this would only be a beginning – but it would offer a research agenda; to apply to problems presently in the forefront of the philosophy of sport the methodological insights here.

Part I
Rules in explaining sport

1 Definiteness and defining sport

I place an ovoid ball onto the grass, and a mile down the road David Campese does the same. But he has scored a try (in rugby) and I have not. We seemed to be doing the same thing, but we were not – in the terminology of the Introduction, these were different *actions*. Importantly, his was a move in a sporting activity while mine was not. But how is this difference to be explained? The context of Campese's placing of the ball was important; that, say, others were trying to interpose their bodies between the ball and the ground and, had they done so, it would not have been a try. So Campese's action can go wrong, or misfire, in ways mine could not. That seems one way to invoke the *rules* of rugby: what marks out Campese's action from mine is the background of rules of the sport. Or so it seems. Here, then, we recognize again the importance of rules in explaining the nature of sport.

Certainly, an insight here is that the actions involved in sport only make sense against a background of rules – only within the rules of chess can one attempt to checkmate an opponent, or succeed in doing so. Similarly, the rules of rugby allow one to score *tries*; otherwise, one would simply be putting the ball down. So those rules are *logically connected* to the possibility of try-scoring; that is, connected to the *action* of try-scoring. Moreover, to win or lose the game or match is related, in all cases, to such scoring. That there are such rules *at all* permits the kinds of action in which, say, winning consists.

To expand that insight: some theorists have sought to completely explain the nature of sport by appeal to such rules – in the literature, a view called *formalism*. Roughly, then, formalism (in this sense) is an account of sport (as for games) which urges that:

> in an important sense the rules of a game are inseparable from its goal. That is, the goal of golf is not simply to put the ball in the hole, but to do so in a quite specified way – by using the fewest number of strokes possible.
>
> (Morgan 1995: 50)

We are to imagine the *specification* done by the rules; moreover, to see this as a complete account of sport. More explicitly, for formalism:

the various derivative notions of a game are to be defined exclusively in terms of its formal rules. What it means to engage in a game, to count as a bona fide action of a game, and to win a game is to act in accordance with the appropriate rules of that game.

(Morgan 1995: 50)

Two aspects to such formalism can be distinguished. The first, explored in this chapter, takes formalism to *define* sport, or to offer a definite and determinate account of the nature of sport, *exclusively* in terms of its rules. So the first emphasis is on *determinacy*. The second aspect, explored in Chapter 2, recognizes that the rules (supposedly) achieve this determinacy: the emphasis is on the *rule-governed* nature of sport.

Thus Part I as a whole explicitly brings together two fundamental ideas, readily discerned in attempts to define *sport*: that the attempt of formalists to characterize sport in terms of its rules alone must fall foul (1) of the nature of rules and rule-following – that rule-following cannot 'close off all options' in the way it is sometimes assumed that it could; and (2) of the role (within philosophy) of the kind of definiteness assumed by, for instance, formalist 'definitions' of sport such as that by Bernard Suits (1978), discussed below.

Arguing for these two points here involves recognizing and exploring the central role, within sport, of its rules; and especially the *constitutive* character of some rules, such that as above they bring into being the possibility of the relevant action (say, try-scoring). But this line of argument cannot warrant a formalist-type conclusion, for the rules alone are not sufficient – rather, they must be *applied* in this or that situation. In summary, there are at least three points here:

- First (discussed in this chapter), general objections to the *need* (within philosophy) for definitions apply when formalists try to define *sport*: (a) we can understand what sport is without being able to define it; (b) any definition cannot really add to knowledge (beyond knowledge of the meaning of a *term*), since one must know how to deploy the ideas independent of the definition; (c) candidate definitions must be tested, which requires recognition of that to be defined *prior* to granting the definition; and (d) such candidate definitions are either susceptible to counter-examples (showing them false) or ultimately circular – in neither case could they fulfil the role assigned to them.
- Second, the idea of a definition (say, of *sport*) that is in principle inaccessible is inherently problematic: such a definition could not inflect my understanding of what sport is, or of whether or not such-and-such was sport, since (in this conjecture) I do not *know* the definition – it is inaccessible! And this is a fundamental objection both to inaccessible rules and to this conception of definiteness (also for this chapter).

- Third, the conception of rules deployed is problematic, both in assuming (falsely) that rules could always be so formulated as to cover *all* cases, and in taking the application of a rule to be a purely mechanical matter – hence, as amenable to another rule. Yet this view must lead to a regress, with a rule needed to apply that rule, and a rule needed for the new rule, and so on (discussed in Chapter 2).

Further, the discussion here is not circumscribed by the cases, from formalism, actually discussed. Since the primary target is a set of assumptions about determinacy – and, in particular, the philosophical credentials of such determinacy – other positions deploying the same assumptions are also assailed.

The issues

To make the discussion more concrete, we will consider the (widely discussed) account of sport by Bernard Suits, selected as a simple and clear example both of an attempted definition of *sport*, and of assumptions about the kind of determinacy appropriate to philosophical investigation – and also the determinacy provided by such investigation (compare McFee, forthcoming). Moreover, Suits's definitions of both *games* and *sport* include explicit mention of *rules*.

Suits, then, offers definitions of *games*, and of *sport* (as a subset of games). Often, the insights lying behind each characteristic in Suits' scheme are brought out most clearly by noting what cases that condition (or characteristic) is designed to *exclude* – bearing in mind that, as we shall see (p. 21), a satisfactory definition of *sport* must have an 'exact fit': what it rules *in* must all be sports, and none of what it excludes must be, or it will be flawed as a definition *for that reason*. To repeat, Suits's positions, in combination, are used here as a concrete example of a formalist account of sport, without taking issue with the fine detail of either.

For Suits, *games* are to be defined by four ideas, each explaining some key feature of games. These are:

1   *A pre-lusory goal*, a notion which needs a little explanation, below.
2   '*Means*' by which that goal might be achieved; that is, the permitted ways to achieve the pre-lusory goal – roughly, you win the game if you achieve the pre-lusory goal using the permitted means. Although this leaves open the question, 'Permitted how?', it is important to distinguish the means since, typically, the relevant means will not be the most straightforward way to achieve the outcome: in Suits's own example, one cannot legitimately win a race if one crosses the line first only by shooting the person in front of one through the head (Suits 1995a: 6).
3   *Rules* which circumscribe those means, which proscribe certain means (tripping an opponent in the race, or shooting him) and prescribe others

(constitutive rules). Games typically have other rules too, which Suits (1978: 37) calls 'rules of skill', indicating how to play the game well. Suits's examples here include 'Keep your eye on the ball', 'Do not trump your partner's ace'.

4   A (or the) *lusory attitude*: one voluntarily agrees to attempt to reach that goal using only those means, and not others at one's disposal. Since the rules *prohibit* certain means, Suits takes this attitude to involve acceptance of less efficient means – and this acceptance of such means is *voluntary*, for one is choosing to play the game. Finally, those who do not accept the rules of (say) chess could not attempt to checkmate opponents: that is, play the game. So the lusory attitude is '. . . the knowing acceptance of constitutive rules just so the activity made possible by such rules can occur' (Suits 1995a: 11, 1978: 40).

To summarize this account of *games*, Suits (1978: 41) fixes on one general feature, writing that 'playing games is a voluntary attempt to overcome unnecessary obstacles'.

In explaining what he means by *goals* here, Suits (1978: 36, 1995a: 8) distinguishes three kinds of aims or goals, most easily seen by considering a competitor in a running race:

*   Pre-lusory goal – the simplest version of, say, crossing the line first: this is a *'specifiable achievable state of affairs'* (Suits 1978: 36, 1995a: 9: original italics), such that we can determine (in principle) whether or not our competitor finished first.
*   Lusory goal – here our competitor will achieve the pre-lusory goal (cross the line first) but must do so within rules: for instance, he or she will not have taken any short cuts, nor hitched a ride on a passing motorcycle.
*   Goal in participating: for example, enjoyment, fame, money. . . . These may be goals *of the competitor* but they are not strictly goals *of the activity* at all – they are extrinsic to that activity.

Suits takes the simplest version of a goal, the first in our list, as the one needed for the definition, since other aspects of the second are captured by his reference to the means being within the rules, while the third has no place in an account of the nature of games *as such*, although it might play a role in the sociology of game-playing.

Sport was explained by Suits as a subset of games with the following additional characteristics:

1   *Skill* – sports cannot be games of pure chance, even if there are some chance elements. This explains why most sports involve efforts to achieve equal distribution of chance effects: for instance, changing ends during a football match, so that any advantage in playing in a particular direction is shared equally. Or, in cricket, tossing for who bats first: the

winner of the toss chooses if his or her side will bat or field. Since an advantage may be gained here, its allocation is based partly on the skilled decision of the captain; but the right to that decision is a matter of chance, as it cannot be left to skill, nor equally distributed.[1]

2   *Physical skill* – the skill must be physical, or games like chess would be included (contrary to the position in Cuba, where chess is regarded as a sport). Some chess is physical, of course – pieces of wood are moved, and so on. But this misses Suits's point, for this is only accidentally true: chess can be played without this paraphernalia, with players simply calling out their moves.

3   *Stability* – this contrasts sports with fads involving physical skill, such as the hula hoop. Of course, this is a pretty loose condition; what counts as *enough* stability? But it seems right that what lacked stability would not be a sport; and that acquiring this stability might be one way for an activity to move into the *sport* category. Further, one way to check on the status of an activity would be by asking, 'sport or fad?', as Suits invites us to do.

4   *'Wide' following* – again, there seems something right here; indeed, the International Olympic Committee uses something like this sort of regulation to decide what activities can be put forward for consideration to become Olympic sports. As with the idea of stability, we have no clear idea of what a *wide enough* following is. Still, it seems correct to disallow as sports activities which lack such a following – those which had just been invented, for instance; we should wait to see if the new activities 'take'.

Suits's account seems correct in recognizing sport's *physical* requirement, and its connection with skill. That these are not just trivial requirements can be introduced with a parallel example: for 'sport on the Internet' might seem to undermine the force of this requirement. But compare 'We met on the Internet' with an answer using a previous technology, 'No we have never met – we are just pen pals'. What is implicit in the idea of *meeting* (as normally understood) would be undermined when the physical requirement is not fulfilled. Nor is this just a verbal classification: to return to our case, if we call both kinds – physical and electronic – *sport*, we must concede that sport comes in two very different kinds; that is, the physical kind (which I follow Suits in thinking *genuine* sport) and the non-physical or virtual kind. This second, then, would be golf on the Internet, not, for example, bridge. To motivate the difference here, notice that golf on the Internet misses something crucial about, for instance, what is required for skill in golf. The possibility of wheelchair golf, for instance, suggests a contrast here – with golf not using a wheelchair. But such a contrast would be unintelligible for the virtual version.

Further, this highlights a typical response to talk of the impact of changing technologies on what is or is not sport – clearly Suits wrote before there was Internet golf. Either, as here, his account of sport serves to mark a contrast which must be preserved in the changed circumstances or – as when a new technology just affects the detail of sport: say, the introduction of aerodynamic javelins – the change does not touch his account.

Does Suits's picture of sport simply amount to a stipulation of what he *counts* as sport? This is certainly not its intention. Rather, it reflects the present situation; but, since it operates with abstract conditions, it does not fix activities as sport or non-sport in perpetuity – a fad for some activity involving physical skill could acquire stability and a sufficiently wide following, and hence be a sport. And, of course, a contentious case, or borderline case, in terms of these conditions would be a borderline case generally. Has Kabaddi (a territorial game from India) a wide enough following? Arguments for and against, say, the inclusion of Kabaddi as an Olympic sport exactly reflect Suits's account: those arguing for Kabaddi would urge that it presently had such a following, while those opposing its inclusion would deny this. So Suits's account of sport *does* seem to have a 'fit' for the notion of sport: here, what is genuinely problematic in the world of sport comes out as problematic on Suits's picture. Moreover, in sport, rules typically prescribe and proscribe behaviours, in relation to the aims of a particular sport – Suits's account successfully highlights this feature.

Discussion will focus on four areas of criticism, each suggesting more general problems for the assumptions about determinacy and rule-following embodied:

1   Suits thinks or assumes that definition is possible and desirable (p. 22), contrary to some general ideas from philosophy;
2   Suits thinks he has a definition (pp. 24–7);
3   Suits's account integrates rule-following into definition, importing assumptions about rules (pp. 27–8: see Chapter 3);
4   In these assumptions (and so on), Suits misses the philosophical point (or lack of it) of definition (pp. 28–31).

These criticisms grow from general philosophy, since the view of determinacy they oppose is also grounded in a general view; namely, that, since *logical* connections are all-or-nothing,[2] the finding of counter-cases can rule out (as not reflecting logical relations) any claims that are exception-bearing. We then arrive at conditions individually necessary and jointly sufficient (see pp. 21–2); moreover, doing *this* is making progress in philosophy.

Here, I use the simplest version of Suits's ideas, even when he modified these ideas,[3] since, first, others (for instance students) often consider this version; second, it makes points in a most direct way; third, if the criticisms of Suits' *project* of definition are sound, more complex versions will fare no better.

Before addressing the four criticisms listed above, we should recognize three fairly general methodological points here:

1 The need to introduce or prepare each point in philosophy more generally, so some of the discussion is not immediately about sport (nor
Suits);
2 The discussion is (mostly) not about details of Suits's claims – even
when these claims are the topic, the discussion reflects more general
points;
3 The 'positive thesis' (developed in response to the fourth line of
criticism) depends on a distinctive view of philosophy.

Therefore our discussion will often be abstract; and, when it is not, its *real*
focus will still be on general issues concerning assumptions about determinacy.

Why define?

It is useful to comment briefly on why a definition might be sought (or
hoped for) and what a definition is. For many who ask for definitions expect
that, if definitions could be got, they would aid understanding; moreover,
that when one lacks a definition of some crucial term or idea, one does not
understand. This attitude explains why, say, students often begin essays
with (putative) definitions – they assume both that the definition will aid
understanding, and that to lack the definition is to not understand. My
current topic would clearly be an important issue for those who hold this
view: by their own lights, they do not understand *definition* until they can
define it!

The thought, then, is that a definition shows the contours of the particular concept, shows what does and what does not fall under that concept.
First, and less formally, a definition is a *concise yet comprehensive characterization of whatever, having an 'exact fit'*. Each characteristic is important:
something not fairly concise would not count as a definition (three fat volumes would not do), and it must be comprehensive in not leaving any cases
out – otherwise it could not offer the kind of clarification hoped for above.
This explains the idea of 'exact fit': if the definition indicates that such-and-
such is a so-and-so, then it *is*; while if the definition indicates that it is not,
then it *is not*.

Our second, more formal explanation begins from there: definitions are
sets of conditions *individually necessary* and *jointly sufficient*. As these are
technical notions, a simple example may help (McFee 1992: 16–17). Consider, say, a triangle, defined as:

1 a plane figure;
2 with three straight sides;
3 completely bounded by those sides.

Each condition is *necessary*, since if one is *not* fulfilled, the figure is *not* a
triangle. (For example, failure of condition (3) allows an open box shape.)

Taken together, these conditions are jointly *sufficient*; if all are fulfilled, one definitely has a triangle. Conditions individually necessary and jointly sufficient ensure an *exact fit*: with fewer conditions (as above), there is no guarantee that the figure will be a triangle, while if one adds more conditions, the fit becomes too tight – it includes some triangles, but not all. For example, adding a fourth condition 'sides of equal length' applies to only equilateral triangles, not to others. Moreover, since *triangle* is a technical expression, it can be defined, even if the account sketched here is not completely adequate – its purpose is simply to explain the technical ideas.

Further, this account of definitions allows us to test putative definitions: is there exact fit? If not, then it is not a definition.

At this point, we can state clearly the general philosophical theses urged here, reflected in the first two criticisms of Suits. For both the following claims are *false*:

1   that if one does not have a definition of such-and-such, then one does not understand such-and-such;
2   that if one has a definition of such-and-such, then one understands such-and-such.

Yet these claims sustain the enthusiasm for definitions. Further, I shall urge that one cannot in fact define terms of sufficient complexity to be philosophically interesting – into which category both *game* and *sport* surely fall. If these points are accepted, Suits must be wrong both in hoping for a definition and in thinking he has one. Let us scrutinize the arguments here.

A definition (of *sport*) is neither possible nor desirable

We now know what a definition is, and why it might be *thought* useful. But is there reason for optimism here about this role for definitions? It seems not. First, one can understand without being able to define (contrary to (1) above). This is easily demonstrated via examples: for instance, *time* – we can do all we need to with the notion of time (for example, tell the time, note when we are late or on time, discuss the International Date Line, and so on); so we do understand *time*, even though we cannot define it. Here, finding even *one* concept which one understands and yet cannot define shows that one's having a definition cannot be a *requirement* for understanding: more loosely, we *can* understand such-and-such without being able to offer a formal definition of it.

Second, putative definitions must be tested against one's experience: I must be able to recognize *bachelors* (prior to your giving me a definition of that term) to see if your putative definition is correct – or even plausible. So definitions do not really aid understanding. Testing the truth of putative definitions requires that one understand before one has the definition. Your account of, say, *sport* must be recognized as correct – I can only do that if I can recognize sports prior to or independent of the definition. Further, since the meaning of expressions in the definition must be known, the definition is not a neutral starting place; if I have no undefined starting place, the search for a *complete* definition will go on for ever. But if there is an *undefined* starting place, definition cannot be as fundamental to understanding as was assumed: it would not be for the starting place. So what definitions offer requires a background of understanding prior to the definition (in line with the point above): but, having such understanding, the definition offers little new (contrary to (2) above) – at best, it offers a new *word* for some already understood. (A useful parallel: I teach you to play chess, but without telling you names for the pieces. Now my telling you that the piece you have been calling 'the horsey' is actually a *knight* does not make you a better chess player.)

These considerations prove that definitions cannot have the fundamental role ascribed to them. But having a definition might still be thought a Good Thing. Against that idea, I urge that such definitions are actually impossible. My strategy consists in showing how to assail any putative definition. Since genuine definitions must have exact fit on the term in question, candidate definitions can fail in one of two ways: either (a) by lacking exact fit – by being too tight (excluding what should be included) or too loose (including what should be excluded; as when a definition of *music* as 'organized sound' thereby includes the Morse code); or (b) by being circular – so that they explain A in terms of B, B in terms of C, and C in terms of A. In this case, they are not specific enough to have a fit at all. (The consideration of examples here, to see how they fail one or other test, can be left to the reader.)

These points count against a *general* requirement connecting definability to the possibility of understanding, but they do not obviously give us what we need. For these points only show that definitions do not have the fundamental role in *general* understanding sometimes assumed: they show us nothing (yet) about philosophy.

The first way of assailing a putative definition involves finding a counterexample or counter-case to the (putative) definition; and this powerful method is widely used in philosophy. It illustrates, of course, the assumption about definiteness embodied in the search for definiteness: that one counter-case shows the definition to be wrong. Yet it also highlights an assumption about the nature of philosophy – about the all-or-nothing relations that (on this view) philosophy explores (see pp. 28–31). If we ask of such a definition *what is its job in philosophy?*, the answer is supposed to be self-evident: that searching for conditions individually necessary and jointly sufficient just *is* doing philosophy – because such conditions are *conceptual* or *logical* conditions (and hence philosophy's business). But we have not shown the benefit, if any, of locating such conditions.

The gain is supposed to lie in clarity: we have given reasons to doubt its credentials – there is no need of such clarity, not any real likelihood that a definition will provide it. Further, there are alternative strategies here (in particular, using examples and contrasting cases) which seem more promising, in the abstract.

Moreover, in that light, we also recognize what makes such ideas or assumptions about definitions *dangerous*: that having a (so-called) definition, and thinking that having a definition ensures understanding, we will conclude that we understand – and then put aside any attempt at really looking for understanding.

Here, then, we have seen why Suits (and anyone) *should* neither want a definition, nor expect to find one; the argument sketched has been wholly general and abstract. To make it more concrete, we turn to features of Suits's own definition, and to our second kind of criticism.

Mistakenly thinking one has a definition

Suits's strategy, recall, was to define *sports* as a subspecies of *game*. He offers the following:

> To play a game is to attempt to achieve a specific state of affairs [pre-lusory goal], using only means permitted by rules [lusory means], where the rules prohibit use of more efficient in favour of less efficient means [constitutive rules], and where rules are accepted just because they make possible such activity [lusory attitude].
>
> (Suits 1978: 41)

He goes on to summarize: 'playing games is a voluntary attempt to overcome unnecessary obstacles'. Earlier Suits (1978: 34) explains:

> to play a game is to engage in an activity directed towards bringing about a specific state of affairs, using only means permitted by the rules, where the rules prohibit more efficient in favour of less efficient means, and where the rules are accepted just because they make possible such activity.

(Notice that we must look to Suits's own work to understand the technical terms here ['pre-lusory goal', 'lusory means', 'lusory attitude'], rather than expecting to find them in common usage.)

Faced with such an account, and its amplification (see pp. 17–19), we know how to test (or assail) it: first, can counter-examples to Suits's (putative) definition be found? That is, are there cases which it predicts are games but which are not, or cases which are games but it precludes? If just one such can be found, Suits is *wrong* – this is not an exact fit for *game*. At first glance, there seem to be two kinds of counter-examples.

First, there are activities involving voluntary efforts to overcome unnecessary obstacles, but which are not games. One might well explain mountain-climbing this way – unlike those who go to the top of a peak to hunt or to manage their goat herds, the mountaineer has no ulterior purpose: the climbing is, in that sense, unnecessary. And we can certainly envisage mountaineers who have rules in the relevant sense. But mountaineering does not, at first blush, seem like a game. Similarly, while exercising in the gym, I might decide to complete a fixed number of repetitions of a particular exercise: failure to do so will mean I have not met this (local) goal, although the more general goal – say, in terms of my health and fitness – will still be met with slightly fewer repetitions. Here, the rules I set for myself make life difficult for me: I could stop earlier, and be equally happy in terms of that general goal. So, superficially, this activity meets Suits's conditions. Yet it does not seem to be a game. Indeed, it cannot *follow* that simply by setting for myself some unnecessarily high limits to some task I thereby transform that task into a game – even in a metaphorical sense! (If Suits then insists that these *must* be games, he makes the account circular.)

Second, there are activities which *are* games but where the idea of 'unnecessary obstacles' makes no sense, the idea of *obstacles* here only having application within the game. For example, what unnecessary obstacles are there on the path to checkmate, in a chess game? Beating one's opponent by checkmating him cannot here be compared with, say, using the chess board as a club. No 'obstacles' here seem explicable *independently* of the game; hence there seems no sense in which they are unnecessary since, without them, there could be no game. Similarly, when children play a 'pretending' game, the reason that the cowboys do not shoot the indians with real guns and real bullets does not seem to depend on the desire for 'unnecessary obstacles' (and neither is it covered in the rules, at least on any normal understanding of what those rules are – the question of real guns never arises).

Further, other details also seem problematic in the same way: for instance, the pre-lusory goal of gymnastic vaulting can probably be taken as, say, getting over the box – but what about gymnastic floorwork? There seems no straightforward way to specify what is required without reference to the sport. And its Olympic status *seems* to guarantee that it is a sport.

So Suits's attempted definition does not seem exempt from the usual criticisms: examples of the first kind suggest that the account has too loose a fit, while those of the second suggest it is too tight. And, even were these *examples* contested, the *possibility* of such counter-cases cannot be excluded.

Moreover, are aspects of Suits's account circular? That is, for any, must we appeal to the idea of a *game* in order to understand it? If so, this is not a genuine definition – and Suits is *wrong*. The account might seem circular: lusory means, lusory (and pre-lusory) goals, and so on, could not be explained independently of the idea of *games*. Hence, to explain *games* in terms of lusory means, and lusory attitudes (and even a pre-lusory goal), is to explain games in terms of . . . games! Indeed, the term 'lusory' seems to recognize just that point.

In addition, as noted above, two of Suits's conditions for *sport* (the ideas of stability and of a wide following) do not readily allow investigation of their application (or not) in a particular case. Here too there is the suspicion of circularity – that a *suitably* wide following is one suitable *for a sport*; and similarly for the degree of stability. So, again, aspects of Suits's definitions seem susceptible to standard kinds of objections, noted earlier.

How might Suits respond to criticisms of these sorts? First, Suits (1978: 84–7) specifically addresses the case of mountaineering: his argument is that Edmund Hillary insists on *climbing* the mountain – that he would not take an escalator if it were offered him. This seems right, but does not obviously make mountaineering a *game*. Notice, too, that if a Nepalese had previously reached the peak of Everest, while out looking for goats, the fact of his having reached the top of the mountain would not mean that he *climbed* the mountain! Suits rightly stresses the constrained nature of the activity: but that does not ensure that this is a *game*, and not some other kind of constrained activity. Second, the example of gymnastics is one place where Suits (1995b: 17) now concedes 'I was wrong': he now identifies two kinds of sports, only one of which – and not the kind instantiated by gymnastics – is a species of game. Of course, this simply means that we cannot regard *sports* as (by definition) *games* with certain properties. And that might set us off looking for some other set of properties for the non-game sports, or we might look for what sports have in common, given that game-hood is now (conceded to be) not a necessary condition for sport-hood. Third, consider his imagined game of *sweat bead* – on which the pre-lusory goal is that three beads of sweat shall run down a particular forehead, this sweat to have been elicited within fifteen minutes, without threats of violence to the person or 'aspersions on his person or professional reputation' (Suits 1995a: 13). He rightly insists that this highly idiosyncratic game might become a sport if it achieved a wide following (and stability). And the fact that a particular person is involved need matter no more than the fact that the Eton Wall Game must be played against a specific wall. But, again, his insistence that there are rules here, and a pre-lusory goal, leaves us some distance from its being a game: in particular, it seems *cruel*, even with the prohibitions of the rules – more akin to gladiatorial contest (if a psychological one) than game. In all these cases, then, Suits has a thought-out reply, but it primarily amounts to deploying other features of the definition, or to endorsing his ability to recognize sports or games. Neither strategy can give confidence in the *safety* of his definitions.

It is far from obvious, then, that Suits could not meet some or all of these specific objections. The difficulty is that, in doing so, either his account becomes *stipulative* – he tells us what *he* will count as sports, dismissing as not really games or not really sports what common sense treats differently – or it becomes *unhelpfully vague*, by which I mean that it cannot fulfil the tasks Suits assigns to it *by his own lights*.

So Suits cannot evade the standard problems for definitions. However, giving up the search for definition is not giving up clarity; for clarity can be achieved in a number of ways, especially by giving examples and by considering contrasts (perhaps in particular contexts). For instance, if we are genuinely puzzled about the nature of sport as it finds itself involved with the school curriculum, we may profitably compare *sport* with *physical education*, and contrast them, rather than try to define either. For not all the features ascribable to sport will have a place in either relating it to, or distinguishing it from, physical education – as we might see when we contrast *sport* with some other notion (say, *recreation* or *leisure*). Again, the best method of explaining what we mean by sport in a particular context may be to exemplify it: for example, by cricket. Then the reader both knows some key features for that context – at least if the example is well chosen – and has a starting point to look for more of the same, with perhaps some sense of where this will necessarily be different! Moreover, such procedures will not lead us into the error identified earlier, of thinking that one had achieved clarity (through a definition) – and hence giving up the search for it. So rejecting this view of determinacy is not rejecting the need for clarity. Rather, it is recognizing how clarity might best be attained.

Recall, though, that accepting these criticisms of Suits will not negate the insightfulness of his account: for instance, as locating the sorts of considerations we might raise to argue for or against a putative sport – say, in relation to its claims to be included in the Olympics; for example, through checking for stability (to rule out fads) and for wide following – even if we cannot say *how* wide!

Rule-following and definition

Faced with issues arising from apparent counter-cases, Suits can fall back on some of the notions central to his account – although doing so will court the accusation of circularity. In particular, he can appeal to the place given to rule-following. For instance, the goal he identifies as central to games (the pre-lusory goal) is not the one dependent on the rules; rather, it can be given a broadly behavioural explanation (for instance, crossing the line in the race – where we have not yet enquired if the trip included using a motorcycle!). But he also recognizes that what counts as meeting this goal within the rules is determined by those rules. So there is here an assumption about rules, connecting them to determinacy (see Chapter 2 pp. 44–7): the rules make plain whether or not a particular behaviour is or is not in accord with those rules. But, as we shall see, that is not possible: rules do not foreclose on possibilities in this way, nor can such foreclosing be achieved by yet more rules.

Were that the way to go, however, it would suggest that all that was wrong here was that the analysis had not been carried out thoroughly enough:

in this vein, Klaus Meier (1995) thinks that Suits's mistake (or one of them) lies in not having *enough* kinds of rules (see Chapter 3 pp. 54–6).

For another kind of objection, which will be important later in respect of *rules*, the issue turns less on whether a definition could be *found* than on the consequences or lack of them of failing to find such a definition – or of determining that such definitions were impossible: namely, the rejection of the *task* ascribed to such definition.

The philosophical point (or lack of it) of definition

The thrust of Suits's accounts here is that a definition of *sport* would be philosophically valuable; and that, even if we cannot find a definition, our search can be clarifying. Moreover, Suits takes himself to have found such a definition.

He must grant, of course, that this definition is not known to most of us, even those who think or write about sport. (More exactly, it only becomes known through Suits's own endeavours.) But what exactly is the benefit in recognizing a definition, or arriving at it by Analysis,[4] if the idea thus defined was already used and understood? That is to say, what philosophical work does the *search for definition* do? Here, a contrasting view would urge that what is relevant must be in plain sight, at least for those who understand the key ideas (or use the key terms with understanding).

In this vein, it is worth mentioning (not least because Suits does!) that Wittgenstein famously tells us to 'look and see' (PI §66) whether there are properties common to all *games*. Some commentators assume that, having done so, we will *not* find common properties – among games, or elsewhere. Such an argumentative strategy might look suspect, a kind of dogmatism. For we cannot *know* that these properties will not be found, in advance of investigation (or so it might seem). If I look and see, might I not come up with something in common? As Baker and Hacker (1980: 327) put it, 'how could we prove it, let alone see it?'. Might we not *find* a common property, or uncover it by Analysis? And this is precisely how Suits responds for the term 'game' – he claims that 'Wittgenstein himself did not follow . . . [his own] excellent advice and look and see' (Suits 1978: x). Had Wittgenstein done so, Suits thinks, he *would* have found a definition of the term 'game', the very one Suits himself claims to identify.

Moreover, even if no such a common property were found *yet*, how can that warrant our concluding that there *is* no such characteristic (or set of characteristics)? To do so is like concluding evidence of absence on the basis of absence of evidence – or so it might seem. Further, as Baker and Hacker (1980: 332) note, most philosophers who have raised such objections 'have found Wittgenstein's answers either non-existent or inadequate'.

Before continuing, we should recognize a potential confusion here, so as to avoid this complication: putting the issue here in terms of *finding* makes it seem an empirical matter. The injunction to look and see might suggest an empirical claim, best answered by a thorough search, judged on its thoroughness – as it would if, for example, I denied your claim that there were mushrooms in such-and-such field. But that cannot be right: our concern, like Wittgenstein's, is philosophical. None of the philosophers to consider here take this as something a survey, say, might determine (*pace* Kamber 1998: 35); and rightly so. In particular, codifying the use of the term 'sport' in English (were this possible) would not automatically help. Determining how the term 'sport' is used in English takes us only so far – and not always in the right direction: as Wittgenstein was fond of noting (for example, PI §79), the right advice is often, '*Say* what you like', with the emphasis on what contrasts one is respecting. Such codification would require us to look for, and recognize, cases of *sport* (and, perhaps, only sport). But which exactly are these? In (mis)taking the question for an empirical one, the difficulties of *what* one looks at – and how one knows both what to look at and how to look at it – are exacerbated; and these were the very questions from which we began.

To return to our main thread: one is now in philosophically deep water. As Baker and Hacker (1980: 331) put it: 'Whether the objects falling under a concept share common properties is only of any philosophical interest on the assumption that this question bears on our understanding of concept-words.'

But why should it be? Indeed, our earlier discussions should make the prospects here not hopeful. They also suggested both that I might understand without a definition, or without the (imported) assumption of determinacy, and that having a definition need not aid understanding. Could that understanding nevertheless be rooted in a definition (or a set of necessary and sufficient conditions) of which I am unaware? Clearly, *we* do not explain the term 'game' by reference to some set of common properties, since we do not know them. Yet, an opponent might retort, how can we *know* that there is nothing in common among all games? Might we not *find* something (like Suits[5]) when we look and see? That returns us to an earlier objection: is this assertion (that no such property common to all games *could* be found) not just dogmatism?

In fact, this objection entirely misses Wittgenstein's point. He is not just claiming that there *is* no property common among games. Instead, even *were* a common property revealed by analysis (PI §69; §91), it cannot be what determines what we mean or understand by the term game since we (or, anyway, I) would not know it – I had not done that Analysis! So Wittgenstein's attitude to the term *game* is not dogmatism. Instead, what is amenable to the 'look and see' request must be in plain sight, rather than discoverable only by Analysis. That is why it is 'completely expressed in the explanations that I could give' (PI §75) together with those I would accept. Thus my use or understanding of the notion *cannot* be grounded by any such set of common properties here, since – when I am reflective about the cases (and therefore consider candidate counter-cases) – *I* do not know any such set of conditions. I cannot mean by the concept *game* something hidden or concealed since I would not be prepared (nor able) to explain the concept in terms of that hidden 'something', nor recognize as correct an explanation in those terms offered by another. Just as one cannot *follow* a rule one does not know (however much one's behaviour accords with it; Chapter 2 pp. 44–5), a definition I do not know cannot be what grounds *my* (or your) use of the terms 'game' or 'sport'. Moreover, such definition cannot be *required* for philosophical purposes. Indeed, there is really no job left for it to do. Yet, *ex hypothesi*, I use the term *sport* (or *game*) effectively – as effectively as those who claim they have a definition.

Suppose one could define 'game' or 'sport': what would follow? Nothing need follow, for me. If conditions individually necessary and jointly sufficient for the application of a term are not known to me (as they have yet to be uncovered by Analysis) but I still use the term correctly, *I* am not employing those conditions. So any other strategies were not on the right track.

Yet what of the objection that a *deep* Analysis, rather than a superficial glance, might uncover hidden necessary and sufficient conditions? This objection cannot be sustained by those who accept that the term *game* is understood by people who do not know this *deep* Analysis (and that must be all of us if the *deep* Analysis has not yet been undertaken!). Further, one has no motive to insist that there *must* be some common property if one approaches the matter neutrally – that is, without a *prior commitment* to the existence of some common property.

These wholly general points impact directly on Suits's discussion both because he explicitly sees himself as answering a challenge from Wittgenstein, and because this line of argument undercuts Suits's *project*, rather than simply its detail. We seemed to know what games were prior to, and independently of, Suits's account of games – we did not check that there were unnecessary obstacles, say, before deciding. It does not make sense to say that one is *following a rule* when one is ignorant of that rule – at best, one's behaviour conforms to it (Chapter 2 p. 44). Can it make more sense here to appeal to a definition of which one was ignorant? Implicitly, Suits here appeals to a definition we might uncover by Analysis. We have seen that there cannot be any general basis for such an appeal.

Perhaps, though, some special feature here explains why *sport* is not amenable to definition. For instance, various writers[6] have urged that (for example) *art* cannot be defined because it is not, say, a natural-kind term. The implication is that natural-kind terms (*camel*, *gold*) are definable, contrary to at least some of the general objections to definability above (see pp. 22–4). Getting clear on that topic might help us find a role of *the search for definition*, if not for the (impossible) definition itself.

Granting this claim about natural-kinds does not undermine the points urged here: *sport* is manifestly not a natural kind term either. For instance, William Morgan (1994: 213) is typical – if more explicit – in taking sport as 'a social rather than a natural kind'. So even were this true of natural-kind terms, that would not be a disaster here. Yet, in reality, the general objections both to definability as such and to the philosophical *use* of definability (or definiteness) apply as much to natural-kind terms as to others – although this fact can be obscured by the account given of *natural kinds*, where (roughly) that *X* is not definable shows that *X* is *not* a natural-kind term (after all, and despite appearances to the contrary). But this is just sleight of hand: the lack of definability follows from the possibility of exceptions to any proposed condition; and the objection to the *philosophical use* of definability is independent of (even) the point that (say) biological terms must apply on some biological basis. In fact, this idea chiefly supports it; since I manifestly do not know the biology of what holds camels together, nor the precise chemistry of gold. At the very least, using the term 'camel' or the term 'gold' does not appeal to it. Even if I did know these bits of science, that knowledge would be as potentially changeable as any scientific thesis.

So this is not a strategy here, neither in general nor for the specific case of sport – for there was no suggestion that *sport* was a natural kind (that 'sport' was a natural-kind term). But it was worth seeing the futility of the strategy, since it is sometimes deployed, especially by sports scientists, in related contexts.

What is in common?

The thought argued against here is that there *must* be something in common to justify our calling both A and B, say, *sports*: for what is the basis for such a thought? We have seen it as primarily an *assumption*; and one drawn from a particular view of the nature of philosophy. We have also given reasons to think that the assumption cannot be made good, or discharged. So there seems no good reason to think that all instances falling under some general term necessarily share some common feature(s). In particular, might there not be other possible models here? For example, if A shares some features with B, and B shares some with C, that might warrant our regarding both A and C as, say, sports even though they had nothing in common.

By contrast, Klaus Meier (1995: 31–3), in aiming to *sort out* once and for all some central classificatory questions (for example, 'Are all sports also games?'), assumes that there is a *clear*, and once and for all, answer here. So that one, and only one, relationship (of inclusion, exclusion, or whatever) exists between, say, sports and games: on Meier's version, only one Venn diagram could be drawn. Meier then uses the techniques this desire imports, such as the use of (putative) counter-examples, to demonstrate the accuracy of his view. But his assumption that there *must be* such divisions, and his use of certain methods to expose them, is really just a commitment on his part – and one we might well reject. Thus our objection has been to the procedure (and its assumptions) rather than to the detail.

In conclusion, the prospects for formalism do not look good by the end of Chapter 1, since one of the two strands of formalism – that concerning definiteness – has conclusively unravelled and, with it, any other positions which make the same assumptions. Will the other strand fare better? It is to that issue we now turn.

2 Rule-following and formalism in sport

Arguments against determinacy in Chapter 1 showed that the *project* of formalism is misplaced: it could not be realized and (even if it were) could make no contribution to philosophical understanding of sport. But that chapter also distinguished a second aspect to the project of formalism. Having thus put aside the 'determinacy' aspect, we turn here to the 'rules' aspect of formalism.

Again, our conclusions are largely negative, but this does not mean that there are no insights here. On the contrary, we are drawn to formalism because the root thought is insightful. That root thought relates the possibility of sporting *actions* to the rules of sports. For only in the context of the rules can one perform that precise action – say, scoring a six in cricket.

This context does not require inclusion of all that could be said about rules (even if there were such an *all*, and even if we knew it), nor does it pick up the full variety of different uses of rules, some of which may be fairly hard to distinguish – but where the contrasts are sometimes crucial. Also, there are many uses of rules not considered here directly, even though they might be of importance in sport; especially, 'rules' of skill (*pace* Suits 1995a: 19), and 'rules' of tactics or strategy within a game or sport.

As remarked in Chapter 1 (p. 15), some rules for sport proscribe or prescribe behaviours; in particular, the most efficient means to a pre-lusory goal might be proscribed. We think, then, of rules saying what *thou shalt not* do. To recall the variety here, note two less usual cases: (a) sometimes the proscription is achieved by listing permissible means, so that anything not explicitly mentioned is not permitted. Our example has been the list of objects, and so on, that players may take on the rugby field. Sometimes, by contrast, (b) not all rules need to be explicitly stated: consider two different examples, from road traffic control. First, in the UK, a sign for 'national speed limit' (some drivers, mistakenly, called it 'no speed limit') – we need collateral information to know what the regulation is. And it might be changed by the legislature. Second, the inference to what is permitted at a traffic light in the USA (at least, in California) – that you can make a U-turn, unless there is a specific sign precluding it. In this case, then, a general rule applies unless there is an explicit modification. But there is no rule-formulation at the particular junction.

In general, then, there is no *one* way that a particular rule *can* – let alone *should* – be formulated, when it is formulated. A signpost may be one way to formulate a rule, a verbal form another, with no general reason to prefer one over the other. But, for sport, there has often been the search for a *canonical* formulation of a particular rule, in words, no doubt partly so that one rule is used by all players. There is a connection, then, to the idea of 'codification' of rules (see Introduction). Yet often that formulation is taken as *canonical* in a stronger sense: as *the right way* to formulate that rule, the way that catches the *real* rule. But this is an illusion for reasons we will come to. (Also, on rules and rule-formulations, see Chapter 3 pp. 68–70)

With these general ideas mentioned and put aside, we turn to our consideration of the formalist project.

Formalism: explaining sport in terms of rules?

As noted in Chapter 1, formalism[1] in this context is an account of sport (as for games) which urges that:

> the various derivative notions of a game are to be defined exclusively in terms of its formal rules. What it means to engage in a game, to count as a bona fide action of a game, and to win a game is to act in accordance with the appropriate rules of that game.
>
> (Morgan 1995: 50)

So formalism begins from our insight that rules constitute the actions comprising our game or sport. Further, it takes those rules to *define* the game, and to do so *exclusively*: that is, without further supplementation. Suits's account seems readily amenable to this sort of reading: the rules proscribe the means at hand, and *lusory* means must be used in order to win. Yet lusory means just are those permitted by the rules – those that, if adhered to, result in the satisfaction of the lusory goal (that is, the pre-lusory goal by lusory means). Thus we know what game is being played by referring to its rules; and 'same rules' will imply 'same game'. On the face of it, then, the role for such rules means that someone not abiding by the same rules as me is playing a different game from me.

Clearly not all rules can have this importance placed upon them: some rule-breaking is explicitly allowed for, when rules of a sport incorporate penalties for that kind of rule breaking. If a bowler in cricket delivers the ball with a bent arm, contrary to the rules, the delivery does not count (it is replayed, and the batsman cannot be dismissed by it, although he may score from it) and one run is added to the tally of the batting side. This behaviour is thus recognized as occurring; and its occurrence dealt with via the penalty. If formalism is not simply to *define away* counter-cases, it must offer some account of the difference between these two kinds of rule-related situations.

As we shall see, the problem here concerns whether, if any rules of a game are broken, participants are still playing *that game*. Or whether formalism is necessarily committed to the idea that one cannot cheat and still be playing the game: that *cheating* and *playing the game* are logically incompatible. Called for this reason 'the logical incompatibility thesis' (Morgan 1995: 50), this idea is superficially implausible. The whole point of cheating must lie in advantage *within* the game. We might wonder who could possibly accept such an idea (until we recall that philosopher Nelson Goodman [1968: 187] thought that an orchestra getting one note wrong had not really played, say, Beethoven's *Ninth Symphony*). Here, then, we are struggling towards the common-sense view that players who fail to abide by a rule, or even cheat, may still be playing the game (what else are they playing?). And we are struggling *against* the views of certain writers on philosophy. Certainly, the contrast between playing the game and playing fairly (see D'Agostino 1995: 43) must be acknowledged. Then perhaps some of the rule-related structures reflect only on playing fairly; they have no role in making a particular sport or game the activity it is. That in turn suggests that a positive insight into the application of rules might come from considering whether, or how, one can (a) *cheat* or (b) *break a rule* (say, the handball rule in football/soccer or by bowling a 'no ball' in cricket) but – in either case – still be within the game.

The device regularly invoked (especially by formalists) contrasts regulative rules with constitutive ones: that is, distinguishes those rules which modify already existing practices (*regulative* rules) from those upon which the existence of a practice (in our case, a game or sport) is logically dependent – its *constitutive* rules – which do not so much determine what players do as part of the game, but rather create new forms of action. Thus:

> [t]he rules of football or chess, for example, do not merely regulate playing football or chess, but . . . create the very possibility of playing such games. The activities of football or chess are constituted in accordance with . . . the appropriate rules.
>
> (Searle 1969: 33–4)

As D'Agostino (1995: 45) puts it, applied to sport, the contrast is between those rules that define an activity (constitutive) in contrast to 'penalty-invoking rules' (regulative). So that, say, the possibility of scoring a try is created by the constitutive rules of rugby, but the prohibition against passing forward operates differently – I will be punished if I break it (and am caught) yet the rules of rugby accommodate this transgression.

This picture gets right the force of *constitutive rules*: that one can only (even) attempt to score a try given the rules of rugby or to checkmate someone given the rules of chess – without rugby or chess, those actions become impossible. So at best formalism is primarily a thesis about constitutive rules: at least, *not* one about regulative rules.

Moreover, the formalist intention (manifest for Suits) involved offering a concise yet comprehensive account of sport, having an exact fit – such that activities recognized as sport by the account clearly were, and those the account denied sport-status clearly were not. That is, an exceptionless account of sport is sought. Note, therefore, the inbuilt assumption of definiteness: that an exceptionless account of sport (or of games) is possible and desirable. And the concerns of others (for instance, Meier [1995]) with the relations between games and sports directly reflect this demand for determinacy – visible through Meier's use of Venn diagrammes. If sport is not amenable to this kind of definiteness – as Chapter 1 suggested – or if such definiteness is not required (for some agreed purpose), this project may be misconceived.

Criticisms: the adequacy of formalism?

Does breaking any formal rule of a game 'invalidate' that game? Certainly it would be very frustrating to play chess or tennis against an opponent who constantly broke the rules, even if he or she was penalized for doing so – but especially if he or she were not. Thus, it would be frustrating to have one's shots in tennis called 'out' when they were not, or for an opponent to be serving from inside the baseline. So, in line with formalism, excessive rule-breaking does 'undermine the game': we are not playing cricket if *none* of its rules is abided by; but neither are we *playing* it if every one of the regulative rules is regularly contravened – not least because that will disrupt the flow of the game if/when the umpire acts on the contraventions. (Of course, it would be equally frustrating if the opponent constantly changed the rules, so that what had been called 'in' before was now called 'out'.) In this sense, rule-breaking, and especially cheating, can undermine the game – we have agreed to play *this* game; thereby to abide by both its regulative and its constitutive rules.

However, the possibility of such widespread rule-breaking can be overstressed. As we will see (Chapter 7 pp. 121–2), one cannot regularly behave like this – anymore than we could lie *all* (or most) of the time (compare Leaman 1995: 195). Nevertheless, the logic of formalism requires that contravention of the *key* rules means one is no longer playing the game *at all*. This follows from the place of those rules in the formalists' (putative) definition of sport: its being a definition requires that it have an exact fit (Chapter 1 p. 21), or that the conditions – here, these *key* rules – be individually necessary and jointly sufficient. But recognizing a condition as individually *necessary* here is claiming that, without the satisfaction of that condition, we do not have an example of whatever: as the failure of one of the conditions for *trianglehood* would mean one did not have a triangle. To apply, if these rules really provide a necessary condition for, say, tennis or cricket, the person not deploying them seems no longer to be playing tennis or cricket.

But the formalist position here looks dogmatic: it seems to identify only two classes of case, with no real justification. Further, doing so precisely commits oneself to the determinacy of any reply. By contrast, D'Agostino's view seems to highlight three categories of behaviour, not two. At one extreme here is behaviour that is *permissible*, which accords with the rules; and, at the other, *unacceptable behaviour* (such as a handball in soccer) that contravenes them and should always be penalized when detected.[2] But, on this view, there is also *impermissible but acceptable* behaviour (D'Agostino 1995: 47): that is, behaviour tolerated in practice (say, to keep the game flowing), even though proscribed by the rules.

Formalists, then, need the constitutive/regulative distinction (or something like it) to avoid the unwelcome consequence that rule-breakers are not, after all, playing the game. But, as Morgan (1995: 56) perceptively puts it, D'Agostino's thought was that 'our intuitions about which rules are indispensable to the practice of a game [or sport] are often at variance with what formalism has to say'. Hence, this defence cannot really save the formalist account of sport (or games).

How should we proceed? An example is helpful, to consider the constitutive/regulative contrast: is the 'no contact' rule in basketball a constitutive rule (or merely a regulative one)? At first glance, it seems constitutive, because under one of its original thirteen rules 'shouldering, holding, pushing, tripping or striking an opponent was not allowed' (see Ebert and Cheatum 1977: 4). As summarized by Mumford and Wordsworth (1974: 19), 'There will be no contact between opponents.' So a sense of *no contact* seems to make basketball the game it is – a game lacking this idea would not be basketball. But this rule does involve penalties if infringed, which makes it seem regulative. So is the contrast between the constitutive and the regulative hard and fast?

In effect, the discussion now concerns this distinction. As we will see, Morgan (1995: 53) contends that the contrast *is* hard and fast, but that constitutive rules *do* regulate, although 'without the pain of penalty'. On this view, D'Agostino has somehow misdrawn the contrast. In explanation, Morgan quotes Searle (1969: 34), whose use of the term *constitutive rule* seems to licence this reading: '[c]onstitutive rules constitute (and also regulate) an activity the existence of which is logically dependent on the rules'. The thought is that 'the constitutive rules are doing considerably more than furnishing new conceptual specifications of behaviour' (Morgan 1995: 53). Of course, this is what was hoped for – but how is this move to be warranted, since clearly Searle's say-so is not enough? As it stands, Morgan has merely repeated what he hopes a fuller account of constitutive rules will deliver. But does this version offer the same distinction? The contrast *seemed* to be between those rules that regulated and those that did not; but now it will be between those that penalize and those that do not. And does this really deal with the problem noted above? The no contact rule in basketball will be penalty-involving, even though it seems fundamental to the character of basketball.

Two standard responses here both take the form of close philosophical argument,[3] built around the question: *can two sports differ only in their regulative rules?* For formalists, the answer is 'no' – after all, the constitutive rules make it the sport it is. So two activities with the *same* constitutive rules will be the *same* sport (or game), even when the regulative rules differ. But is this correct? Antiformalists such as D'Agostino (1995: 46) will argue that these might be different activities, and hence conclude that formalists have misrepresented the distinction between regulative and constitutive; while moderate formalists such as Morgan might offer a commentary on the distinction, to preserve the formalist account. (Both will stress the place of an *ethos* for sport; Chapter 3 p. 59.)

The example, too, is shared. Consider two games (G and G′) otherwise the same, and resembling football (soccer), but where the first has and the second lacks a 'handball' rule. Formalism requires that these be the same game (since their constitutive rules are the same): anti-formalists such as D'Agostino (1995: 46) will urge that these can be different games. But the chief target (as above) will be undermining the formalist defence by showing that the constitutive/regulative distinction is unsustainable.

The appeal here begins from what is intuitively (or pre-theoretically) obvious from the case: where 'our intuitions are likely to be radically at variance' (D'Agostino 1995: 46) with the formalist conception. So formalists cannot share such intuitions. Might we fill-in the considerations to suggest that these are indeed different games, because games with different *values*? The two games considered (G and G′) are not the same if we can contrast them – say, in terms of the values underlying them.

A key thought here asks about the *motivation* for the inclusion of a handball rule in soccer: if players are generally using their feet, heads, knees and chests to control the ball, a player using his or her hands gains a sizeable advantage. So, roughly, the rule is to preclude that advantage. Thus the rule is explained by appeal to considerations of fairness. But now this (regulative) rule seems embedded in the values of soccer-playing – it seem more than a mere adjunct to the game. Of course, we might suspend the handball rule on certain occasions – say, when playing with children – or modify it to take account of circumstances: perhaps, in an informal soccer game, one is allowed to touch a ball kicked hard in such-and-such a direction, when the alternative is a long chase for the ball across the park. These are not the cases at issue. Rather, in *this* example, each game should be taken as complete in itself.

So we could conclude that they are not the same game or sport (at least in some circumstances), despite sharing constitutive rules – contrary to formalism. Thus, as Morgan (1995: 53) notes, D'Agostino 'maintained that G and G′ . . . are different games, not withstanding that constitutive rules of both are identical'. Equally, regulative rules (understood this way) can have a bearing on what values underlie a particular sport. So are they really the rules earlier characterized as regulative; that is, as those which modify already existing practices? For the practices themselves depend on the values invoked here. So there seems no basis for dividing the rules that neatly and exhaustively leaves one class as purely regulative and the other purely constitutive (with no 'penalty-invoking' function, even if with a regulative one).

In any case, this example suggests that the application of the constitutive/ regulative distinction is problematic. The assumption seemed to be that either the same distinction will be drawn (in the same place, if this is different) in all cases, or that there is no distinction. But this example suggests that uniform treatment will not be possible.

Some defence of formalism

A sophisticated formalist – here represented by Morgan – has a reply, divided into two parts, from imagining two cultural contexts. First consider the two activities (G and G′) in a social context very different from ours, where (for instance) football is revered. Here, Morgan (1995: 53) tells us, 'sheer deference to the game itself', or 'unabashed regard for the rules' (Morgan 1995: 54), will mean that the players of G′ do not use their hands, even though there is no penalty for handball. For it is 'a game of skill in which the use of one's hands plays a limited and at best incidental role' (Morgan 1995: 53).

In this culture, will matches at game G′ differ from soccer matches? Three points are important. First, a situation where rule-breaking *never* arises will be uninformative: if regard for the sport meant that players would not use their hands *whether or not* there was a prohibition against doing so, there might be no genuine difference between the two activities as, say, the spectators encountered them. Is there a rule never transgressed, or no rule at all? *We* cannot be certain. Second, and relatedly, if the example *specifies* that members of this culture never act so as to transgress a handball rule, had there been one, it specifies that the matches will be indistinguishable. But this is not the same as the games being identical: that the behaviour of one side *conforms* to a particular rule differs from saying that players *acted on* the rule (see p. 44). *We* might not know which game was being played, but the players would. So the 'fact' of indistinguishability is irrelevant. Third, the case involves an odd idealization: the reality of many soccer matches is that there are cases of handball which are accidental, but where – since one side would otherwise gain an unfair advantage (say, by scoring a goal) – the referee justly penalizes the activity. Were such an 'accident' to happen while game G′ was being played, there could be no penalty. But then, as the anti-formalists hope, the games will be visibly different. (That cannot be Morgan's intention.)

Again, where did members of this culture get the idea that a good way to proceed involved avoiding even accidental contact with the hand or lower arm – of the kind that would be penalized in football, and therefore (I take it) in game G – rather than simply ignoring such cases.

The trouble with this account (as Morgan concedes) is how close his version comes to saying that, in this culture, handball *is* a constitutive rule of game G': Morgan (1995: 55) actually says that 'to respect the game itself is to respect the constitutive rules of soccer'. But, as it stands, *that* cannot be right – for the point at issue is whether or not game G' *is* soccer, since game G obviously is.

Part of the problem (reflecting D'Agostino's view) is that, at least super- ficially, a game or sporting activity which permitted handball would not be soccer; and for that reason. In Morgan's example, players who grant that the use of hands is permissible then *decide* or choose not to do it. But in what sense is it *soccer* if this is an open choice?

Morgan's answer might turn on his view of the role of constitutive rules. As he points out, for him, there is *some* sense in which constitutive rules regulate, since 'in laying out all the conditions that must be met in playing the game, the constitutive rules . . . place quite real strictures on what one can do as a player' (Morgan 1995: 53).

Is what D'Agostino specified as a regulative rule here being treated con- stitutively? If so, this seems to suggest that the contrast is problematic (one of D'Agostino's contentions, recall) and that, *if* rules must be one or the other, Morgan is simply not discussing the same example.

Suppose the distinction between constitutive and regulative rules were sound [D'Agostino (1995: 46) denies this]. Then rules could only be one or the other, not both.[4] That idea seems built in to the formalist thesis that one can break regulative rules and still be part of the same game, where this does not hold for constitutive rules. But, in granting that games G and G' differ only in their regulative rules (in the example), are we assuming a constitutive force to the handball idea? As we have seen, Morgan seems to assume this. Yet surely the right way to imagine the other game (G') is rather as one might play soccer with a child who had never heard the handball rule and so does not see that touching the ball does infringe the skill, and so forth.

Morgan's idea was to use the first imaginary culture to 'soften up' antiformalist resistance. But his argument remains unpersuasive. To com- plete the argument, consider Morgan's second (imaginary?) culture, which resembles ours in that rule-breaking is widespread. How could the case be made that, appearances to the contrary not withstanding, these are still the same game? Morgan asks us to note what *changes*, from the first to second of these cultures: it is the regard for the rules, expressed as regard for the 'nature' of the game. So *that* is what has disappeared as we move from one context to the other. Then, for Morgan (1995: 54) the case becomes clear: there is only one game in this culture because 'G' is a defective instance of

G' (Morgan 1995: 53) – the fundamental contrast, then, is between a *differ-ent* game and a *defective* game.

In at least *some* circumstances, Morgan is correct: *there*, we understand the second game (G') only as parasitic on the first (G). In that preferred case, these are the *same* game (same constitutive rules), and the second game is some kind of (deliberate?) modification of the first. Yet this cannot save his position, since the counter-view is only that the two games were not obviously identical: which means that they will not be the same in *all* con-texts – and, in fact, Morgan (1995: 54) concedes this, when he writes of only 'virtual complete identity'.[5]

Treating the case in Morgan's manner involves contextualizing the issue in ways we need not. *Sometimes* – say, in order to consider sport at its zenith of performance, with all its (codified) rules in play (as I put it; Introduction p. 5) – elite or professional sport should be regarded as the *real* sport, its rules the *real* rules. *Then* a failure to abide by those rules will have the implications the formalists highlighted: one no longer plays that sport (or game), but merely a 'defective instance'. But we should recognize the con-textual nature of such a conclusion: we come to it only when the context imposes on us a concern with 'sport at its zenith of performance' (and even *this* might not be true). On other occasions, these cases might (with justice) be treated differently. This is the philosophical point: that we should reject *some* idealizations of what sport (*essentially*) is.

Against the insistence that game G' is *necessarily* a defective instance, we should recognize such a conclusion as simply prioritizing one context for playing the sport over others: but why prioritize one over the other? (Com-pare someone claiming that the order 'Slab!' is elliptical for 'please, bring me a slab here and now' [PI §20]. Which is the elliptical one?; and why? We cannot say.)

In line with our earlier point, the mistake lies in concentrating exclusively on elite sport. For, to repeat, sport is played in many contexts – in the park with one's friends as well as on the professional stage, and so on. And these are all *the sport*. Often, the *philosophical* assumption of a definiteness (here, a definite *answer* to the question: is this such-and-such sport?) makes us doubt that, say, the game of soccer in the park is really soccer. On the other hand, it is not obviously some *other* game.

At first glance, then, there seem to be sets of differences (with fuzzy borderlines) between (a) cheating or rule-breaking at *this* game; (b) playing a modified game (football in the park); and (c) playing a different game. [For instance, William Webb Ellis is popularly credited with originating the game of rugby (rugby football) in 1823 when, during a traditional football match of the time at Rugby School, he picked up the ball and ran with it. So he is an enabler for new 'versions', creating new sports.]

If the park example offers the right way to think about Morgan's version of this case, we see *both* how game G' is derivative – it seems a modification of soccer: roughly, soccer without that rule – and how this activity is *transformative* (that is, supports D'Agostino's position) because within this new game (G′) the *action* of handball is impossible: roughly, touching the ball with one's hands does not, indeed could not, count as *handball*. For *ex hypothesi* (for D'Agostino) *handball* is not constituted by the rules of this sport, nor is touching the ball with the hands penalized by the regulative rules.

Morgan might dispute this: for him, once the constitutive rules indicate the importance of using feet, head, and so on (and not hands), the fact that there are no penalties for using hands does not really indicate that one ought not to do it – even though there is no penalty. But in what sense can there be a prohibition here without a penalty; or vice versa? In sport, to be prohibited must imply some downside to the action. For otherwise the prohibition has no teeth. If we imagine that there is a prohibition – even a moral one – we are granting (at least) a kind of penalty. But then the case is not D'Agostino's.

It can seem difficult to move forward here. In summary, the confusing intuitions one might have are:

1   If handball is not included in one of them, G and G′ seem different games – games with different underlying values or aims or intentions.
2   If when playing in the park (with the handball rule dropped 'in some circumstances') we are not playing football, what are we playing? Here, the idea of a defective instance might seem applicable: we changed the rules *from* those of soccer, or *modified* soccer.

On the face of it, the first intuition supports a D'Agostino-type position; the second might support a Morgan-type. But why do we have to choose? Better, what forces us to choose? The answer: a conception of reality as determinate and of philosophy as revealing it to us. It might seem that these either *are* or *are not* the same game – the difficulty would then lie in deciding which. But this is a philosophical thesis (concerning definiteness), not a fact about the world. To explain that idea, though, we need to think in more detail about the constitutive or regulative force of the rules (see pp. 43–4) and about the nature of rules and rule-following (see pp. 44–7).

Here a *contextual* answer is needed as to this sport's *key* features: that is, the ones where contravention seems like 'no longer playing the game'. For that might vary from context to context, and such an answer allows us to recognize both insights. To move forward here, consider again a question the asking of which was, according to John Wisdom (1965: 88), Wittgenstein's greatest contribution to philosophy: *Can you play chess without your Queen?*

In what contexts might such a question be raised? To repeat an earlier case (see Introduction pp. 4–5), I give my grandson a Queen's 'start' in a chess match – are we playing chess? Clearly, no easy answer is satisfactory. My victorious grandson will certainly claim a victory *at chess*: and, equally, we are not playing draughts, or solitaire, or bridge. Still, if the best player in the world gives me a Queen advantage, in a simultaneous display, and (*per impossibile*) I win, I will claim my victory as *at chess* only in a highly qualified way. In these situations, we know what to say – we know the sense in which one can and one cannot play chess without one's Queen. But no answer here is hard and fast, no answer is exceptionless, or fits all situations.

Constitutive and regulative uses of rules

As we saw, Morgan (1995: 53) takes the contrast between the constitutive and the regulative to be hard and fast, between two kinds of rules. Certainly there is something right in the contrast. The regulative rules impinge on me while I am playing, although there may be a slight spillover here (say, my 'bringing the game into disrepute', where I may be punished for transgressions related to the *nature* of that sport). What is typically regulated is any advantage I seek to gain by contravening the rules. So, Maradona's 'Hand of God' goal against England in 1986 at the World Cup in Mexico should have been disallowed – and he should have been penalized – just because he gained an unfair advantage by contravening the rule. Seen in that way, the rule functioned regulatively: there were penalties, and these were within the game – the penalties themselves were permitted by, and therefore part of, the rule structure within that activity.

Yet we saw, earlier, that the handball rule in soccer could often seem constitutive. There, the argument seemed merely concessive: to grant regulative force to constitutive rules. Yet the difficulty here is more profound. For it is assumed that rules are either regulative or constitutive – or the distinction is not hard and fast. But that assumption assigns rules to one camp or the other, or denies there are such camps. And any such strategy grants the view of definiteness mentioned above, by taking (say) constitutiveness as a (fixed) feature of the rule. Instead, we should recognize regulative and constitutive *uses* of rules, granting that a rule may be used in a regulative way in some contexts – as we have seen that the handball rule in soccer should have 'regulated' Maradona's 'Hand of God' goal – and yet may also be used constitutively, as it was in contrasting the two games (G and G′ above).

Wittgenstein articulates the insight here as a fluctuation between criteria and symptoms (PI §354, also Z §438), so that what are sometimes criterial are treated as only symptomatic because they *are* sometimes symptomatic. As we might expect, the difference is contextual: each use responds to a different question, arising from a different context. A clear if simple example is provided by the standard metre (when there was one), a metal bar in Paris. Suppose I assert, 'That bar is one metre long': on some occasions, I am answering a request concerning the length of the bar. Then my reply is bipolar – I might be right or wrong (say, if the bar has been heated without my knowledge). Here, the question is empirical – the answer reflects something like a symptom. But, equally, I may be explaining what a metre is. Now, when I exclaim, 'That bar is one metre long' I am not telling you anything about the bar: roughly, I am explaining how the term 'metre' should be used. Then my claim is not bipolar: the length of that bar is logically tied to metre-hood – it functions as an *exemplar* of metre-hood (Baker and Hacker 1980: 290–2). Or, roughly, its role there is criterial: we use it to explain what is meant by *one metre*. What is worrying, of course, as Wittgenstein notes (PI §354), is that this 'fluctuation' between the two kinds of question can pass unnoticed. And that is exactly what happens when a rule sometimes having a regulative use also has a constitutive one, or vice versa.

Moreover, we can see when (typically) each of these uses would be appealed to. Each might be seen as answering a different kind of question about the rules, or the sport – just as the two remarks about the metre-rule differed, despite being in the same words. If the question asked about the penalties involved, or those that should have been (in Maradona's case), the handball rule is treated regulatively. Now finding rule-breaking will take that breakage to be encompassed by the rules – *regulated* by the rules! But when a question asks precisely what *actions* were performed, the rules are treated on their constitutive understanding; then any contravention may indeed mean that the actions were not performed – that the game was not played (Chapter 7 pp. 121–3).

Our method of reinstating a broadly constitutive/regulative distinction comes to this: that these are *uses* of rules, which different contexts bring to the fore. Then we can see why breaking constitutive rules of a game amounts to not playing that game. For if, in the context, the rule is granted a constitutive use, failure to abide by it will indeed be failure to play that game. So something like the regulative/constitutive distinction is maintained, but for *uses* of rules, not the rules themselves (although sometimes, for convenience or economy, we will speak of constitutive and regulative *rules*).

Some general considerations about rule-following

Here, it is worth saying something explicit about rule-following by laying out briefly eight general considerations, often missed in discussion of rules in relation to sport. The first distinguishes behaviour that *accords* with a rule from behaviour that involves *following* a rule: following a rule amounts, roughly, to behaving in this way *because of* the rule. Thus, my behaviour might accord with the rules of chess, but be the result of pure luck – I am simply making pretty patterns with the pieces of wood. So we cannot just assume that behaviour which accords with a rule is rule-following behaviour. As Searle (2002: 190) puts it, 'I don't just *happen* to drive on the left-hand side of the road in England. I do it *because* it is the rule of the road.' As Searle recognizes, a key feature of rules such as this is that they have 'world-to-rule' direction of fit: the rules influence the behaviour.

Second, and relatedly, the fact that mere conformity with a rule must be distinguished from rule-following implies that one cannot follow rules of which one is ignorant – if my behaviour conforms to the rules of, say, chess, I am not automatically playing chess (hence, following the rules of chess): roughly, to be following the rule, I must be behaving in that way *for that reason*. This is a version of one of the points, deployed in Chapter 1, against Suits's account of sport: the kind of features to which he appeals will not be known by those supposed to be employing them – for instance, his insistence that sports-players 'make life difficult' for themselves. Here, the rule will sometimes be fairly explicit: as a novice chess-player might refer to a diagram of the knight's move before moving the piece. But one can follow the rules much less explicitly. Sometimes, one simply knows the rule. Moreover, in many cases, the rule may play no active role in the agent's deliberation.[6] This would be especially likely if the rule were well-habituated: for instance, experienced drivers in the UK do not refer explicitly to rules of the road before driving on the left – although perhaps an extended period in the USA *might* require one to do so (explicitly). More usually, though, the *presence* of the rule in one's behaviour is clear at the level of justification: I invoke it to explain my doing *this* (driving on the left) rather than *that*. Or, at the least, I agree when *you* invoke it. Again, I cannot (in these ways) *justify* my behaviour by reference to rules of which I am unaware.

A third consideration is that rule-following cannot itself be a matter of rules. How *do* humans follow rules, say the rules of chess? There is a temptation to think that a second rule makes one follow the first rule and so on, but this leads to the regress, on which a further rule is needed to explain the following of the second rule, and one for the following of *that* rule, and so on, indefinitely. Realizing this cannot be right precludes looking for some explanation in the psychology of rule-following: as Wittgenstein was fond of quoting from Goethe, 'In the beginning was the deed' (OC §402). We must just say that humans can follow rules; view ourselves as creatures capable of seeing rules as rules, and acting on them. (This is part of seeing ourselves as *persons* and as *agents*: see Introduction pp. 5–6.)

Fourth, rule-following is not the slavish adherence to rules: rather it is action, where the person has 'learned how to go on' in respect of that rule, learned what constitutes following it. In line with the previous point, this should be seen as something humans can (learn to) do.

Fifth, often, what needs explaining is action which departs from following a rule – reference to the signpost explains why I came this way, while going some other way may need explanation. (Notice that the explanation need not be psychological at all.) So what turns a post with a plank on it by a roadside into a signpost? The answer is that humans take this object as a signpost, treating it in certain central ways, for example, by following it (PI §85, §87). Moreover, if I am following a signpost, my behaviour in going that way is explained: nothing more needs to be said. So only deviations from the path stand in need of explanations (true for figurative as well as literal deviations). These points should guard against trying to understand how something is *done*, when the only possible answer has the form, 'people can just do those sorts of things (perhaps, once they've learned to)'. We cannot explain *how*, say, we typically raise an arm – it is just something we can do. This exemplifies a general point from Wittgenstein: that the hard thing in philosophy is 'to begin at the beginning. And not try to go further back' (OC §471).

Sixth, rules are typically normative, concerning what *ought* to be done, or not done. And, moreover, normative *all the way up/down*. For instance, in chess (one of Wittgenstein's favourite examples, and officially a sport in Cuba), there are the rules of the game, rules for changing those rules, rules for changing *those* rules too, and so on. Further, each set of rules indicates what *ought* to happen (or not happen). The same is true, although not always so clearly formalized, for sporting activities: and, of course, its rules are (partly) constitutive of a particular sporting event. Again, the Olympic movement has rules for changing its charter, and so on – so there is another normative structure here too.

Seventh (and to be argued later: see pp. 47–52), rules are not completely specifiable, since all rules admit of exceptions (compare PI §§84–6). Hence, the (widespread) response of changing the rules, faced with difficulties in a sporting activity, is worrying. For instance, faced with too may false starts in competitions in the short races in athletics, the rules are changed so that 'only one false start per race in events up to 400 metres will be allowed rather than one false start per athlete as in the past' (Mackay 2003: 18). Now, changing the rules would be a sensible step in *all* cases only if the problems were caused by rules being badly formulated: that is, if there *was* a clear rule, which was not (yet) on the statute books. However, this situation cannot obtain, since rules are always 'open' in new situations.

Relatedly, various (mistaken) assumptions here feed the view that rule changes could enforce the *spirit* of the game, so as to always make, say, referee's discretion unnecessary in *every* case by modifying the rules – *mistaken* because any rule admits of more than one interpretation. (This is a point to which we will return in Chapters 6 and 7.) In effect, our argument will be that, in order to see how a rule applies in a particular situation (when it does), we must know what occurred – but that is something we cannot determine in a way that is context-free (or occasion-free).

As a simple example, suppose we feel that the wearing of nose-expander strips is not contrary to the *spirit* of rugby although, as imagined, the rules are constructed by listing what a player is allowed to take onto the field, with (at present) nose-expander strips not on the list. Perhaps this is a case where – although the rules are presently silent – those rules in fact permit the player to use the strips. For their use seems consistent with the use of other aids, such as scrum caps. So perhaps this is not, after all, an exception to the present rules – but clearly that conclusion could be contested and it would be unsatisfactory if different referees or umpires decided differently. Moreover, we have no principled way to resolve the matter: the present rule (as I imagine it) simply enumerates what is permissible. It might therefore seem attractive to modify the rules: say, by adding the nose-expanding strips to the list of permissible objects. Yet this strategy, while dealing with *this* case, would still leave other issues on which the rules were silent, where discretion would be needed. That is to say, issues where another rule change (or rule addition) might seem in order. But, of course, there can never be a point where all the loopholes were closed or all the exceptions excluded. Recognizing this is recognizing our seventh insight into rule-following.

Eighth, explanation of a rule (or a rule-following situation) is essentially in a context, so that more might always be said, if asked (a) a more focused question or (b) a question by a more focused individual – where these come to the same thing. For instance, in this vein, the term 'constitutive' does not seem an especially helpful categorization: lots of sports-playing contravenes (or *apparently* contravenes) various rules without ceasing to be that game. Various kinds of deliberate contravention are crucial; but we can play to other rules in some circumstances (although in some circumstances we might concede that we were not *really* playing, say, cricket, but some four-handed version) and some contravenings also count (both because my side can be punished *within* the match if I contravene a rule by, say, bowling wide and because I will lose my title [in boxing] if I am disqualified).

Some implications for formalism

The central thought here develops our seventh point above, addressing both aspects of the formalist project: it concludes both that any system of rules will encounter exceptions (that rules cannot, in principle, be devised to cover all cases) and that such gaps can never be filled completely by yet more rules, or by reformulations of such rules. The argument is complex, but in essence comes to this – rules cannot cover all cases because there is no *all*, no finite totality of cases. So, whatever rules were set up (and however carefully), a situation could always be envisaged where either those rules were silent or where they produced an answer intuitively contrary to the *spirit* of the game. (Later some real examples are briefly discussed: Chapter 6 p. 104.)

We will sketch an argument for the general claim here; but we are simply showing how exceptions might arise – clearly, these loopholes might then be covered, but doing so just exposes us to other, different loopholes or exceptions. As we will see, that argument will recognize the *occasion-sensitivity* (or speaking-sensitivity: see p. 49) of descriptions, explanations and rules.

Of course, I am not suggesting that the exception-inducing cases are *likely* to occur – or even that they will *eventually* occur in practice: their logical possibility alone precludes rules ever having the kind of all-encompassing determinacy the formalist project assumes.

But we cannot argue simply in terms of rules, for the centre of the argument concerns the nature of descriptions of the world – and especially of true descriptions. At issue is whether, faced with a description of an event which left open or ambiguous *whether*, if at all, a certain rule applied, we could *always* produce a disambiguation of that description which clarifies the matter – as when, eating the Indian meal, we offer an (apparent) 'disambiguation': 'But that is another kind of hot.' Our conclusion will be that this is not always possible.

Disambiguation seems to offer some *natural* or *obvious* way to distinguish cases. But is this really always so? Consider an example from Charles Travis (1997a: 89): 'the leaves are green', said of painted leaves – now, is this just plain true or plain false? Part of the difficulty is that we cannot decide *which*, since it seems natural (on a particular occasion) to say one and, on another occasion, to say the other. And if we cannot decide *which* is to be (obviously) right, then neither can be *obviously* right.

Faced with the disambiguation option, then, we turn our attention to one of the apparently disambiguated pair: if we can generate occasion-sensitivity in respect of it, then the disambiguation strategy looks unhelpful. For it suggests that, however good we are at plugging the gap we started from, yet other gaps might arise. Thus we could talk of, say, 'painted-green leaves' – but this too might be problematic; for instance, some otherwise green leaves might be painted green. These would then be, as it were, double-green.

So our strategy is, for *each* different 'sense' of the term 'green', to find it still amenable to occasion-sensitivity. Of course, one cannot prove that such still-contentious cases can always be found, but it looks promising. As Travis (1994: 175) notes, there is a wide variety of cases here, including the sense 'green' to mean inexperienced ('But that is a different *kind* of green!'). Still, even sticking to some version of (roughly – but much turns on *how* rough) *green-coloured* and *leaves*, there are green leaves painted green as well as brown leaves painted green; we also have leaves dyed; and naturally occurring green leaves. In this last camp, there are those uncontentiously green, and those contentiously green ('Isn't this one a little yellow?'; 'Hasn't that one started to turn red?'). And many more. For some purposes, what I am happy to call 'a green leaf' – and right so to do – will not count for you: you needed an example for your biology class, and neither my painted leaf nor my yellowing (but still green) leaf fits the bill. And you have no truck at all with my jade leaves!

Suppose that we hope to deal with our problems by legislation: so that a new term, 'flurg', says of a leaf precisely what you said in saying (on a particular occasion) 'The leaf is green' (compare Travis 1997b: 119).[7] But this 'is a dead end' (Travis 1997b: 119), because even flurg-saying must now be confronted with 'novel cases, which it may count as describing correctly or not' (Travis 1997b: 119). So that we cannot escape occasion-sensitivity with this kind of stipulation.[8]

Even if disambiguation sorts out *a particular* case, I could not be sure that it could sort out *all* such cases. For any level of grid, why might a yet finer mesh not be needed to avoid, once and for all, unclarity or ambiguity? If this is so, we need the idea of an ultimately fine mesh – but we lack any basis for such a conception. Further, if disambiguation works for these purposes or in this context, we could view it as dealing ('completely') with the issue in this context: and our puzzle is the one *now*, the one in this context. But that makes the puzzle, and the relevant disambiguation, occasion-sensitive.

The point of disambiguation, recall, was to find a *single* version of a rule – or a single description of what happened – to apply exactly to this situation. If I cannot successfully disambiguate – either in a rule or in the description of a situation – I cannot find a *single* reading of the rule (or description): without it, the rules cannot define uniquely one situation; and hence I cannot hope to formulate rules that deal with *all* possible cases. For no description would uniquely identify a range of cases within which no problematic instances could arise. And this occasion-sensitive account of understanding precludes precisely those possibilities of disambiguation.

An occasion-sensitive view of meaning and understanding

The argument, then, draws on considerations in the philosophy of language, which can be introduced with an example drawn from Travis (1989: 18–19), asking us to consider the following situation:

> Hugo sits reading the paper. At his elbow is a cup of black coffee. Across the room is a refrigerator, empty except for a puddle of milk at the bottom. Hugo's partner, Pia, says, 'There is milk in the fridge.' To see that this utterance is occasion-sensitive, consider two cases. First, immediately before the moment described above, Hugo – whose fondness for white coffee is legendary – had looked sadly at the coffee cup. Seeing his look, Pia makes her statement: in doing so, she says (falsely) that the fridge contains milk which might be used to whiten Hugo's coffee. In the second case, Pia had previously asked Hugo to clean the fridge – now she finds him reading the paper, drinking coffee and *still* the fridge is not clean! So Pia utters the sentence, saying (truly) that the fridge contains the puddle of milk.

Notice that the utterance *amounts to* something different on the two speakings just presented – we see this clearly in recognizing that, in the first, what Pia says is false while, in the second, it is true. And nothing else has changed: the word 'milk' still means *milk*, the word 'in' still refers to the inside of the fridge, and so on. Moreover, the indexicals ('here', 'now', etc.), and such like, are not the issue. Pia is talking about *that* very fridge, and at *that* very time. (Not, for instance, looking at the television and commenting on a fridge in California.) In these cases we see the word 'milk' making 'any of an indefinite variety of distinct contributions to what is said in speaking it, and, specifically, to the truth condition for that' (Travis 1991: 242).

And what is true here (of what Pia says) is true more generally: however carefully one builds in details of this situation *only*, other 'readings' of it – and hence other ways of treating it – are always possible (Travis 1996: 454–9). For 'it is clear how a list of such contrasting examples could be continued indefinitely' (Travis 1985: 221), showing (for any case) how it might be read differently by citing circumstances where that makes sense. This is called *occasion-sensitivity* or 'the speaking-sensitive view of words' (Travis 1991: 242). Of course, the primary point here is nothing to do with *words*: instead, it concerns 'the way the world is' (or 'the way things are'). We might both say the world to be such-and-such – then we both speak the truth (independent of the words we use). Given the debt to Travis, as well as the complexity of the issues, I will largely continue to discuss his examples, with a fair amount of quotation. (At the least, this offers a puzzled reader a clear location for an alternative source of discussion.)

Here, three points are important. First, the view is heavily contextual: in some cases, the hearer may not know how to take an utterance, although it *is* in fact clear once the context is taken into account – while it might have misled me, it is not *misleading*. Suppose I work as assistant to both a marine biologist and a cook (McFee 1992: 121; Travis 1984: 78–81); both are interested in red fish – the cook in a surface-swimming red fish, the biologist in a deep swimming one. Now the instruction, 'Bring me a red fish', is clear once I know which of my masters uttered it. Although I might end up confused (I don't know who said it), it is not *confusing*: I might be unable to fulfil the task but – in this case – what I am being asked is perfectly *clear* (Travis 1989: 18–21), in the sense of prescribing one behaviour as a satisfactory response. But particularizing the matter offers this clarity: I know who said it *then*. There may be no *prior* way to guarantee in which of these worlds we find ourselves but (in practice), as participants, we will not be perplexed.

Further (and second), the issues raised cannot simply be treated as amenable to solution through *disambiguation* – which may have been a first thought faced with both the 'milk' and 'red fish' cases mentioned earlier. Could we not just speak more exactly of 'surface-swimming fish' or 'milk suitable for whitening coffee'? Then, the thought might go, the speaking-sensitivity has disappeared: what I *hear* determines which fish to bring – or whether it is *true* that there is milk in the fridge – with no need to explore the details of the occasion or the speaking. But we have seen a number of reasons why this answer is inadequate:

1   *What is said* was always clear in these cases: once we know what occasion this is, or what 'world' we are in, the order or claim becomes clear (and clearly either satisfied in such-and-such way or true/false [respectively]). So there is really no *ambiguity* to be remedied.

2   There is no *natural* or *obvious* way to distinguish cases. My *red fish* story might seem to support the misunderstanding: in trying to simplify the case I indicated how the expressions might be taken. But that is a *red*

herring (!): in general, there is no precise number of possibilities here – for this reason, my artificial cases (with, seemingly, only two outcomes possible) may induce recognition of speaking-sensitivity while clouding our understanding of it.

3   If there really were just two options here, we should be able to say *which* is the correct one on a particular occasion, which we cannot. As Travis (1997a: 90) puts it, this amounts to urging that, say, both of the utterances ascribed to Pia have the *same* truth-value: both are true (or both are false). Thus, for example, someone might urge that she is speaking the *truth* when she says there is milk in the fridge (because it is messy) so she is also speaking the truth when she asserts 'there is milk in the fridge', meaning that Hugo could whiten his coffee: in both cases there *really is* milk in the fridge! But why is *this* the preferred outcome, rather than the other reading of what Pia said? Each seems to reflect what, on that occasion, she said: so why select one as true? As Travis (1997a: 90) notes, 'one must choose in a principled way. What the words mean must make one or other disjunct plainly, or at least demonstrably, true.' And there seems little hope of this.

4   If we take some term in English to be ambiguous (and therefore amenable to disambiguation), 'there must be a way of saying just what these ambiguities are: so a fact as to *how many* ways ambiguous they are' (Travis 1997a: 90: my emphasis). And, again, there seems no hope of finding some *fixed* number here.

5   Further, the 'new' terms, now suitably disambiguated, are still amenable to speaking-sensitivity – as when the cook would ask for a surface-swimming, *red-skinned* fish if he were making fish tacos and a surface-swimming, *red-fleshed* fish if he were making fish stew. Having disambiguated the expression 'red fish' once, I am still left with two occasions, with different satisfaction conditions, where I bring red fish; and on which the word 'red' means *red*, 'fish' means *fish*, and so on. And the artificiality of the case should not disguise its power for us. For we cannot in general *predict* how certain expressions might be used; moreover, we cannot *predict* which of the many understandings (Travis 2000: 4) of a particular situation is the appropriate one for a particular occasion – although (consonant with earlier points) we would typically understand it when we encountered it!

Third, in highlighting one set of contextual features, this position seems merely to demonstrate the inadequacy of the concepts presently deployed – that, say, an ideal language might do better. But that notion of an ideal language is a fiction, because there is no finite totality of conditions to be met in describing a particular scene; relatedly, even if a particular issue could be accommodated by, say, modifying what was urged (so that it covered exclusively *some* of the cases originally envisaged: for instance, by specifying *which* kind of red fish), the problem simply recurs – there is no *basic* level of description or explanation here (see McFee 2000a: 130–1). So that we cannot simply 'disambiguate' (see 3 above) *down* – or *up* – to that level: there will always be a sense of, say, the term 'green' which may escape such disambiguation.

Each of these points has a direct bearing on the view of the completeness of rules. For, by the first, there is no suggestion that the rule is unclear in the situation in which it *is* deployed; by the second, no amount of disambiguation will deal with all cases which could offer exceptions to that rule; by the third, the introduction of new concepts (or new rules) cannot deal with all problems. In this case, it is easy to return to our slogan (see p. 47): that there is no *all* to permit consideration of *all* cases that could lead to exceptions (or cases where rules are silent), no finite totality of cases to consider.

Another way to make the points here focuses on the idea of *completeness* for a set of rules:[9] for in one sense they are *perfectly* complete – namely, in dealing with the actual cases, in an actual context. They are only incomplete in failing to deal with *all* cases, actual and possible. But this cannot be a deficiency in the rules here, since no complete list of such cases is possible, in principle. Yet that, of course, is what formalism requires of such rules. So these considerations make *rules* especially unsuitable as elements in a (genuine) definition, contrary to the claims of formalists (Chapter 1 p. 27).

Rule-following and understanding

We should conclude that the model of rule-following assumed by our formalists is mistaken: it cannot be applied in practice, since any sets of rules may be confronted by new circumstances to which their application (if any) is unclear. And this difficulty is inherent: it cannot, even in principle, be resolved by modifying the rules. Moreover, and for these reasons, rules cannot offer the kind of closure hoped for – in particular, the hope that the application of a rule will always be transparent is a vain hope.

But the use of rules in defining sport is built on just such a hope. For it is assumed that whether or not a rule applies in a particular situation – and, if so, how; and with what outcomes – will be clear and determinate. Indeed, were it not, there could never be a definition in terms of such rules, since there could never be a determination of whether or not the fit of the (putative) definition was exact.

We have seen, then, that the second strand of formalism (as presented by Suits) fares no better than the first – and for similar reasons: it too imports an unreasonable request for definiteness, couched as a requirement of all philosophy. But might some modified formalism, or some related alternative succeed? To address these issues, we turn, in the next chapter, to just such accounts.

3 Rule-following and rule-formulations

The first two chapters have identified two kinds of assumptions which might bedevil any account of sport which focuses exclusively (or even largely) on its rules: these concerned the kind of definiteness appropriate to philosophy and the open-ended nature of rule-following. And our specimen account of sport was Suits's formalism. Yet, to repeat, the argument was not with Suits as such, but rather with tendencies that consideration of his work exemplified.

However, my account of the problems for some such formalism might seem misplaced. So this chapter considers two (and a half) revealing replies that might be offered on behalf of formalism – although, as we will see, all transform it to some degree. The first, typified here by ideas from Meier (pp. 54–6), might be called *more of the same* – it seeks to meet challenges to formalism by identifying further rules, or further *kinds* of rules. Hence it remains true to the formalist project. We will see, though, that it cannot represent a satisfactory strategy. Moreover, consideration of the second (broad) kind of response raises two particular issues which take us onward, while considering the importance of an appeal to sporting practices and the relation of rules to rule-formulations.

Concluding this chapter (pp. 66–8), I turn to how many such views depend on misplaced assumptions of determinacy (again derived from mistaken conceptions of philosophy and – especially – of language). At the centre of the mistake here lies confusing rules with rule-formulations.

To be clear, my thought is not that these are the only possible two or three alternatives to formalism in the literature. Rather, they are the ones that build on the account of rules in a direct and explicit way.

The target throughout this chapter is clear: to ask whether our conclusions about the inadequacy of the project of defining *sport* by reference to its (acknowledged) rule structure might be contested if other accounts of sport (than Suits's) were considered. Centrally, we recognize that our objections cannot be overcome by adding more rules, or more kinds of rules (p. 55), nor by looking for some feature of the rule-following context (such as an *ethos*: p. 58) which either *augments* (p. 63) or *clarifies* the project of formalism: at bottom, the appeal to ethos (in either form) imports the same assumptions about determinacy as its formalist 'ancestor' (pp. 66–8).

Formalism extended: the idea of more kinds of rules

Contrary to my analysis, it might *seem* that formalism is simply beset by sets of counter-examples, cases where formalist thinking to date – say, as manifest by Suits – does not correctly draw the line between sport and non-sport. (It might even seem that inventing and dealing with such counter-cases was *the* business of philosophy.) Then one response to any questioning of the adequacy of formalism might draw yet more distinctions within the kinds of rules involved, maintaining the central feature that the appeal was still to *rules* – hence this was still (modified) formalism. For example, Klaus Meier's 'auxiliary rules' specify and regulate 'eligibility, admission, training, and other pre-context requirements' (Meier 1985: 70 quoted 1995: 28). Later, Meier (1985: 71 quoted 1995: 28) offers three examples:

> first, rules pertaining to the participant's safety or exposure to physical stress, such as 'all football players must wear a helmet with a fixed faceguard' or 'no player may pitch more than three innings in any one age-group baseball game'; second, specific empirical restrictions placed upon participants concerning such attributes as age, sex, or weight; third, an entire grouping of arbitrary restrictions selectively imposed for a variety of social or political reasons.

In explanation of the third class, Meier (1995: 28) says that it:

> includes such things as the deliberate exclusion of professional athletes, representatives of the Republic of South Africa, or a limitation of no more than three athletes from any one country in a particular sports meet.

These considerations do bear (in different ways) on sport and sporting events:[1] it would be a mistake to dismiss all of them as having no such bearing. Considerations of these kinds can *seem* fundamental to (some) sporting contexts without turning neatly into constitutive rules, regulative rules, or even 'rules' of skill. Then, if one is already a formalist, the strategy of adding yet more rules – or even more kinds of rules – must seem the right one.

Some apparent counter-cases to Suits's version of formalism might be accommodated in these ways – by seeing that rules of sports apply to (at least some of) these circumstances. For instance, it seems central to some sports that competitors are of approximately equally weight (that there would be little competition were this not so) where this was neither constitutive of the sport – you could certainly break this rule with impunity, although the outcome might be dull – nor need it be penalty-involving. Moreover, some cases in the third category seem obviously *relevant* – the decision to boycott South Africa in its apartheid days was (one might think) a *sporting* decision: apartheid was applied within sport[2] and contravened some fundamental *sporting* ideals. So the addition of auxiliary rules might, in this way, meet such an apparent counter-case: considerations not (obviously) covered by Suits.

Meier's concern is clearly that some problems for formalism arise because not *enough* is included within a traditional view of the rules of a sport. But, as cases remind us, there must be limits here. For example, eighteen college-level athletes were suspended from competitive participation in sport by the National Collegiate Athletic Association (NCAA) for 'abusing their textbook allowances, breaking NCAA rules . . . According to NCAA rules, schools may buy books for athletes only if they are 'required' for classes they [the athletes] are actively taking' (*Los Angeles Times, Sport* 2003a: D2).

Thus one student, Scott Stevens, broke these rules by using 'his book allowance to acquire a biology book that was recommended, but not required, by his professor' (*Los Angeles Times, Sport* 2003a: D2). This outcome might seem unjust – and perhaps a little silly. The point here is that, although rules of the Association, these are not rules of the sport. If one does go down the road of auxiliary rules, one must be wary of including too many regulations that are not part of the sport.

But why – other than an attachment to formalism – should we choose this option? For instance, even Suits (1995a: 19; quoted Meier 1995: 29) denies that some of the 'rules' Meier believes in (auxiliary rules) are best seen as rules – or, at least, as rules like the others under consideration: 'the rules to which judges of performance address themselves are . . . rules of skill rather than constitutive rules'. What turns on calling them *rules* here? It may be better to ask: '*Rules* instead of . . . what?'. The beauty of rules here *seemed* to lie in circumscribing the activity – that its rules sort out what was and what was not an example of such-and-such a sport. But we already have two different reasons for thinking that hope to be vain: no set of rules would cover all cases, and the (assumed) determinacy was not required (for philosophical purposes).

So, first, all of these are not best seen as rules, even when there are formalized rules in the offing – because there are 'rules all the way up' (rules, and rules for changing those rules, and rules for changing those rules: Chapter 2 p. 46). And there are alternative ways to accommodate them: for instance, following D'Agostino in referring to an *ethos* for sport (see p. 56). Second, not *all* these issues could be resolved by augmenting rules. (And, if not, then formalism is wrong on that point.) For there is no *all* here – no finite totality of cases or situations.

Were the problem simply that the account of rules was not *rich* enough, with this generating the counter-examples to (say) Suits's formalism, attempting to answer this problem within the structure of formalism would make sense. So, if the criticisms just amounted to a few counter-examples, the 'more of the same' idea might be a legitimate strategy. But, even were that granted, we would still have the criticisms of the *project* (Chapter 1 pp. 28–31): in particular, the criticism that it misconceives the level of determinacy needed (or possible) *for philosophical purposes*. Indeed, the mistaken understanding here makes it seem that the criticisms amount to a set of counter-cases or counter-examples.

More importantly, criticism of the model of rule-following is *fundamental* (Chapter 2 pp. 44–52): no rules can fill *all* gaps, because there is no finite totality of gaps (from Chapter 1). So, however many insights it may generate along the way, this strategy is bankrupt.

Alternatives to formalism – the *ethoi* position

However, the literature contains another strategy, with D'Agostino (1995) a classic case, and Morgan (1995) a more recent and more subtle exponent. On this view – in addition to an importance accorded to rules – important weight is given to an *ethos*, explained as 'that set of unofficial, implicit conventions which determine how the rules of that game are to be applied in concrete circumstances' (D'Agostino 1995: 48–9).

For the game as represented by its rules, in their pristine state, differs from real instances of the game: D'Agostino (1995: 47) cites the contact/non-contact nature of basketball, as the fans encounter it at (say) a game at Staples Centre (where the Los Angeles Lakers play, in the NBA). That is, the rules (beloved by formalists) maintain their purity by contrast with the game as played and watched. But this separates the game from its rules, which is surely a mistake. Instead, as Morgan (1994: 216) suggests, 'When we prick the rational core of a practice like sport, we find not something natural, pure, inviolate, or necessary – not an essence – but something social, impure, and contingent' (Morgan 1994: 216). In (supposedly) missing this, a Suits-type formalism requires us to explain in what activities the game or sport consists, in ways (in principle) impossible – this insistent idealization of sport D'Agostino (1995: 44) calls its 'Platonism'.

Recognizing such idealization suggests that formalism could be modified to a more realistic view of rule-breaking; and especially of the penalties involved, where presently it 'effaces the distinction . . . between playing and playing fairly' (D'Agostino 1995: 43). So this formalism fails by ignoring 'the role which the ethos of a game plays in defining various game-derivative notions' (D'Agostino 1995: 47). For what, say, *foul* in basketball really means must address the notion of a *foul* as it is applied in the game, not just what the rules suggest. Hence one insight needed to combat formalism lies in recognizing how the formalist overlooks the contrast between acceptable and non-acceptable rule-violations. Thus 'in real life, we talk of a fair result of a game of basketball . . . even if rule violations occurred' (Loland 2002: 6). But this would become obscure if every rule-violation were treated equally.

Moreover, the objection to some activities not contrary to the rules becomes clear if that objection resides in the ethos. For instance, in high-level soccer in the UK, when a player is injured and players from the other side have control of the ball, (a) they will typically kick it out of play, to allow the injured player to receive assistance, and (b) the side of that injured player (who receive the ball after it has been kicked out of play) will return possession of the ball to the side that had it at the time of the injury's recognition. But, in a match in the English Premiership between Arsenal and Sheffield Wednesday, a player not familiar with this convention 'caught the ball and scored a goal' (Tamburrini 2000: 16). It was clear to the fans that something untoward had occurred; but '[t]he referee condoned the goal, as no formal rule had been violated' (Tamburrini 2000: 16). Moreover, this goal proved decisive in an important match. The manager of the 'winning' side, mindful of the convention here, offered to replay the match. Although this suggestion was not ultimately adopted, it indicates the firm nature of this particular conventional restriction: it was, we might conclude, part of the ethos.

An ethos-account, then, can do justice to features of rule-following or rule-breaking not captured by a blunt statement of the rules: recall the idea ascribed to D'Agostino (Chapter 2 p. 38) that the values of the two games (G and G′) might differ although their constitutive rules were the same; and that this difference might be recognized in recognizing the *ethos*. The ethos thus conceived plays a role 'in *defining* various game-derivative notions' (D'Agostino 1995: 47: my emphasis): that is, the project is still conceptualized in terms of definition.

One task, then, is to explore the *ethoi*: that is, to observe our institutionalized application of the rules of sport, and to describe that application carefully and systematically – that could remind us of features we recognize, but are neglecting. It might also give greater richness to our accounts of sport, by seeing some of what occurs as *part of* the sporting event – hence, moving aware from an idealized, and pared down, view of what sport *really* is.

For instance, we are familiar with 'cheats prospering' in the 'real world' of sport. For example, in a match against Turkey in the 2002 World Cup, the great Brazilian footballer, Rivaldo, 'feigned the most extreme pain, pretending ... [a Turkish player] had volleyed the ball into his face. All the world (including Fifa) could see the ball had struck Rivaldo's knee' (Mitchell 2002: 7).

Discussion of the *nature* of rules in sport should have such cases in view. This particular case might seem like a bad refereeing decision. Yet players might do this sort of thing while agreeing that it was wrong. As the former England rugby player Brian Moore (2003: 49) commented, in matches with France: 'The only rule was never to retaliate when the ref could see. Was it fair play? Were England playing the game? No, but it worked: which was good enough for me.'

Such instrumental accounts implicitly accept that there *is* a prohibition against such play, independent of rules against it; one not simply avoided by avoiding the referee's notice. But what is the nature of that prohibition? Does it bear at all on the *nature* of sport?

As we will see (Chapter 6 p. 105), it makes sense to grant a prohibition here *even though* (a) the rules of the sport may be silent or (b) the traditional 'reading' does not support such a prohibition – by arguing [re (a)] that there is a *principle* at work, or [re (b)] that the traditional reading is wrong. (Of course, this point is independent of what we think of, say, the actual case of Rivaldo.) So there is a sense of how the game should be played – a sense in which (as Moore describes it) England were not 'playing the game'.

This view, then, tries to look outside (formal) rules and rule-formulations to, for instance, what does not *need* ruling out. Often, appeals to the *spirit* of rules seem to just invoke such an ethos. Recall the use (for example, in rugby) of enumeration: that is, the use of, say, lists of what items are permitted on the field (Chapter 2 pp. 46–7). Such rules are especially problematic, having as it were *just* rules, with no *spirit* of the rules to which appeal might be made in tricky cases. For instance, this might be replaced by, say, some specific exceptions, combined with appeal to an ethos. Thus, a rule precluding the taking of a machine gun onto the rugby field would not be needed, although it might seem worth excluding, say, knuckledusters from the scrum. That there might be justified exclusions not listed, but nonetheless excluded, seems to depend on an ethos. One might agree, then, that the critique of formalism shows 'that sport is best understood with reference to the social and cultural contexts within which it takes place' (Loland 2002: 6). For a richer account of sport will follow from less idealization, and greater recognition of sport's embeddedness in its context.

We have treated the views of D'Agostino and Morgan as variants of a single *ethos* position. But important differences between them indicate positions of different kinds. And, since our concern is with trends or tendencies represented rather than with individual authors, we can begin with broad brush-strokes. Any attempt to map the terrain here should say something about these differences. Yet both accounts share with Suits a set of fundamental mistakes concerning rules and determinacy inherited from the *project* of formalism, as we will see (pp. 66–8). That is one way in which the critique of formalism *might not* represent the most useful starting point!

Again, our argument here does not require considering the ethos position as a whole: showing its dependence on already discredited conceptions both of determinacy and of rule-following gives reason to reject it. So a part of this critique simply highlights that this account cannot *ultimately* offer more than is imported from its assumptions (taken over from formalism or from a dated view of philosophy – *essentialism*).[3]

Two versions of *ethos* account

The broad contours of an ethos account draw heavily on D'Agostino's version. Recognizing the distinctiveness of Morgan's view involves distinguishing two different answers to a fundamental question; hence two ways to deploy the idea of an ethos here. The question is: *why should we act in accordance with the ethos?* How can it function normatively to indicate what one ought to do in such-and-such a sporting situation? The central issue, then, is how an ethos account explains the difference 'between impermissible and unacceptable behaviour and the disparate way in which it treats each' (Morgan 1995: 60), since this was *one* (or *the*) issue on which Suits-type formalism was supposed to founder.

As we have seen (Chapter 2 pp. 36–7), part of this issue comes to *the problem of penalties* (D'Agostino 1995: 45): how can rule-breaking be penalized, if to break the rules is (really) to be playing another game? An answer insisting on a rigid contrast between constitutive rules and regulative ones would be suspect in the eyes of those like D'Agostino (1995: 45) who deny such a hard and fast contrast. But, more than that:

> players and game officials have . . . conspired to ignore certain of the rules of basketball . . . in order to promote certain interests . . . e.g. to make the game more exciting than it would be if the rules were more strictly enforced.
>
> (D'Agostino 1995: 47)

So that we have, instead of a dependence on formal rules, 'an unofficial *system* of conventions which determines how the official rules of the game will be applied in various concrete circumstances' (D'Agostino 1995: 47). On this view, then, we ought to behave in line with the demands of *ethos*, rather than rules: recognizing this is (supposed to be) acknowledging the reality of sport, rather than its idealization.

This gives us a sketch of the ethos at work, highlighting its (potential) normative impact, by showing that '[t]he ethos of a game . . . distinguishes between those official judgements that are acceptable, and those which are unacceptable' (D'Agostino 1995: 47). This description of the ethos in operation introduces two rather different ways in which it might be understood: as Morgan (1994: 226, 1995: 60) rightly characterizes them, a normative and a descriptive 'reading'.

On the descriptive reading, understanding the ethos teaches 'what social standards and norms we presently use to judge and watch the games we judge and watch' (Morgan 1995: 56). That seems to amount to observing the 'unofficial *system*' (above) in operation. But does this really tell us about the games themselves, or only something about (say) our reception of them?

The difficulty for the descriptive reading lies in getting normative force from the social and cultural context: we should be alive to the issue (or danger) of confusing 'social description with normative justification' (Morgan 1995: 51). Suppose we have, for instance, full details of the corruption (and such like) in respect of the bidding for, and organizing of, the Salt Lake City Winter Olympics (compare Jennings and Sambrook 2000: 19–48). Defects at this level are no guide at all to what *ought* to have happened – or, more perspicuously, what *Olympism* requires. The demands of sport may not be actualized. If we treat the context as providing a description of what goes on, we cannot get the normativity: for what happens on a particular occasion can be (normatively) flawed. And this is one reason why appeal to what actually occurs can be unhelpful.

However, appeal to the idea of a *practice* may seem to give a new lease of life to a version of descriptive account here (as perhaps when authors speak of *moral practices*) or to justification by tradition, sometimes invoked via the idea of a language-game.[4] Typical views hold that such practices have a force '[a]s philosophers we must not attempt to justify' (Malcolm 1963: 120). So the connection of ethos account(s) to the idea of 'sport as practice' (Butcher and Schneider 2003: 160–1) should be recognized: reference to an ethos is one way to say what practices offer, and vice versa – which puts a yet greater stress on the aspect of the practice as something simply *done*, something standing in no need of an independent justification. Moreover, standard objections to this kind of position (regularly voiced when the notion of a language-game appears in philosophical writing), applied (as here) to *sport*, can be found in respect of its other manifestations.

A similar appeal to practices, justified by tradition, has been visible in the United Kingdom recently, in appeals for countryside pursuits: in rehearsing some of the misconceptions in this example, we expose some of those inherent in the appeal to practices. Three such considerations are:

- The appeal to ethos, practice or tradition alone provides at best weak argumentative support: compare Nielsen (1982: 69), in respect of the idea of religious belief:

    > that at all times and at all places, even among the most primitive tribes, there have been sceptics and scoffers, people who, though perfectly familiar with the religious language-game played in their culture, would not play the religious language-game . . .

    Of course, such views cannot be rejected simply by pointing to their conflict with the dominant tradition. Further, the descriptive version of ethos or 'practice', reporting the actual judgements of people, takes us only so far. As the case of long division should remind us (Baker and Hacker 1985b: 71–2), such a statistical notion cannot generate normativity (that is, how people as a matter of fact behave cannot tell us how they should). For suppose most long division is done by children, learning the principles. Then it makes perfect sense to say that the majority view is mistaken: the consensus is beside the point.

- The concern is only to defend *some* pursuits; that is, there is an inherent value component. Here, the concern might seem to relate simply to *humane* treatment. Yet what counts as humane here? To apply, suppose we agree that sport is 'culturally valued' (Alderson and Crutchley 1990); still, is the valuing warranted? For it cannot be enough to grant that a group *does* value something – as above, we must ask if it *should* do so.

- Valuable, in what way? Again the comparison with the countryside issue has something to tell us. For the objection to, say, hunting foxes with dogs is often assumed to be that this activity is cruel to foxes. But this is mistaken: the issue is not cruelty to animals. What is centrally objectionable about hunting foxes with dogs is that people take pleasure from it. Thus, if it were shown that foxes were a pest, or vermin, killing them might be necessary (for human comfort). (Let such an argument simply be granted here.) Then we would simply look to humane treatment, in line with the point above. Instead, what is repulsive about the practice is that people take pleasure from it. So that we should not be *that* kind of person, nor teach (or train) others to be so: thus this practice might tell us about ourselves – it might tell us something bad! And, again, that would give us a reason to *reject* the practice – as here.

In these three ways, a tension exists between what simply describing the activity or tradition could offer us and what is needed to *explain* the normativity of rules by reference to such an activity. That it *has been* done in the past does not guarantee that it *should* be done.

Is a pure ethos account guilty in this way of 'discarding the formal rules as a standard of legitimation' (Morgan 1995: 60)? It must seem so, if this view involves 'deploying . . . ethos as a legitimation device' (Morgan 1995: 59). But that will be problematic when the ethos is conceptualized descriptively; which is perhaps why, for D'Agostino, the normative force of sports playing requires formal rules and ethoi 'jointly' (D'Agostino 1995: 49).

Ethos: a normative account

Rejecting the descriptive reading, Morgan distinguishes his views from D'Agostino's by explicitly highlighting their different accounts of how the ethos legitimizes rule-following. For D'Agostino, 'the interests of the insti-tutionalized forces . . . presently frame our compliance or non-compliance with the rules' (Morgan 1994: 226). By contrast, Morgan's own account will give more weight to a justificatory force here, by appealing to 'the distinctive rationality and the array of goods and virtues that define sport-ing practices' (Morgan 1994: 226).

Of course, the position criticized may not be D'Agostino's own; but he certainly writes as though the matter were descriptive – as though it might be resolved with a survey! For example, of determining 'the conventions which guide game officials', we are told '[o]ne must make this determination empirically' (D'Agostino 1995: 47). Such concerns, justly characterized by

Morgan (1995: 56) as 'what social standards and norms we presently use', easily seem descriptive. This cannot offer a profound understanding of games because it 'confuses games with their social setting' (Morgan 1995: 56) – it leaves a sport-shaped hole in the theory (Chapter 8 pp. 131–2).

As Morgan notes, one danger here is relativism: if we simply describe the activity (here, the sport) as it goes on in the society, other societies may (perhaps, will) support different descriptions of 'what goes on'. Giving each equal weight may lose the normative force of what should happen, thereby succumbing to the relativistic thought that, here, anything goes (Chapter 10 p. 168). Equally, there is a danger in looking for normative force in ways that ignore social contexts: indeed, this is often what the accusation of *idealization* (or, worse, *essentialism*) amounts to.

A difficulty in the other direction is that – to the degree that one's conception is genuinely normative – we no longer really describe the practices (naturalistically). Thus, Morgan (1994: 224–5) characterizes his view of *ethoi* as:

> those attitudes, commitments, values, goods and virtues that are necessary to sustain the ways of life embodied in sporting practices. In its most basic sense, the ethos furnishes a compelling reason to make the gratuitous difficulties of such practices the central point of engaging in them. More specifically, it supplies a reason to take seriously and pursue diligently the standards of excellence that infuse the aim of the game, a reason to try to win in whatever way the game demands.

Then these are not just what has happened in the past. We are not really *describing* any extant practice: rather, this appeals to some idealization of the way its rules (and so on) have developed conceptions of what should happen for us, rather than to the real past of the sport – that leaves unclear how the rule structure is dependent on the practice.

To introduce a picture of rule-following meeting such a challenge, Norman Malcolm (1995: 6) urges that 'a rule does not determine anything *except* within a setting of quiet agreement' (my italics). So that, outside the context of a practice, rules are inert, determining nothing. But, in that setting, they do! This, then, is one thread of a view such as Morgan's: that a kind of 'community agreement' is crucial, because presupposed by the possibility of rule-following. In summary, then, for Morgan, the ethos or practice provides normativity to his account, doing so roughly via community agreement (see Chapter 4 p. 74).

If this is roughly right, it allows us to distinguish three kinds of contrast to Suits-type formalism, not two. Originally (see p. 56), we added the ethos account to the *more of the same* account (from Meier): but one of our *ethoi* accounts of rule-following behaviour in sport replaces formalism with the ethos picture (D'Agostino) while the other aims (roughly) at supplementing formalism with ethos (Morgan). So we should recognize D'Agostino's account as *now for something completely different*, rather than a defence of a modified formalism. (In this light, a Morgan-style view might be *something old, something new*.)

A formalist account 'supplemented by an account of the ethos (the social context)' (Morgan 1995: 50) might seem impossible in principle: is not the notion of an ethos *inimical* to formalism? Put roughly, Morgan's position is, rather, that reference to an *ethos* helps make sense of the formalism without being separable from it – his appeal is still to the deep logic of the sport, embedded in its rules. Thus Morgan (1994: 249 note 41) claims to stake his formulation 'on the acceptance of the logic of game playing itself', in contrast to Suits (1978: 144), who grounds his account in rule-acceptance. Because – for Morgan – the nature of the practice relates to the logic of sport, this use of an *ethos* does not undermine his formalism.

Perhaps such considerations concerning its descriptiveness make D'Agostino's view unsatisfactory: it cannot readily offer the normative justifications that it promised. Morgan seems clearly right that *pure* practices cannot provide normativity. So do we really need to give any credence to all *three* views here? But then only *pure* practices can offer the fact of their existence in their defence or justification. So a view giving due weight to the *fact* of the practice or activity will contain insights, even if (for some purposes) we reject it.

One difficulty throughout is recognizing what should make a person reject one account – and, especially, reject it in favour of another – rather than just acknowledging whatever insight the account embodies. This argumentative point is best served by trying to develop a coherent position in response to one's own major issues or perplexities (rather than seeking to cover all cases; or to immunize one's account against counter-cases). Later (pp. 66–8), I sketch reasons to put aside the project to which these three accounts offer answers. For now, though, note how Morgan (1995: 62) summarizes his view:

> I have argued . . . that the standard account of formalism [by which he means roughly Suits's, but with his modifications], which defines a game in terms of its formal rules, is quite capable of settling what constitutes playing a game, and playing a game fairly.

Its doing so assumes that, faced with a dispute about what constitutes a game, one can read off 'the underlying purpose of the game by considering its rules' (Morgan 1995: 62). These quotations encapsulate three ideas for later discussion:

1 Is the term 'defines' here indicative of commitment to the project of determinacy (see pp. 66–8)? And are there other indications?
2 Is this really formalism? Morgan (1995: 62) answers 'yes', since this account grants 'the primacy of the rules advocated by formalism'. But

one might wonder whether, in order to fulfil its requirements by its own lights, it must incorporate non-formalist notions; or if it will prove to be mistaken by failing to do so (Chapter 4 p. 82).

3   The issue of reading off 'the underlying purpose of the game by considering its rules' (Morgan 1995: 62) – see pp. 64–6.

Pursuing this discussion takes us quite some distance from sport (directly) and for quite a time: but doing justice to the complexity of the issues requires it.

Rules and the purposes of sport

A key thought (Chapter 2 p. 45) was that a rule cannot determine its own application (PI §§201–2): that, in context, someone knowing perfectly well the rules of, say, soccer might still face an open question as to what (rule-followingly) to do at any stage of the game. For what that rule amounts to here is *contextual* (and therefore occasion-sensitive [Chapter 2 pp. 49–51], where others might appeal to an ethos). While the rules cannot do the job alone, can the kind of *rules-plus-ethos* favoured by Morgan?

The thought here is to augment one's understanding of the game by appeal to its purpose, or goal, or underlying logic. In his summary, Morgan claims to find the game's underlying purpose from its rules. In its dependence on rules, then, this account is still fundamentally formalist, but going beyond simple formalism in granting that reference to an ethos answers some central questions: here, questions of how the application is determined, if not by the rules (alone). Morgan (1994: 224) cites with approval the idea of rules as making 'clear the "aim of a game"' (Searle 1969: 34 note). One could broadly agree with this, as part of the insight behind, say, Suits's commitment to the 'lusory attitude' (Chapter 1 p. 18): that, in general, one plays games voluntarily in the sense of choosing to commit oneself to the rules (even when, say, the stronger pressure seems to be the screams of one's children). First, games will typically be framed in terms belonging to that game. The rules of bridge, for example, include 'declarer', 'trump', 'follow suit' – notions which must be explained in learning bridge (at least for those without knowledge of complementary card games, such as whist). So making sense of the game is partly *internal* to it, since one must understand what actions rule-relatedness permits. Second, teaching someone to play, for instance, bridge involves teaching that person both to play correctly and to strive to win. So we have overlapping insights here.

For Morgan (1995: 50), it is *not true* that 'one cannot read off the purpose of a game by citing the rulebook, its system of rules'. This double-negative conceals a difference as to *why* it is not true that one cannot do so. For Morgan, there *is* such a purpose – 'the major point of sporting endeavours' (Morgan 1994: 211), identifying 'the social logic of these practices' (Loland

2002: 4). He thereby concludes that one *can* read off its purpose from those rules, properly understood.

But rules of sports cannot *show* a purpose because sports cannot *have* a purpose ('by definition') if one thinks of that purpose in *other* than an internal way. And certainly the most natural way to think of purposes is *extrinsically*. Then, it is false that you *cannot* read off the purpose from the rules, but equally false that you can. For the problem lies in the idea of *purpose*, not the possibility of *reading off*.

Of course, if the purpose of the game is purely internal, one *can* read off something of that purpose by reference to the *nature* of the sport. But we have shown a distinctive *nature* (or essence) to be unavailable to the theorist of sport (Chapter 1 pp. 28–31). Hence reference to a *nature* for a particular sport here must be treated differently. Clearly sets of underlying constraints in most sports, with some connection to rules, seem characteristic of that sport. For example, in cricket, there is a rule against the bowling of wides – the bowling side is penalized (in quite a mild way) if the deliveries bowled are too far from the batsman; that is, too far to allow him a reasonable chance to hit the ball, given his (assumed) skill-level. At its *heart* or in its *nature*, then, cricket has a conception of giving the batsman a reasonable opportunity to display his skill (Chapter 7 p. 112). To this degree, something can be read off from the rules together with our understanding of them. But doing so is seeing cricket's *principles* (in a sense due to Dworkin 1978: 72, 1986: 15–20), not looking in a confused way at its rules. Or so I will urge (Chapter 6 p. 105). In part, my reasoning there applies, to a case such as this, the insights from our discussions into the occasion-sensitivity of rules.

For (say) Morgan by contrast, there is 'what the rules really say', the logic of the game, the goal of the game. For me, these are *either* versions of the view of determinacy I have been rejecting (as essentialism) *or* amount to something close to my own view, which (as we will see, pp. 80–2) puts less weight on the idea of a practice and more weight on the logic of action. And one feature differentiating these responses, of course, is their take on the role of individuals: I am content with the idea of *individual* agents in ways many theorists of practices are not (McFee 2002: 124–32). But this will be fundamental when we inquire in what sense the rules of sports must be shared: my answer invokes a logical requirement for shareability, not the practical requirement for being presently shared (the kind of community view highlighted above). Again, I happily concede that *sports* should have 'a wide following' (from Suits; Chapter 1 p. 19); for me, though, this requirement has a quite different nature. In reality, for Suits too, sport inherited the requirements that relate to rules from the status of sports as a species of *games*, with the 'wide following' requirement modifying this account. My account stresses individuals as agents – a community of the like-minded or the like-tongued is not assumed (although these might still be argued for); further, the stress is on *agency* (see Introduction pp. 5–6) – nothing further is needed to explain the fact that persons can 'do stuff', beyond recognizing that they are persons;[5] moreover, the requirement for *publicity* is a requirement for the objectivity of normative conditions (as will be urged: Chapter 5 pp. 77–8), not for their being practically shared.[6]

These sections have explored the insights behind other (than Suits's) ways to fulfil a broadly formalist project. The ethos position had something right: roughly, that different practices lead to different *forms* of normative behaviour – that is, the practices inflect (at least) the *forms* of behaviour; and that much in sport is circumscribed, but not by rules (for example, 'how high one throws the ball in tennis' (PI §68). But, as we shall see, these insights are better captured in other ways. Moreover, there is a yet more fundamental line of criticism of its project.

More fundamental criticisms

If the considerations of the previous sections have weight, the addition of an appeal to *ethos* might not look attractive as an alternative to formalism. (And these might be strengthened from the concerns with ethos and normativity; Chapter 4 pp. 75–82.) But a more fundamental line of objection can be mounted, taking Morgan as our example once again.

We have seen how the aspiration towards a 'rational demarcation' (Morgan 1994: 225) of sports was misguided. Either Morgan's *ethos* account is an attempt to write in – by means of *ethoi* – what he thought is missing from an account of rules in the manner of Suits's formalism, or it leaves those rules (and their application) open, but tells us that *in practice* ethoi close this opening. If his intention is the first, he is hoping (against hope) for what cannot be: one cannot fill in the gap between rules and applications or instances. As we saw (Chapter 2 p. 52), one cannot fill it with rules, and neither can one can fill it with *ethoi*. The reason in both cases is the same: that there is no *specific* gap to fill, no set of *all* applications or cases to cover. On this version, we see explicitly how the gap is assumed because a view of determinacy is imported.

On the contrary reading of Morgan's account, highlighting the other alternative, the supposed gap will now be left open: roughly, this amounts to living with the gap. But this would accept what one *has* as second-best: that a better arrangement would be found *if only*. . . . This too is contrary to the arguments throughout this work – lacking any idea of *completeness* here (Baker and Hacker 1980: 79–81: see Chapter 2 p. 52)[7] we have no reason to think such an account incomplete.

Another, more fundamental line of criticism here arises from recognition that Morgan inherits from formalism the flawed project of such demarcation: roughly, the aspiration to define *sport*. Morgan's own summary (quoted above) characterized his as a project that 'defines a game in terms of its formal rules' (Morgan 1995: 62). But this shared assumption of determinacy is also visible elsewhere. Consider the argumentative strategy for the two games (G and G′), which were – roughly – football and football-without-handball respectively (Chapter 2 p. 38): there Morgan urges that the (apparent) two games *definitely* are the same game. His technique involved insisting that appearances to the contrary are explicable: for instance, in cases where G′ is a 'defective instance'. Our interest lies in his motivation, and in the assumptions he imports.

First, it is important for Morgan that these are definitely the same game because, otherwise, this is a counter-case to the formalist picture of the relation between rules and games. Implicitly, then, he accepts the view of logical connections as all-or-nothing – that, *if* there is a counter-case, the (putative) definition is wrong. For only on that view is this a worry. Second, there is no room here for variety among different cases; or even a variety of different contexts. For Morgan, there must be only one game in the example – and that conclusion should be absolute: at the least, game G′ either definitely *is* or definitely *is not* the same game as G. Third, the dispute is of philosophical importance; hence, the outcome of finding that this is, or is not, the same game must be thought to do some philosophical work. And that *work* must somehow reflect on the soundness of the concept *game* – hence, the soundness of all concepts.

Formalism seems to begin with Frege's completeness requirement for the soundness of concepts: 'To a concept without a sharp boundary there would correspond an area that had not a sharp boundary-line all round' (Frege 1960: 159). But that is really no area at all! So this picture captures (and explains) the requirement for determinacy. Rejecting this analysis, the friends of an ethos approach declaim:

> Frege says unto you of old: a concept with vague boundaries cannot be called a concept at all; but I say unto you: such a concept may serve just the same purposes as a concept with a sharp boundary.[8]

That is, they advocate '(sharp) rules plus a smudge-operator'. But that merely tinkers with a picture of determinacy for rules and concepts that (following Wittgenstein: Chapter 1 pp. 28–31) I am attacking wholesale. Adding an ethos, and reference to the essentially social character of sporting activities, leaves the same underlying assumptions. For the point cannot simply be that 'the demand for completeness of definition for all our words would be utopian . . . as long as concepts fulfill the practical purposes for which they were devised' (Baker and Hacker 1980: 432).

That is, we cannot simply regard philosophical demands on our account of sport as setting the standard impractically high, so that we have something roughly right, or a first approximation – as the ethos account took its stand against idealization. For the picture of being *completely right* remains unchanged. So such a model for completeness reimports (traditional) determinacy as a *possibility* in a way that makes no sense. The position rejected presupposes 'a distorted conception of what it is for a set of rules to be complete (or incomplete)' (Baker and Hacker 1980: 432). As implied previously (Chapter 1 p. 30), the concept 'game' is not in any way defective – on the contrary, as Wittgenstein argues, the concept is sound *without* being amenable to definition of the traditional kind, or any other! But acknowledging this point involves giving up the assumptions noted above about definiteness.

Thus, Morgan's procedures (for example, his 'two-games' argument: Chapter 2 p. 38) show his commitment to a *goal* of definiteness – and this is not just a fact about Morgan's position but a prerequisite of *any* such position. This suggests, then, that such a strategy for avoiding simple formalism is as bankrupt as the *more of the same* strategy, and for the same reason: each shares formalism's mistaken picture both of rules and of determinacy.

Rules and rule-formulations

Part of the confusion into which, if I am right, Morgan has got himself comes from misconceptions concerning the difference between rules and rule-formulations. Faced with questions or issues about rules and their scope, Morgan soon treats them in terms of particular rule-formulations – the codified rules of sport. As we saw (Chapter 2 p. 56), one problem arises if we (always) treat the version of soccer played by professional as *real* soccer, with other occasions providing defective versions: but fuel for this problem is provided once rules are always identified with some codification of them. (As widely recognized in practice, minor rule changes, even in constitutive rules, do not necessarily constitute the playing of another game: *modification* of the Laws of Cricket is possible – although, in extreme cases of rule changes, it might constitute a new [-ish] game: on technology, see Chapter 6 p. 101.)

Of course, as Baker and Hacker (1985a: 42) note, '[r]ule-formulations are not rules', although the relation is complex. We make a mistake either by too closely identifying rules and rule-formulations or by too forcefully separating them: in some cases we need this contrast, in others we do not. First, in some contexts (or for some purposes), rules should be distinguished from particular formulations of those rules. Then the rule itself might be formulated in a number of ways. At its simplest, the very same rule can be written in different languages: on the face of it, this is a different formulation of the same rule. But then we have moved away from identifying *the rule* with, say, what is written in the 'laws of the sport': say, the Laws of Cricket. For what is written will be one rule-formulation; and not necessarily (by this point) the only one. So we can usefully ask whether, say, a Laws of Cricket published in French really does state ('formulate') the lbw rule, or whether something is lost in translation.

Indeed, the point may be even stronger here: a particular string of words with another use might be *mistaken* for a rule-formulation: 'Any sentence used to formulate a particular rule can also be used for other purposes; typically, it can be used to report that a rule is in force' (Baker 1981: 60).

Saying that handball is not permitted in soccer is sometimes *stating* the rule and sometimes *reporting* its being in force. This follows from our insights into rule-following (Chapter 2 pp. 49–52): not all the verbal formulations that look like rules will function, in a particular context, as *rules*. In fact, the only grounds for classifying a string of words as a rule-formulation (hence, what is said in them as a *rule*) is their *use* as a rule: they are sentences (or some such) *used in a particular way*, not sentences with miraculous normative properties.

Second, in some contexts (or for some purposes), close ties between rules and their formulations will be important, such that they are not distinguished for philosophical purposes. Wittgenstein (PI §87) led the way here, treating signposts (clearly rule-formulations) as though they were rules, although 'we do not call them "rules"' (Baker and Hacker 1985a: 57). We should recognize the variety of rule-formulation, and hence the variety of rules – or, perhaps better, the variety of rule-related contexts. Signposts do not have the form usually associated with rules, even though 'we *use* them in the same way as rules' (Baker and Hacker 1985a: 60). So not all rules are visible through rule-formulations – and, in particular, many are not found codified in the 'laws of the game'. In part, a generous reading of ethos might pick up some of these – or an account of the *principles* underlying laws (Chapter 6 p. 105).

In a dispute between representatives of D'Agostino and Morgan, both might agree on the reprehensible character of such-and-such behaviour (say, shooting a member of the opposing team: D'Agostino 1995: 47; Morgan 1995: 51), such that it *cannot* be part of the game. Both concede that the codified rules do not mention it. One insists that this behaviour is excluded (or proscribed) as a consequence of the ethos, not of the rules, while the other claims that the 'logic of the game', drawn from its rules, supports the exclusion. How can each proceed? One may find rules where the other does not: say, that such-and-such is just drawn from 'an unofficial *system* of conventions' (D'Agostino 1995: 47: original emphasis – I would emphasize *unofficial*). But this debate is about where to find rule-*formulations* (for a particular purpose). If our sporting activity proscribes the behaviour, we might take that as a rule – even if the rule-formulation is found in the way the game is taught.

This point is important when considering how, in various games or sports, finding a different rule-formulation will *sometimes* be enough to imply that a different rule is in place – hence (perhaps) a different game under consideration. (We can imagine this as the strategy of those who claim games G and G′ are different: Chapter 2 p. 38.) This exploits our first point directly. But, on other occasions, this will not be so: recognizing a different rule-*formulation* will be no more than that. Indeed, this too follows from our first point: if the rule may be variously formulated (say, in words or in pictures), having one of these rather than another cannot make a difference.

Of course, whether or not (in a particular example) we have the same rule may be a matter for debate. But we recognize some considerations for such a debate: will the two formulations be equivalent in practice, at the level of sophistication at which the game is being played? (It might be irrelevant that, under some circumstances, these rules would proscribe or prescribe different behaviours if, as the game is played, such differences would be ignored, say.) Do the two formulations sustain the same basic values? Again, if (say) one 'version' is concerned to preserve or extend *fairness*, the 'other' must be too.

Our third point extends this second: that no rule-formulation can capture all the cases that a rule might come up against. This follows from our earlier point (Chapter 2 pp. 47–9); that new circumstances can always arise – such that the application of a particular rule will be rendered problematic. Further, this matter cannot be resolved by reformulating one's rule: any rule necessarily can face such new situations. So rule-formulations give the illusion of a clarity not possible – they seem to imply that one can always determine, from the formulation, whether or not a rule is being implemented. This is manifestly not true. One example here concerns codes of professional conduct (see McNamee 1995: 146–52): their successive refinement *seems* rooted in the idea that a perfect formulation is possible – that is, a formulation that deals with all conceivable cases. But this assumes exactly the kind of definiteness whose possibility I have denied.

Here, two contrasting theses are urged: first, the unrefined code probably deals with all or most actual cases – and a concern with *all possibilities* is unwarranted. But, second, one cannot *in principle* deal with *all* possibilities, since as we saw (Chapter 2 p. 47) the idea of a finite totality of possibilities makes no sense. Just as we do not know what to make of a bird which explodes or quotes Virginia Woolf (Austin 1970: 88[9]), so there are surely cases where – faced with a rule-formulation – we do not know what to say; and nor should we. For these are not cases our concepts confront.

Again the main project of this chapter has been to defend our conclusions about the inadequacy of the project of defining *sport* by reference to its (acknowledged) rule-structure against other accounts of sport (than Suits's). The *more of the same* position – unsurprisingly – offered nothing new; both the other versions, in sharing the commitment to the *model* of definiteness (and hence to the *project* of definition), do no better. The *now for something completely different* position could not fulfil its own goals, since a descriptive account of *ethoi* would not capture the normativity of rule-following. A solution that looked promising offered (a) a constraint on current practice (in the 'logic of the game') and (b) a more sophisticated account of the nature of ethoi. In the end, though, the *something old, something new* position imports the same assumptions about determinacy – and hence is similarly flawed.

The centre of this chapter might have *appeared* to be a debate between a set of theorists (Meier, D'Agostino, Morgan) and a view from another theorist (Suits). This appearance is deceptive: the theorists merely concretely instantiate particular kinds of position – ideally, classic (and familiar) ones. As a result, confrontations with their views are less often followed through than would be necessary were they the real topic. Yet the upshot is primarily to highlight flaws in a project they all share, to some degree or other, diagnosed in terms of a conception of definiteness within philosophy.

4 Practices and normativity in sport

This chapter contains an extended discussion of a response of the ethos position to the normativity of rule-following, although remaining some distance from engagement with sporting practicalities. Exploring the views of D'Agostino and Morgan allowed us to sketch two areas of primary divergence, based on two accounts of how the ethos legitimizes rule-following: 'For D'Agostino, it is the interests of the institutionalized forces that presently frame our compliance or non-compliance with the rules' (Morgan 1994: 226).

By contrast, Morgan's own account gave more weight to a justificatory force here, by appealing to 'the distinctive rationality and the array of goods and virtues that define sporting practices' (Morgan 1994: 226). So the differences were, first, that Morgan's conception is normative rather than descriptive (Chapter 3 pp. 61–2); second, Morgan roots his account of normativity in an account of practices, from Alastair MacIntyre.

For Morgan, the account of sport remains formalist, since he claims to stake his formulation 'on the acceptance of the logic of game playing itself' (Morgan 1994: 249 note 41); we have raised some doubts there (Chapter 3 pp. 64–6). A fuller consideration of Morgan's version of an ethos account, the *something old, something new position*, requires investigation of the account of normativity offered, since Morgan urges that his account does justice to the normativity of rule-following which – as we saw (Chapter 3 p. 63) – was fundamental to what the ethos (allegedly) offered. For, recall, Morgan is critical of D'Agostino precisely for his failure to provide such a basis for normativity. Here, I simply sketch the position, giving its ancestry in the writings of MacIntyre, and present some elements for a critique. This has more general relevance, given the widespread use of MacIntyre's ideas throughout the study of sport. (Notice, though, that would not be criticism of MacIntyre, were his project different.)

A view of practices

A publicly agreed or established way of behaving in line with the rules – which I and others recognize (or agree on), by and large – imports a distinction between what *is* right and what seems right to me (see PI §258). This just recognizes the necessity that the *requirements* of any rule be independent from what anyone *takes* these requirements to be. Indeed, since normativity consists in the maintaining of such contrasts between genuine and apparent justification, losing them will be 'a sort of mental suicide' (Putnam 1981: 122: also quoted Morgan 1994: 219) because, as Putnam notes, doing so will not treat seriously our distinction between *asserting* or *thinking* and merely *making noises*. But how might such a distinction be maintained?

A popular answer (for instance, Morgan 1994: 131 ff.; Butcher and Schneider 2003: 160) begins by offering some standard quotations from MacIntyre. So, first, a practice is presented as:

> any coherent and complex form of socially established co-operative human activity through which goods internal to the form of activity are realized in the course of trying to achieve those standards of excellence which are appropriate to and partly definitive of that form of activity, with the result that human powers to achieve excellence, and human conceptions of the ends and goods involved, are systematically extended.
>
> (MacIntyre 1985: 187)

Further:

> A practice involves standards of excellence and obedience to rules as well as achievement of goods. To enter a practice is to accept those standards and the inadequacy of my own performance as judged by them. It is to submit my own attitudes, choices, preferences and tastes to the standard which currently partially define the practice.
>
> (MacIntyre 1985: 190)

The last sentence here is crucial: the practice operates normatively over my choices and the standard thereby created 'partially defines' the practice – so the constitutive force of the practice is recognized. And it will come as no surprise to find MacIntyre (1985: 188) referring to chess to explain how the 'standard' within the practice operates.

MacIntyre's emphasis on *internal goods* – as social goods, which are practice-specific – is to be applauded: such goods cannot be achieved except through engagement with the practice, and only those who take up the practice can recognize them (compare Chapter 8 and Chapter 9). Moreover, for MacIntyre, these internal goods provide standards of excellence within the practice (to which we can aspire, and which we can aim to surpass). Moreover, as MacIntyre (1985: 189) suggests, it follows that '[t]hose who lack the relevant experience [of the practice] are incompetent thereby as judges of internal goods'.

Granting that sports are practices in this sense, then, will be granting 'the essentially social character of the activities in and through which goods definitive of the activity . . . are required and developed' (Jones and McNamee 2003: 42). But how *exactly* does the social character of the practice impinge? On one popular reading, the link is through a (general) community view of the justification of rule-following activities,[1] such that 'only a member of a rule-following community can follow a rule' (O'Hear 1991: 44). Then the following of a rule – by a particular individual on a particular occasion – *always* requires a background provided by a rule-following community (to which that person is seen as belonging).

Here, introducing the *practices* of a community answers those difficulties of justification that would arise (or so it seems) for rule-followers in isolation. One cannot give oneself a present, despite people regularly using this expression: since (say) the cash was mine all along, the book I buy is a purchase of mine, not a present (PI §268). Similarly, one cannot *sell* an object to oneself, nor *buy* it: given that one owned it initially, there is no change of ownership. And these points speak to the public character of rule-following: a person *alone* can no more engage in rule-following than that person can engage in buying *and* selling alone (RFM VI §45) – in this sense, rule-following presupposes the rule-following community. Part of this thought is that rule-following behaviours have a *temporal* dimension: granting such-and-such as rule-following behaviour *now* implies both that (in typical cases) the rule could be followed at a later time – indeed, repeated applications of the rule are envisaged – and that doing so draws on regularities of my behaviour in present and future cases, although it may also *create* the possibilities of doing just those *actions*; say, the possibilities of (rugby) try-scoring.

Once rule-following is taken, for these reasons, to require or presuppose a community in these ways, it only remains to articulate the details of the community; or to explain exactly what it provides, so as to ground the requisite normativity. And this again MacIntyre does. Or so it seems. The passages quoted above introduced the relation of the practice to its excellences, and to the ideal of internal goods. It is useful to contrast MacIntyre's discussion of external motivating 'goods': the child learning chess for sweet-money. As MacIntyre (1985: 188) points out, a crucial fact is that these external goods (here exemplified by money to buy sweets) could be acquired in other ways: they are not specific to the practice. So they cannot be the goods *of* the practice. In a similar vein, the notion of virtue is presented as internal to practices: a virtue is

> an acquired human quality the possession and exercise of which tends to enable us to achieve those goods which are internal to the practice and lack of which effectively prevents us from achieving any such goods.

> (MacIntyre 1985: 191)

So the value of the practice and the activities it justifies come together. Thus this conception of a practice answers our justificatory doubts. Or so it seems.

Ethos, practice and normativity

Pictures of this kind are widely deployed by writers on sport, and generally positively. Much turns on how this idea of a *practice* is understood, of course: but exploring that topic would take us too far afield. We have noted in passing, though, how some criticisms deployed against a descriptive account of *ethoi* mirror criticisms standardly offered of a kind of Wittgensteinian thinking – that stressing (independent) language-games. Moving forward here also addresses other ways in which Wittgenstein's insights might be understood and deployed. For the (mistaken) community view of rule-following, too, has been offered in analysis of Wittgenstein.

At least three issues suggest that – on the popular community reading – a view such as MacIntyre's is problematic as an account of the normativity of rule-following. First, are there any practices in MacIntyre's sense? Second, to what degree does this account evade the charge of relativism (noted in Chapter 3 p. 62): that is, does it render practices immune to criticism? Third, and in the contrary direction (see p. 81), does securing the normativity make redundant any reference to *the practice itself*?

So, first, what guarantee have we that any activities actually fit the bill of MacIntyre's abstract descriptions of *practices*? MacIntyre cannot guarantee this – since his constraints are powerful, no activities might meet those constraints: for example, the description stresses *internal goods*. Of course, we are told that 'we are all familiar with ... [the concept of an internal good], whether we are painters or physicists or quarterbacks or indeed just lovers of good painting or first-rate experiments or a well-thrown pass ...' (MacIntyre 1985: 191). Further:

> Tic-tac-toe is not an example of a practice in this sense, nor is throwing a football with skill; but the game of football is, and so is chess. Bricklaying is not a practice; architecture is. Planting turnips is not a practice; farming is.
>
> (MacIntyre 1985: 187)

This list might make it seem *easy* to distinguish practice (in this sense) from non-practice – the practices have goals of excellence that are internal: bricklaying is not (typically) undertaken as its own reward; and, although there are excellences of bricklaying, they relate to the virtues of upright walls, and thence to the virtues of durable structures, or some such. But were that the right reading, how much weight rests on the assumption that the excellences of practices are actually *excellent* (that is, good)? For not all human activities with internal excellences seem excellent. Yet they might be thought of as MacIntyre thinks of practices – for example (despite the denial from MacIntyre 1985: 200), *torture* as it is understood by the character Severian in Gene Wolfe's novel *The Book of the New Sun* (Wolfe 1980), as an end in itself: it certainly has excellences internal to the practice. If we decline (in principle) to grant that torturing is a *practice*, the account becomes stipulative towards positive excellences. But can we correctly identify what is actually positive? If not, this principle will lead us astray. If, instead, the 'empirical facts' (MacIntyre 1985: 200) preclude there being *virtues* in such a case, we return to a descriptive account. So a tension remains between the normativity of the practice and its exemplification in human life. (MacIntyre [1985: 23] may be unbothered since, for him, '[a] moral philosophy . . . characteristically presupposes a sociology'; and that sociology will [presumably] describe the practices theorized – as normative – by the philosophy. But that simply repeats, in a new form, our question about the relation of one to the other.)

Our second, and related, issue concerns whether or not (on this view) practices are immune to criticism. MacIntyre thinks they cannot be, for conceding that they *were* so immune returns us to the language-game position dismissed earlier (Chapter 3 pp. 60–1). In fact, MacIntyre (1970: 67–8) suggested just this sort of criticism, when he wrote: 'beliefs and concepts are not merely to be evaluated by the criteria implicit in the practice of those who hold and use them. . . . There are cases where we . . . can criticize what he does'.

Moreover, MacIntyre explicitly raises his own criticisms, both at micro- and macro-levels; for instance, respectively, of the technically-great chess player who – because he focuses only on extrinsic goods to be got from chess – cannot achieve the goods specific to chess (MacIntyre 1985: 274), and therefore can be censured, and in granting that 'there *may* be practices . . . which simply *are* evil' (MacIntyre 1985: 200). Further, '[t]raditions do on occasion founder, that is by their own standards of flourishing and foundering' (MacIntyre 1985: 277), where this comes about partly through interaction with another tradition.

But is MacIntyre consistent here? He takes the ethical life of a society to make sense only within the rule-related practices of that society: this might seem to relativize any judgements to the societies – more bluntly, to make them only amenable by critique by 'insiders'. And MacIntyre certainly writes sometimes as though he were content to describe extant practices; he writes of 'moral philosophy, as it is *dominantly* understood' (MacIntyre 1985: 236): in context, this does not suggest that the dominant view might be confused or otherwise problematic. Moreover, the emphasis within MacIntyre's account of practices on *internal goods* seems to support the thought that no external criticism is possible.

Luckily, our concern is not with the detail of MacIntyre's work (let alone with his own views of it). Our interest is only in whether such a practice account of normativity could be applied to sport. For instance, whether, on a MacIntyre-type view, the internal goods of sport are 'goods that can only be realized inside the very practice of a shared, just ethos of the sport in question' (Loland 2002: 113) – if this is right, we can criticize the practice if that ethos is not *shared*, not *just*, and so on. And one constraint on any such account was that its practices should be amenable to criticism, since that possibility was at the heart of normativity.

So can practices (on MacIntyre's conception) really be criticized or sub-verted? The need for a normative dimension suggests a 'yes' answer, but the need for a 'standing place', outside of the particular concerns of particular societies, might speak against it. Perhaps the only suitable answer involves recognizing this tension: the drive towards a satisfactory general normativity here – which would permit criticism of practices – runs counter to any (broadly descriptive) account of what practices there are.

Recall that, in distinguishing his account of ethos from D'Agostino's, Morgan (1994: 225) urges two *different* conceptions of ethos. So here, asked about the detail of *ethoi*, we might turn to the actual happening in the world of sport (suggesting the descriptive view of the ethos); asked about the constraints on rule-following, we might offer the 'logic of the rules' picture, with its associated normativity, drawn from our abstract conception of the nature of practices. But such a position lends itself to equivocation, deploy-ing one kind of answer when faced with one sort of question, the other when faced with a different one – and all the time treating the topic as univocal!

Such a strategy cannot suit Morgan (say), because it does not meet his requirement for an account which 'defines a game in terms of its formal rules' (Morgan 1995: 62): the equivocation would prevent any such defini-tion. However, in discussing the contrast between regulative and con-stitutive *uses* of rules (Chapter 2 p. 43), the fluctuation between criteria and symptoms (PI §354) was deployed: here, it suggests that, asked different *questions* about human activities, we might expect different bases for the answers. That may offer a way to rehabilitate the insights from the practice account.

Customs and rules

The formulation of practices under discussion *seems* to give weight to the fact that people do behave in these ways – and have, in the past: 'that this game is played', in a quotation modified from Wittgenstein (see PI §654).

But that leads to our third criticism of the practice-account, since the requirement for a practising community seems misplaced. Instead, as Baker (2002: 64 note) eloquently puts it:

> whether or not there is a practice must be the *minimum* requirement for the possibility of distinguishing following the rule from thinking that one is following the rule. It is certainly *not obvious* that this depends on the existence of a custom within a *community*. What is required is the *possibility* of teaching the rule to others.

Thus, the extant-ness of the activity is no (necessary) part of the idea of a practice – or, better (since the term *practice* might suggest that the activity *is* actually engaged in), we do not need a set of practices in that sense. As we have seen in respect of appeals to countryside traditions (Chapter 3 pp. 60–1), the mere fact of being extant is normatively inert.

Such a view also carries weight against any normative account of a practice, at least if understood on the community view, because that view still gives weight to the (prior) existence of the activity, instead of focusing squarely on the normativity requirement. Since the normativity requirement for rules is satisfied, as Baker says, by being able to teach the rule to others, *this* is the condition that needs consideration.

Of course, the point is not how one *learns* the normative distinctions, conceived as a history of one's coming to recognize them, but (somehow) on their foundation. That is, the requisite teaching might be achieved by various methods: one might even imagine someone coming to the understanding for himself, as though finding a new word (see PI §257). Yet then, to continue the image, we ask, how did he manage to locate 'the post where the new word is stationed' (PI §257)? This asks how the regularities of behaviour introduce – or, better, *create* – normativity.

This difficulty is visible even in some perceptive discussions of rule-following: thus, Baker and Hacker (1985b: 42) write of '*regularities* of behaviour of sufficient *complexity* to yield normativity' (original emphasis). But, clearly, this cannot explain how such normativity arises. Instead, it merely recognizes its connection to patterns of behaviour.

The thesis that rule-following is a practice is sometimes attributed to Wittgenstein (on the basis of PI §202): but that misreads the remark – he actually wrote[2] 'hence also "following a rule" is a practice'. The force of the scare-quotes here is that this is *rule-following* 'in our specific sense' or 'in the sense we have been discussing' (Baker 2002: 63–4), where the previous context stressed that these were *public* or *communicative* cases: naturally, in that context, following a rule is a community activity. Yet nothing follows, one way or another, about rule-following conceived more generally: Wittgenstein's remark relates to the context *he* specified.

Wittgenstein (PI §199) also points the way forward here usefully when he writes: 'To follow a rule, to make a report, to give an order, to play a game of chess, are *customs* (uses, institutions).'

Some detailed consideration of this passage is rewarding. Wittgenstein is not simply stressing the term *custom* by putting it in italics. Rather, this resembles the use of scare-quotes, better understood as indicating something like 'in a certain sense' or 'in a special sense' (Baker 1999: 203–4).[3] Once this 'special sense' of the term becomes clear, the remark is plain: so, in *this* context or in answer to *this* question, we should refer to the customs, institutions, and so on because . . .

But what is the special sense here? It cannot simply involve emphasizing the *social* aspect of customs, since that would be very odd applied to the giving of *orders* – as Baker (1999: 204) noted, 'there is nothing here [for orders] of the variability which is . . . characteristic of customs'. That is, it makes no sense for a society to lack 'all forms of interaction that fall under the general headings of giving and following orders' (Baker 1999: 204). Hence, this cannot offer a consistent reading of Wittgenstein's point.[4] So this is not simply a requirement for an 'institutional environment' (Wright 2001: 155).

Interestingly, MacIntyre (1985: 206) highlights some of the variety within the notions that might be applied here when, having written of a 'social setting', he comments that this 'may be an institution, it may be what I have called a practice, or it may be a milieu of some other human kind'. This suggests something of the richness to be accommodated. Turning to the idea of a *custom* in this light, we might see customs as lacking 'authoritative codification' (Baker 1999: 205), closer to a *habit* than is often granted. So that, for instance, in England orderly queuing is a custom. (Or, if that is no longer true, it is because children are no longer *trained* that way.) We recognize how much here depends on activities whose mastery we have acquired through 'imitation, drill and practice' (Baker 1999: 205; see Z §419). That is to say, suppose the key feature of *customs*, the feature that made it revealing in this context to speak of these diffuse activities as customs, was that customs were habitual – that they could be repeated, were regularities, and could be acquired through habituation. Then, in general, rules will be introduced when explicit rule-formulation is introduced. The possibility canvassed is that rules are customs in the sense that a rule-formulation might build on established patterns of behaviour by particular individuals – customs in *that* sense. So these customs would precede rule-governed practices, as the mastery of the practical activity of counting is presupposed in the rules for the use of number-words in counting and measuring.

We might choose to characterize rule-following as a practice, under certain circumstances: ones Wittgenstein (PI §202) envisages can take for granted that we are discussing an extant activity. Equally, under different circumstances (or faced with different questions), we might prefer to emphasize the connection between rule-following and habituated behaviour. On this picture, then, the point in calling rule-following occasions *customs* would be to emphasize the primitive nature of *actions* here, as opposed to thoughts or 'interpretations'.

Before briefly addressing such a point to the rules of sport, two possible areas of misunderstanding of Wittgenstein's view as sketched here (following Baker) can be noted. First, giving this weight to *action* might seem to suggest another, different social or community aspect: namely, that the possibility of rules requires the (actual) following of those rules. And that at least requires a community context. Now, Wittgenstein is surely right that the very existence of any rules depends on *some* rules actually being applied *sometimes*; and that one rule being applied only once would not be enough. But granting this – that is, granting that we are rule-following beings – is not granting that a particular rule must have been followed *in the past* in order to count as a rule. As we noted, all that is required is the *possibility* of teaching that rule, given that the 'student' is a (potentially) rule-following creature.

Second, the rejection of *interpretation* may strike some as unreasonable. Yet Wittgenstein's point is that interpretation still leaves a gap: one cannot close that gap by inserting community agreement (see above; and Baker and Hacker 1985a: 243), nor with an 'interpretation', since the interpretation must still be applied in this case – it too has a species of normativity. The issue concerns what is required *in this case*, not abstractly. It is tempting to take the abstract conception of the rule as fundamental. Instead, *acts* of following or contravening rules are more fundamental than giving interpretations – that is, than offering explanations of what the rule requires. For explaining the rule only makes sense for someone who understands that explanation: and that involves understanding that it is indeed a rule – something to be followed (or not). So that, my being able to follow a rule does not require that I can explain that rule to you. For instance, with the offside rule in football or the lbw rule in cricket, my ability to abide by the rule and to recognize contraventions of it might exceed my ability to explain every case to which it applies, and in what ways. Further, you would take my explanation to cover *all* cases of the application of the rule. Whatever was said here would also be open to being variously interpreted. So it is an illusion to think that an *interpretation* is needed to fill the gap between, say, an order and its execution. You only execute my order to shut the door by shutting the door: if you do not see that, you do not understand the order – hence you could not do as instructed. But if you do understand it, you have simply to act on it, doing what (in context) you were told to do. And if you required instead some explanation of what to do, one when you understood the words could still leave you confused as to what to *do*. Certainly, if we assume there must be some such understanding (some 'interpretation') between order and action, we will generate a familiar regress. And the confusion is even more likely with a complex instruction; say, my explanation of the offside rule. For the interpretation will itself be general; and hence could be treated as a further rule (PI §201).[5] That is, as still needing to be *applied* in any particular case. On these assumptions, then, one would simply have introduced gaps between order and interpretation on the one hand and between interpretation and execution on the other – two gaps now! Indeed, Wittgenstein stresses that 'there is a way of grasping a rule which is *not* an *interpretation*' (PI §201), because (in this context) an interpretation *is* (or at least could be, in principle) given in signs – for instance, in words. But what is needed here is just *action*. As he continues, that way of grasping the rule: 'is exhibited in what we call "obeying the rule" and "going against it" in actual cases' (PI §201). Here again, Wittgenstein is returning – with a new twist – to the slogan: 'In the beginning was the deed.' For, as in the discussion of customs above, a human *power* is stressed here: the bedrock is what we (can) *learn* to do, where that learning is akin to training or to the acquisition of habits or customs. And saying this repeats an earlier point: that normativity for a rule is granted in granting that the rule can be taught to another.

Now, the fact that I cannot *justify* what I did (that is, cannot produce an argument that supports the verdict that my action was the correct one) is beside the point: others will judge from my *doings* in particular cases whether or not I understand; and there is room here for discussion of whether my behaviour merely *conforms* to the rule (or custom) or whether instead I am *following* that rule – we recognize that these are different (Chapter 2 p. 44).

Of course, MacIntyre is not travelling in this terrain. Rather, he begins from such normativity: there are standards of excellence from the beginning. So MacIntyre's ideas cannot explain the normativity inherent in a practice but, instead, depend on it. Yet his view is regularly cited as offering just such a legitimation (compare Morgan 1994: 219–20; Jones and McNamee 2003: 42; Loland 2002: 19). And if, at the centre of that dependence, is the community view of normativity, this is the *mythologizing* of practice: 'the tendency to erect . . . the mythological picture of rule-following . . . out of a practice in which that notion [consensus] can be given content' (Wright 2001: 189: my order). For these ideas do not conduce to an explanation here, but presuppose one. The mistake lies in thinking that MacIntyre's account will tell us more than it does (or can).

Having granted that rule-following is a custom, we should not conclude that, since sport involves rule-following, sport too is a custom. Rather, the point of this remark is to show something central, if often missed, about rule-following; namely, its relation to (habituated) activities acquired via training. Since they are trained, rather than learned, such activities are not centrally the province of persons. For persons (unlike trained seals) can genuinely *learn*, in the sense that implies the possibility of understanding. So, while rule-following activities themselves are learned, their core resides – on this view – in the habituated (that is, in this sense of *custom*). And sporting activities could not be habituated in *this* way, since sporting activities are genuine actions (where this is only marginally true of the habituated activities customs describe).

Suppose this picture of following a rule as a custom were employed: where would it leave the normativity of rules in sport? Sports do not grow directly from the sorts of habitual activities discussed – although we might see how some such activities led first to games (say, folk games) and thence to sport. So sport is a human creation in a slightly stronger sense. At the least, though, this picture has no direct impact on how we should understand the following of rules of modern sports. Nevertheless, it emphasizes the weakness of the appeal to sport as a practice: although sometimes presented as almost descriptive of sport (see Butcher and Schneider 2003: 161), this idea amounts to the ascription of certain properties to sport. And those properties could not explain the normativity (apparently: Morgan [1995:

60]) required by a formalist account of sport, and hence could not contribute to 'their rational demarcation' (Morgan 1994: 225).

It seemed as though we needed to understand the basis of the normativity: *how* do rules come to determine what is to be done? And, specifically, how does the general (the rules) make contact with the particular (the specific action, in the context[6])? The sorts of abstract answers that seemed to be required are typified by responding, say:

- 'by means of interpretations' (but we have seen Wittgenstein urging that an appeal to interpretation cannot be satisfactory), or,
- 'by reference to the shared practices (or the precedents) of a community' (but that is not the aspect that where reference to the past of rule-following activities was revealing: see pp. 61–2).

The position here is complex, and contextual. We reject these mistaken answers as part of rejecting the general *question*: there is no one answer here – nor could there be. These (mistaken) issues reflect what Wittgenstein recognized as 'so difficult' in philosophy: namely, 'to begin at the beginning. And not try to go further back' (OC §471). For, if the issue truly concerns normativity, enough has been done when we recognize that our normative practices might be thought of as having their roots in customs, viewed as habituated: we learn to go on in this way or that way. Doing so might steer us away from other ways of looking at such activities. But these are neither specific justifications of particular rules (as the language-game theorists hoped: Chapter 3 p. 60) nor reflections of community agreements. Once this is granted, the reference to a practice is not adding anything (in *this* context). By contrast, reference to an *institution* (Introduction pp. 7–8) might, although the point would be a quite different one, because talk of an institution supports the idea of there being institutional facts: that is, facts which oblige or constrain behaviour, as the fact that I borrowed money from you obliges me to repay it. Of course, these *could* become 'practice-facts' (here, the practice of promise-keeping) but then the positions just converge.

So, the conclusion must be that this use of MacIntyre's ideas cannot fill the gap Morgan indicates (through his critique of D'Agostino). The thought there was that the *normativity* of rules as actually applied had yet to be explained: and one could not do it simply by *describing* that application. If there *is* such a gap between the rules in theory and their practical application, as Morgan contends, a MacIntyrean practice cannot fill that gap because MacIntyre's account does not *explain* normativity, but simply assumes it. So if the project is to explain the normativity, MacIntyre's account of practices is unhelpful. (Of course, if the *project* is radically different. . . .)

My view is that normativity *rests* on the customs (in the 'habituated' sense); but this, again, does not explain the origin of that normativity – and does not seek to. For it has no origin if we think in terms of its having an *author* and (hence?) *authority* (see McFee 2002: 130–1).

In these ways, then, the connection between normativity and human activities (say, as practices) cannot offer any final solution to the project of completely characterizing *sport* (that is, of offering to sports 'their rational demarcation': Morgan [1994: 225]). Rather, we are thrown back on the varieties within sports and sporting contexts, and on the relation of (general) normativity – humans as rule-following creatures – to the specifics of rule-following, or breaking, in sport. But the error lies in supposing that there was some gap here; and that follows from the demands of determinacy.

Conclusion to Part I

Finally, it is worth drawing together the chief threads from Part I: if the project of determinacy is misplaced – in its own right, and as indicating something profound about the nature of philosophy – attempts to deploy that project in the understanding of sport are doomed to failure. This is what we have found, following the trail of our central example, formalism. Further, a distinctive feature of sports (although not of them alone) is their dependence on rule structures. But it is easy to mistake the nature of rule-following – not least in thinking that it has a (single) nature! Yet this misconception (or set of them) combines very naturally with the other: that yields the project of formalism, as it is understood here. And, again, explorations of the nature of rules and of rule-following expose its limitations. We should conclude both that the project cannot be saved in this version and that other versions will be equally improbable once the flaws are recognized to be in the *project*, not its execution.

In pursuing these ideas, we have also begun the exploration of other relevant terrain: in particular, the occasion-sensitivity of understanding and the roots of normativity. In every case, we have simply mapped enough of that geography to reach our destinations – for, consonant with the philosophical positions developed here, the mapping metaphor is misleading precisely in thinking there is a fully determinate terrain to be mapped. Here, as elsewhere, we should be rejecting the assumption of a finite totality of cases or positions to be considered.

We began by granting the importance for sport of its rule structure. But our investigations here might not seem to have generated very positive results as to the *point* or *value* of those structure. In part, this is mistaken: we have learned a lot about the constitutive nature of sport's rules. We will say more when we turn in Part II to a set of primary rule-related activities; namely, those of judges, umpires and referees.

Part II
Rules in judging sport

5 Aesthetic sports, publicity and judgement calls

Part II addresses the place of rules in determining the outcome of sporting contests. As we have seen, that there are such rules at all permits the kinds of action in which, say, winning consists. (These are our constitutive rules: Chapter 2 p. 35.) For example, the rules of rugby allow one to score *tries*; otherwise, one would simply be putting the ball down (just as the rules of chess turn the redistribution of carved wooden items on a chequered surface into, say, a checkmate). And the very different rules of American Football allow a very different action to count as scoring a touchdown. Moreover, to win or lose the game or match is related, in all cases, to such scoring.

So one feature of those rules is their role in determining who wins and who loses. But there seem to be a number of problems here – at least the following. First, there are clear cases where (with the benefit of action-replay) we see that an apparent score was actually not within the rules: for many, Maradona's 'Hand of God' goal against England in the 1986 World Cup would be a prime example. Second, there are cases where the rules seem to penalize unfairly, or benefit unfairly, a given team or player. For instance, when a golfer in the lead in a major tournament is disqualified through an error on his card for which he was not (directly) responsible, or when a golfer is penalized for having too many clubs in his bag – even though he has not considered using any club other than ones he would certainly have retained – we may feel that, while some penalty is appropriate, the actual penalty is too harsh. Here, our difficulty is with the *fairness* of the rules. Third, there are cases where the referee or umpire is called upon to exercise discretion as to how the rule applies in this case (for instance, in deciding if the attire of a player at the Wimbledon tennis tournament is 'predominantly white'); there may even be situations where the rules seem silent, and where discretion on the part of referees seems to be making new rules. For example, when the suitably named Anne White played at Wimbledon in 1985, her attire was predominantly – in fact, exclusively – white; but it was a 'dazzling skin-tight body stocking' (OSM June 2002: 5). The official who commented that this was 'not traditional tennis attire' was clearly correct – but it certainly met the 'predominantly white' condition.

With the rules seemingly silent, the officials were obliged to make a ruling. Such cases relate primarily to how (if at all) the rules were – or should be – applied. Fourth, there are issues about whether the *right* judgement was made of, say, a gymnastic vault or spring-board dive: did the competitor get what he or she deserved? There can be (justified) dispute here. Fifth, there are cases where judging is suspect in other ways. For instance, at the Salt Lake City Olympics of 2002, there was a controversy in the result of the pairs figure skating: as a result, a second gold medal was awarded (to a Canadian pair), and one of the judges was censured (see pp. 98–9). In this chapter, therefore, we will consider how our insights into rules and rule-following – together with some others – might be informative in respect of the application of those rules in sporting situations.

Just about every call is a judgement call

There are obvious difficulties with ensuring fairness of judging or refereeing. The dismissive idea that all referees are blind – regularly asserted by those who think their preferred player or team has fallen foul of unfair refereeing – goes back as far as the sport-like activities of ancient Rome (if not farther), at least if Lindsey Davis (1998: 430) is to be believed. Yet such fairness is clearly central to any satisfactory sporting contest. And many problems here are familiar, explicable (sometimes) as human error. As a recent article perceptively put it, referees in National Football League (NFL) in the USA:

> 'aren't robots in grey shirts or the enemy. They are people.... But, because they are human, I do think they can be subject to personal feelings. They can be swayed by the charismatic aura of star players or burn at the incessant hammering of an edgy coach.
>
> And because they are human, sometimes they simply blow the call.
>
> Maybe that was the case in each of the nine mistakes the NFL admitted were made in a review of a Minnesota-Green Bay game leaked to the media.
>
> (Adande 2002: D1)

Often, when the refereeing is at fault, the situation is complex: hence errors are explicable, since 'eventually human judgement is going to enter into the equation' (Adande 2003: D1). For instance, at the end of a crucial NFL game between the San Francisco 49ers and the New York Giants (on Sunday, 5 January, 2003), players from both sides should have been penalized – as the NFL has since admitted in a news release. In fact, the complexity of the situation meant that the referees mistakenly penalized only the Giants – and, since time had then run out, with the Giants in arrears, that was the end of the game. If, instead, the offsetting penalties had been recognized, the net effect would have given the Giants another chance to kick the field goal that, if successful, would have won them the game. Of course, there is no guarantee that the field goal attempt would have been successful. But, had it been, the result of the game would have been different, with a different team going forward in the competition. Still, there is no malice (nor any other explanation) here – however unpalatable that might be to Giants' fans.

Moreover, the action taken in this case (reported *Los Angeles Times, Sports* 2003b: D5) was familiar: the rules were changed – in this case, the positioning of the officials during field goal attempts. The logic, then, is that it was the rules, not the officials, that were at fault.[1] And we know (Chapter 2 pp. 47–9) that this strategy of rule-changing is hopeless: it deals with *this* situation, should exactly this case arise again, but it will leave other situations open – this is a consequence of the nature of rules! Yet, at least, there is no suggestion here that the umpiring was flawed in principle, however defective it was in practice.

Then, one *might* explain some errors in umpiring or refereeing as honest mistakes. Insofar as that account is correct, it is lamentable – something we should do our best to eradicate – but no more than that. Moreover, it seems eradicable, at least in principle. For the image is of well-motivated umpires or referees, doing their best at a difficult job (perhaps in an environment made difficult, say by the media). As the piece continues: 'I'd like to leave it to human error, but the biggest problem facing the league is the perception that there is more behind the calls than a mere reaction and the tweet of a whistle' (Adande 2002: D1).

Later, the author summarizes: 'We can accept bad. We just can't tolerate agendas' (Adande 2002: D7). As this discussion illustrates, a sharp contrast should be drawn between human error (even if regarded as ultimately ineliminable in practice) and some *motivated* bad judging: here, motivated by an 'agenda'. We are familiar with this kind of worry. For example, problems with the judging of ice skating at the Winter Olympics in Salt Lake City 2002 (noted above and discussed below: see pp. 98–9) likewise highlight the need for reliable judging.

Notice too that the term 'judgement' here should not be taken as *judgemental*: a judgement here is roughly whatever a judge or referee or umpire says (or would say), whether or not it actually identifies such-and-such as good or bad, as legal or illegal (within the sport). Talking about 'judgement calls' for such referees or umpires, then, means simply that what they would say depends on their own judgement, their (informed) view of what has taken place; with the implication that the rules do not decide the matter, either partly or wholly – that there is *room* for the referee's judgement.

It might seem that one way forward would be to avoid depending on referees, umpires or judges: to eliminate the element of judgement. But this is problematic, in three ways. First, there is a justified resistance to it. Thus:

> The NBA has incorporated instant replay to help determine if shots and fouls occur before the end of quarters. Jackson [Stu Jackson, NBA's

> Vice President of Operations] said it has been used more than 100 times this season, with six reversals [of referees decisions] – and that the league is reluctant to expand the use of replay because just about every call the officials make is a judgement call.
>
> (Adande 2002: D7)

Second, it is far from clear that it could be eliminated, even in principle: the reason the idea of a *judgement call* is stressed in the quotation is at least partly that, for many sporting activities, the relation of the rules to what *action* is actually performed ensures that no mechanical means for determining what occurred could be adequate – for instance, the referee must determine whether the player had *control* of the ball (see Chapter 6 p. 103); and this is not simply a matter of how hard he or she is holding it. Third, for some sporting activities – such as pairs figure skating – the whole nature of scoring depends on recognition by judges of the manner in which the actions are performed. Here the element of judgement seems especially ineliminable. On the basis of these reflections, three issues can be identified:

- *Bias of judges* – this is a practical problem only: as we will see (p. 93), the possibility of *bias* shows that unbiased judgement is possible. Thus, for example, we need umpires or referees with no agenda outside the sport, but that should be possible (at least in theory).
- *Objectivity of judgement* – can these 'looking and seeing' judgements ever be objective? (Is there a logical bar?) Again, there is no in principle objection to public and shareable judgements here (see pp. 93–7). Still, it will be worth reflecting on this issue in the context of those sports – like pairs skating – where judgement seems ineliminable.
- *The basis for 'reading' the rules* – how do we ensure that the rules are understood by all judges, referees or umpires in the same way? In particular, how do we ensure consistency across judgement calls? In part, the practical answer must lie in the training and education of our judges or umpires. But what is its theoretical basis? This will be the topic in the next chapter, introduced via some powerful examples.

Does this tell us something revealing about judging or refereeing in general? As we will see, it raises a number of revealing points, some of which have a bearing on the nature of judging or refereeing, while others highlight a fundamental contrast within the nature of sports.

Two kinds of sports?

David Best rightly distinguishes between:

- *Purposive sports*: '. . . the purpose [goal] can be specified independently of the means of achieving it as long as it conforms to the limits set by the rules or norms' (Best 1978: 104). For purposive sports, then, any action meeting the broad aim of the sport within the rules counts as a score – goals, and such like, can be graceful or not, but are still goals.

- *Aesthetic sports*: '. . . the aim cannot be specified in isolation from the manner of achieving it' (Best 1978: 104) – a (gymnastic) vault is not just 'getting over the box': rather, the manner of achieving the aim is crucial.

Unsurprisingly, this distinction between kinds of sports is manifest in the nature of scoring in each kind of sport. Thus, in the first case, it does not matter if, for instance, a goal scored (in football or soccer, say) is an elegant solo effort or a messy goalmouth scramble – both count one goal in the team's tally. By contrast, the aim of gymnastic vaulting – and hence success in such vaulting – depends entirely on the *manner* of getting over the box. So this distinction also permits us to recognize that aesthetic considerations apply differentially across sports. Purposive sports like football do, of course, have an aesthetic dimension – where grace, line elegance and the like are celebrated; but this dimension only becomes important once it is granted that the purposive element is satisfied. Thus *Goal of the Month* competitions look for grace, elegance, and so on among what are *acknowledged* to be goals (see McFee 1986: 166–8). Importantly here, whether or not the aim (in a purposive sport) has been achieved will be a matter of measuring or timing, or of a ball crossing (or not crossing) a line, or some such – all matters *in principle* determinable detached from human judgement (although judges might be needed to determine whether or not it occurred within the rules).

By contrast, for an aesthetic sport such as gymnastic vaulting or diving, the manner in which the action is performed becomes crucial to who wins; and that concern with *manner* can only be finally resolved by some person's looking and seeing. That is, it is determined by the judgement of informed observers. Thus such judges or umpires are assigned a fundamental role (in scoring). So *more* is under consideration than whether the judge was, say, in a good position to notice the achievement; for, in this case, that achievement in the sport can only be rated by our 'informed observer'. Then one set of issues here concerns the role, within aesthetic sports, of judges or umpires: these are posed sharply as questions when, say, one judge is singled out as having *misjudged* an Olympic skating final. We must clarify a variety of issues here relating to objectivity and publicity, as well as bias, to put aside this kind of objection to the (logical) role of judges or umpires, at least in its fundamental form.

The contrast between purposive and aesthetic sports, as Best articulates it, may not be exhaustive, in that it may be impossible to uniquely assign a particular sport to one category or the other. But Best is surely right that it encompasses all sports. For instance, the scoring in ski-jumping awards some marks for distance (purposive), and some for style (aesthetic). So ski-jumping is a straightforward mix of Best's two categories. As this case illustrates, weight might be given to both a manner-related score (as in aesthetic sports) *and* to an outcome-related score (as in purposive sports): this need not be worrying – our thesis was only that scoring in all sports worked in one or other of these ways, so it is unproblematic to add 'or a combination of them'. What is being denied is that there is some *third* kind of sport. And the primary emphasis here is to show how, for aesthetic-type sports, there is necessarily a judgement of the manner in which the activity was conducted, going beyond the simple judgement of whether or nor it was conducted within the rules. Rather, scoring in these sports involves determining the *quality* of the manner of conducting the activity. In context, that can only be done by some knowledgeable person (or group of them) looking carefully at what occurs. That is, the importance of personal judgement is stressed – whatever is the case elsewhere, for aesthetic sports at least scoring will always depend to some degree on looking and seeing.

But, as above, this highlights one (apparent) difficulty: such looking and seeing might have been thought *necessarily* subjective, or *necessarily* untrustworthy. In fact, a huge mistake is implicit in such claims: what permits of (limited) variety is not therefore private, or subjective in the dismissive sense. But to get there requires turning briefly to some general arguments concerning subjectivity.

What is subjectivity?

When asked (in this context) 'What is subjectivity?', we typically intend the term 'subjective' in a pejorative or dismissive sense: as something to be avoided or deplored. For simplicity, I will identify four uses of the term 'subjective' (McFee 1992: 22–3):

1   Subjective as inner – 'anything goes';
2   Subjective as biased;
3   Subjective as prejudiced;
4   Subjective as personal, involving persons.

Of these, 1, 2, and 3 will be pejorative uses, as – in each case – finding that a judgement was subjective would make one think less highly of, or disregard, that judgement.

Here, we should ask: Are such judgements *necessarily* subjective? For kinds 2 and 3, the answer is 'no': if *I* am biased or *I* am prejudiced, this is implicitly contrasted with someone else who is not. For instance, if I am a biased essay-marker, this means that my students do not get 'what they deserve' for the essay – but this is simply a practical problem: I am marking badly or inappropriately, and the essay should be marked by someone else, who will award it the mark it deserves. In this way, the possibility of bias is a guarantee that any difficulty here is a practical one only – that it could be done in an unbiased way. So the suggestion that *all* marking is *necessarily* biased makes no sense. Thus we can put aside options 2 and 3: they could not explain an *in principle* difficulty for judgements, or any judgements being *necessarily* subjective.

It is important to be clear exactly the nature of the accusation under consideration. Suppose that the account Andrew Jennings (1996: 79–92; Jennings and Sambrook 2000: 205–8, 212–16) offers of the judging of boxing at the Seoul Olympics of 1988 is true: that, for instance, Roy Jones was adjudged to have lost a match against a Korean, Park Si-Hun, despite the fact 'that Roy Jones landed eighty-six scoring blows and the Korean only thirty two' (Jennings 1996: 86). Then it seems right to regard *that* judging as biased: the best boxers did not win the matches – or, better, the boxers who *actually* won the matches (in terms of scoring the most points) were not *awarded* these wins. This is, of course, a very worrying practical dimension of sport. But it makes a straightforward (if important) philosophical point. For judge X or judge Y is being *biased* in his/her judging: we understand that idea just because we can see what it would be like for the judgements to be made in an unbiased way. Indeed, in this case, we can even see who *would have* been awarded the victories, if not for the bias: hence, who *should have* been awarded them. So these cases are not part of, and do not suggest, a discussion about the (logical) inevitability of bias. Rather, the practicality of bias in this or that case shows that unbiased judging is logically possible: it makes sense to aim (or to hope) for such judging.

Thus, this cannot be an argument against the objectivity of refereeing, umpiring or judging as such – in fact, it demonstrates the possibility of such objectivity. So, to repeat, options 2 and 3 in our list can be put aside. This discussion, though, suggests a ground rule: namely, that some distinction between objective and subjective must be maintained; that all judgements cannot turn out to be (necessarily) subjective.

What is needed here is a basis for a judgement to be *necessarily* subjective (not merely practically so); what might that basis be? Clearly, the candidate here will be of sense 1, on which any 'view' is as good as any other.

What is so bad about subjectivity (in sense 1 above)? The answer lies in the connection (or lack of connection) of such judgements to truth, knowledge and understanding. If an area is (necessarily) subjective – in sense 1 – its judgements cannot manifest knowledge or understanding, since it makes no sense to contrast your knowledge with my ignorance or your understanding with my lack of it: any one 'view' is as good (or bad) as any other. Further, there can be no teaching or learning in such an area, since the concept of learning implicitly compares the case of ignorance (prior to the learning) with later knowledge. And this makes no sense if any view is as good as any other.

Two bad arguments for the subjectivity of judgements

To make the discussion above a little more specific, we can turn to two arguments designed to explain why a class of judgements is (necessarily) subjective in sense 1 above.[2]

The argument from personal character

This kind of argument might be summarized as follows: 'My judgements depend on my impressions, coming through my senses: therefore they are subjective.'

Our reply should make two points. First, if sound, this argument would make all judgements (even those by scientists) subjective, contrary to our ground rule (see p. 93). Second, the argument is not sound, since it confuses what is personal with what is idiosyncratic. To see this point, consider colour-blindness: differences here are regular and recognizable, but against a background of systematic perception by the rest of us! The judgements of a colour-blind person can be identified, and contrasted with colour judgements uncluttered by colour-blindness. So that one cannot with justice plead that the traffic light was not red because it did not look red to me. Here, it is not true that any view is equally good.

What moral should we draw from this bad argument? It invites us to recognize a person's role in making judgements: it correctly gives weight to a person – and hence to what he or she has learned or can discriminate. With this thought in place, we can turn to the next.

The argument from diversity

The contention here is that the persistence of disagreement shows judgements in an area to be subjective. If it were not subjective, agreement would be reached (eventually): there is 'one right answer', if only we knew it.

Our response begins by recording that like must be compared with like (Bambrough 1979: 18): for there may be much less diversity in the world than is sometimes imagined – or urged by writers in philosophy. It is sometimes thought that factual claims, such as those concerning the boiling point of water, are straightforward in ways that value claims (say, about the morality of abortion) are not. As Bambrough points out, this does not compare like with like: the massive moral consensus around, say, the wrong-ness of torturing innocent children might equally be contrasted with disputes in the far reaches of physics; for instance, about the number of elementary particles. We must take examples of equal complexity – if a moral sceptic reminds us that there are those who reject moral claims, 'we can offer him in exchange the Flat Earth Society' (Bambrough 1979: 18). That is, we point out the divergence within claims for the so-called factual.

More fundamentally, agreement *as such* is not the issue – we could all be wrong! For what is required here is not human agreement as such. To see that, we should remember that most long division is performed by children learning the skill – hence it makes perfect sense to imagine that most of the answers arrived at are wrong. But no amount of agreement among those wrong answers makes them right.

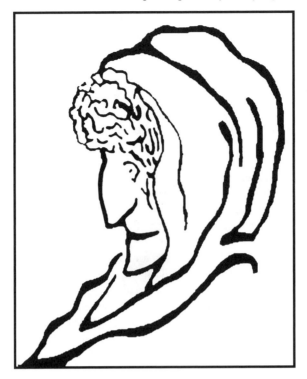

Our next point is most easily introduced via an example: the old woman/ young woman multiple figure, from psychology (above).

As this case highlights, diversity is not an index of subjectivity. This figure can be seen as a picture of a young woman or a picture of an old woman. So there is diversity: but, with such multiple-figures, one's judgement can be wrong (so not anything goes). Any account of the figure must be answerable to the placement of the lines: that any which is *not* must be wrong for that reason. Further, in explaining how the figure may be seen as a young woman ('This is the line of her cheek; this is her velvet choker'), I highlight exactly those features of the design. So here the combination of diversity with the possibility of being mistaken shows that diversity is not an index of subjectivity in sense 1.

Moreover, diversity is to be expected when we reflect on the variety of human experience: for we are recognizing, as Bambrough (1979: 33) put it, that '[c]ircumstances objectively alter cases'. In Bambrough's compelling example, a tailor aiming to ensure that each suit fits its owner must treat each suit (and each owner) differently: but that will be a way to treat each *the same* – each suit will fit!

From this bad argument, we should extract the moral that diversity is not an index of subjectivity; that 'not subjective' is not equivalent to 'one right answer'.

Objectivity and options

Has the foregoing discussion established anything about the objectivity of judgement? To reply, we must recognize the term 'objective' as having a number of uses; in particular as:

1 'One right answer' – but this is not a sense we are using;
2 Detached, neutral – to be objective in this sense is simply to avoid being inappropriately *engagé*;
3 Rational, responsive to reason, public.

Applied to the kinds of judgements made of sporting events, sense 1 is false (as multiple-figure cases show), while sense 2 is methodological rather than substantive. So sense 3 picks out the requisite one here. As we will see, its application to sporting judgement is relatively uncontentious: all that is needed is that one's judgements be arguable – that concedes that one has 'reasons' one might offer to others, which they will notice (even if they do not regard them as reasons for that judgement). Then the status of these (putative) reasons can be discussed.

But what is objective in sense 3 still permits diversity, and is still contentious. For instance, observation (for example, in science, and elsewhere) is *theory-laden*; so that seeing oak trees differs from just seeing trees – and depends on what one knows, or has (say) learned to recognize. The difference does not lie in the patterns of light and shade striking the retina. As a result, 'what one sees' may be both public and shareable, and yet differ from what another person sees. Yet this is not a defect here. Rather, the situation resembles the multiple figure discussed above: whatever one claims about the figure must be answerable to its features, as when I say, 'This is a velvet choker . . .'. An informed discussion of the case can proceed exactly *because* we can both point to its features.

Moreover, this position is central to the ability to criticize the claims of others. For instance, if such-and-such a view is wrong because, say, it has unacceptable consequences (morally, aesthetically), these consequences are *publicly* unacceptable – the 'error' cannot even be diagnosed in a sphere with no right or wrong (Bambrough 1979: 40).

The conclusion to be drawn here is that what is personal (subjective in sense 4) (p. 92) may still be open to reason (objective in sense 3); hence reliable in the assessment of sporting events (in principle).

This discussion has not *proved* the objectivity of this or that particular remark: but my response to a criticism based on that point would be twofold. First, we have put aside any reason for thinking that this realm of discourse is *necessarily* subjective – and, what comes to the same thing, we have shown its potential for objectivity. So one cannot just assume that any comments from this context – say, the judgements of a particular judge of figure skating (see p. 99) – are subjective (in the dismissive sense). Indeed, were an assumption to be made, it must be the one of objectivity.

The second point emerges from this one. For *proving* the objectivity of a particular comment must be done (if it can) case by case: that is, we demonstrate the objectivity of this or that remark or judgement. Or, at least, this is what we attempt. And we do that only when we have reason to challenge or suspect it. Indeed, philosophy could never show that *all* the remarks of, say, a particular judge or referee have the required detachment – we simply ensure that this is possible, and then turn to particular examples. In fact, this is just the procedure we needed to show that a particular judgement was not objective: that seems to unite these two lines of consideration.

With these points about the nature (in particular, the public character) of judgement now safely determined, we can return to the consideration of the nature of aesthetic sports; and especially our consideration of the importance of such judgement for them.

Aesthetic sports: the importance of judgement

Best's presentation of the purposive/aesthetic contrast emphasizes the nature of the goal or target of the sport: that for the purposive it is, and for the aesthetic is not, independent of the manner of achieving that goal or target, as long as it is within the rules. For us, the emphasis falls on the manner of awarding points (and so on): is it simply a matter of determining whether, say, the ball entered the net, or of how far was thrown or jumped, or (again) how long a time was taken to run a certain distance (or, more likely, which competitor covered the distance in the least time)? Or does it depend on the informed judgement of an observer, such as a referee or umpire, determining the manner of the performance of the activity, as it must for aesthetic sports? In respect of aesthetic sports at least, then, there is an additional need for, and role assigned to, umpires, referees and the like: namely, the role of determining the manner in which the activity was performed, and in scoring it accordingly. As a shorthand, I shall say that, for such sports, the scoring necessarily involves the *judgement* of the umpire or referee.

Due weight must be given to the 'necessarily' here: that there is no possibility of determining whether the performance was satisfactory, and (if so) to what degree, generating what score, other than by someone, or some group of 'someones', *looking and seeing*. For what must be determined includes the *manner* in which the actions were performed, and – like our seeing the young or old woman in our multiple figure (p. 95) – this can only be achieved in that way, since it involves recognizing salient features of the actions. Was this triple toe-loop jump in figure skating cleanly landed? Was the height in the air appropriate, and was the leg extension full enough? Of course, some such features will always be invoked in practice: thus, the umpire in cricket must determine whether or not the bowler's arm was straight at the moment of releasing the ball – this being the crucial difference between bowling and throwing. But we can imagine this resolved by reference to video tape, where the straightness of the arm could be measured. The same cannot be said for aesthetic sports. Such judgements for aesthetic sports draw on the knowledge and experience of the judge: one must have learned to recognize these features of the action. And only when the judge accurately determines the manner in which the action was performed – and, moreover, sees it correctly as part of the performance as a whole – will the performer be accurately scored.

Initially, two different (if not unrelated) difficulties should be contrasted: the first might be called the issue of *just deserts*. It was brought out clearly at the Salt Lake City Winter Olympics of 2002, when a judge of the pairs figure skating competition, Marie-Reine Le Gougne, claimed that she was 'pressured' (*Los Angeles Times* 2002: A1) to award her best marks for the Russian pair (Elena Berezhnaya and Anton Sikharulidze). As a consequence, they were declared the winners 'even though many experts believed the Canadian pair of Jamie Sale and David Pelletier had deserved to win' (*Los Angeles Times* 2002: A28). Later, a second gold medal was awarded to the Canadians, and both the judge and her Federation president were banned from international events for three years.

Of course, the detail of this case is contentious: that Marie-Reine was *pressured* to award the high marks to the Russian pair (assuming this to be so) does not mean that she would not also have marked them at the same level without the pressure – perhaps she (also) honestly saw them as the best. In fact, the case returned to public view when a Russian 'entrepreneur', Alimzhan Tokhtakhounov, was 'charged with trying to . . . fix *two* Winter Olympic figure skating contests' (*Los Angeles Times* 2002: A1: my emphasis). One event was the pairs, as described above: the other was the ice dance. Here, the eventual winners, French champions Marina Anissina and Gwendal Peirzerat, were established world champions, and it was never seriously disputed that their performance was the best. But their result too was (apparently) also subject to the intended 'fix'. The difficulty here is that the pressure alone may make the results *unsafe* (in legal parlance): we cannot be *sure* that marks awarded are those the judges thought appropriate to the performance.

Further, it was suggested that 'the superiority of the Canadian figure skaters . . . was so obvious that an investigation followed immediately' (McNamara 2002: E1): but this is certainly not my recollection – the Canadian skaters certainly pleased the (largely partisan) crowd, but was their skating superior to the trained eyes of judges? It may be hard to say. Still, we can simplify the actual example, highlighting what (for our purposes) is essential here. Although we unquestionably want the 'honest opinion' (Loland 2002: 93) of the judges (that is, what each really thinks), *far more* than that is also needed: judges must recognize the features of the sporting events – that makes them informed judges, knowledgeable judges, and also highlights how a particular judgement might be challenged without disputing the fairness of the general procedure.

In the case as imagined, then, the judging was unfair – the result was, in some way, fixed (or, at least, this was intended). In such a case – let us imagine – the ice skaters did not get *the marks their performance warranted*; or, more simply, did not get what they deserved. So the problem here is that, as it were, the appropriate marks are not awarded – we can imagine such a judge awarding marks with her back to the ice skaters (or phoning the scores in from her hotel room!). Of course, this sort of behaviour in judging (should it occur) is reprehensible. But this account of the situation implicitly concedes that there is a fair or appropriate mark – the one these skaters should have received but did not. So this is an example where the judging is done *badly* or inappropriately, where the *wrong* marks were awarded. As such, it implicitly concedes the soundness of untainted judging. That is why my title for it, *the issue of just deserts*, is warranted.

This kind of case – hence, this kind of objection – is not central to our concerns: it highlights the importance of reliable judges, well-trained, experienced and (where possible) not amenable to pressure, or other distorting forces.

A second (possible) difficulty might be called the issue of the *subjectivity of judgements*. What is contentious here is whether the sort of judging called for in, especially, aesthetic sports could ever have the kind of public reliability required. The thought might be that, in some way, judgements of this sort are essentially or necessarily problematic. (Of course, the substance of this problem has been put aside; see p. 93.)

This formulation brings out immediately objections of (seemingly) other kinds, which are really only ways to formulate the issue of just deserts. For it might be urged that, say, my judging of ice dance is *biased* – that I overrate a kind of lyric quality in the dancing, or a certain novelty. Or, again, that my judging of ice dance is *prejudiced*: that I favour ice dancers from, for instance, the former Soviet Union. If either of these accusations is true, then I am not a reliable or appropriate judge of ice dance: the dances do not get the marks they deserve – hence this raises our issue of just deserts. For, notice, the accusation here is that *my* judging is biased or involves prejudice, not that *all* judging does. But this resembles the essay marking mentioned earlier: the fact that I am a biased marker, or a prejudiced marker, only makes sense by contrast with my colleague down the hall, who gives essays what they deserve. So were the objection to judging that it imports bias or prejudice, this is (at best) an important practical objection, to be met by attention to the training and selection of judges. For such objections do not – and cannot – suggest that such judging is essentially or necessarily problematic: rather, they highlight difficulties for *some* acts of judging, not for *all*.

The more substantial objection must claim that all judgement is, of its nature, problematic; but how might such an objection be sustained? As we have seen (pp. 93–7), it seems unlikely that such a wholly general argument could be forthcoming. The outcome, then, is that (in respect of objectivity) aesthetic sports are basically in the same position as purposive sports – both have publicly available means by which knowledgeable judges or umpires can determine the score, and so on. And both must be on the look-out against ignorance, bias, agendas and the like.

6 Principles and the application of rules

For some, '[i]t is only a matter of time before major tennis tournaments are played without line judges' (Henderson 2002: 16). This might be thought a good thing, eliminating human error. But, as we have seen, human judgement is essential in aesthetic sports. Still, it might seem that the difficulties or issues raised for judgements of aesthetic sports in the previous chapter either do not apply to purposive sports, or that (when they do) they can be overcome by appeal to technological solutions; for instance, modelled on the way that some line-calls in tennis are automated. But neither point is correct: there will always be areas of judgement, even in purposive sports, since what event occurred depends on how the rules constitute actions (see p. 91); further, there is a limit to what technology can ever achieve.

It is probably not possible in practical terms to do without the judgement of referees or umpires, even in purposive sports. Perhaps decisions about what precisely occurred in such-and-such a case are often replaceable by some 'technological solution'; as, for instance, when the Cyclops machine used in lawn tennis replaces line judges for at least *some* cases of determining the legality of the serve – we can imagine such a technology extended to cover *all* cases, 'from infrared motion detectors to Matrix-style rotating cameras' (Adande 2003: D8). Yet, even were this possible, not all issues will be resolvable in this way.

For instance, other considerations of this practical kind relate to the gain if (or when), say, the umpires in cricket were replaced by some technological solution of this sort, recently raised in the context of a discussion of the pressure placed on umpires by 'players, crowds, media' (Brearley 2002: 8): for one way to remove the pressure on the correctness of one's judgements would be to make those judgements answerable to a machine, either to its bleeps or to its 'decisions' as to whether a ball was in or a batsman was out. But one might, with justice, harbour reservations about taking that much power out of the hands of persons – where there would be no appeal when the machine beeped that a ball was out. And, of course, one would not have eliminated human judgement if there *were* such an appeal, but to an umpire.

In such cases, though, one practical danger is that we must now *rely on the machine*, which differs from trusting an umpire or referee. As with computers, the machine here is likely to function as a black box: we will not know, nor be able to check, that it is functioning correctly – nor that it continues to do so. After all, an umpire can be asked to explain, in ways a machine never can. Further, we can understand how an umpire might acquire authority. As Brearley (2002: 8) rightly put it, such authority 'comes from good decisions, . . . but it is also earned by an attitude lived out by the umpire, an attitude that communicates such qualities as honesty, impartiality, fair-mindedness, integrity, directedness, and openness'.

Only the first of these is possible for our machine. Should the machine be adopted, it may 'subvert the decisions made by court-side officials' (Henderson 2002: 16): certainly, in challenging them, it will at least represent a different kind of authority. (And, as we will see, the umpire may be required to deal with new or unexpected cases.)

Moreover, trusting the machine will alter the nature of the sport in other ways; for instance, by changing the margins of winning or losing. Consider the use of ever more exact timing in downhill skiing: what now constitutes a narrow victory would, at an technologically more primitive time, have been a tie, a dead heat, or a draw. This may not matter. In addition, the reply might be that there was *always* a difference here – that the difference had now become noticeable (or recordable).

Of course, it might be decided that *real* sports should be of the completely measurable sort – but that would have implications, with a reduced list (compared to, say, the Olympics) of what are and are not sports; moreover, the list might differ markedly from what – pre-theoretically – we thought. For if judgements by umpires can be required, not simply as to whether the ball crossed the line or the batsman grounded his bat, but also as to whether the action was within the rules, such umpiring decisions will always be indispensable. And, as I shall argue, this is – and must be – the situation.

The need to *apply* the rules (even for purposive sports)

Two features are supposed to make the situation clearer for purposive sports than it was for aesthetic sports. First, the outcomes themselves are clearer – it *seems* the question is simply, 'Did the ball cross the line?', 'Which runner crossed the line first?'. (That is, there is an answer in terms of Suits's pre-lusory goals.) This might seem a *purely factual* matter, not one requiring the discretion of judge or referee. Second, all the referee or umpire needs to do is to *apply* the rules of that sport, where such rules will unambiguously determine whether or not there was a score; or, more generally, what should be done.

Doubts have already been raised about the first of these elements. 'What occurred' in a sporting context often cannot be decided independently of the application of the rules of the sport: that is one sense in which rules function as *constitutive*. For convenience, we might contrast the role of the referee or umpire in adjudicating as to what happened with the role in adjudicating on

the application of the rules in 'tricky' situations. In part, the umpire's adjudication on what happened will always be rule-related. Thus determining what happened might involve answering such questions as, 'lbw or not?', 'ball or strike?': and these involve determining not only that the ball was in a certain position, but that this was achieved within the rules. The second half of this contrast, concerning tricky situations, can wait until a little later. For most of the situations in a standard game or match will be ones where, once what happened is known, the application of the rules is unproblematic.

But, to pursue the first element of this contrast (adjudicating what happened), there will be matters where judgement is needed: for example, in American football, a player must have 'both feet down and be in control of the ball' in order that a pass into the end zone be completed (for a touchdown). Here, at least, judgement is required as to whether or not there was *control*: that does not seem a matter readily determined by a machine. Similarly, in rugby, scoring a try requires that the ball be touched down in control, where one contrast is with the touching down being blocked by, say, the body of an opponent. Again, such recognition could not realistically be mechanized. So some level of human judgement is inevitable here too, as it was for aesthetic sports.

The second matter is equally problematic, for (as we saw in Chapter 2 pp. 49–52) rules could not – in principle – cover *all* cases. Then the umpire or referee's application of a rule in a particular case may go beyond what had previously seemed the scope of the rule. In such a situation, the umpire will *seem* obliged to make a new rule – which appears to give umpires too much power (or inappropriate power). In both kinds of sports (aesthetic and purposive), there are questions concerning the role of judges or umpires: in applying the rules of sports, should we perhaps see these umpires as *making* rules (as some writers on jurisprudence have seen judges in the US Supreme Court as *making* law: compare p. 108)?

Moreover, the general difficulty here is that *all* rules must be applied in *all* situations: what behaviours a rule prescribes or proscribes is not automatically clear. This follows from our earlier recognitions about rule-following – that one cannot, say, provide a further rule to explain what following this rule amounts to (since to do so suggests a regress: Chapter 2 p. 45); and that there will be cases where the application of the rule is either silent or problematic (for instance, counter-intuitive).

Some cases?

The central cases, then, are those where the application of the rules of the game seems problematic. In some cases, the extant rules do not seem to deal with the actual situations while, in yet others, there seems to be a clear rule – but the wrong one! (Or, at least, one that generates cases that seem to violate considerations of natural justice; one where a common-sense application of the intention behind the rule would yield the opposite outcome.)

Starting from some examples from J. S. Russell (1999), let us explore some of the varied bases to which decisions by umpires or referees might appeal in practice.

- *Helping out at home* – in an 1887 game, runner Mack, who had success-fully crossed home plate, tussled with the catcher, allowing two further runners to cross the plate: but the rules applied only to *base runners*: having completed his run, Mack was not subject to this rule.
- *Hoak's sacrifice* – in a 1957 game, Hoak (on the batting side) fielded a ball himself, to prevent two members of his team being out. He was penalized for hindering a fielder making a play on a batted ball; but there was 'nothing explicitly in the rule book to penalize an offensive player for intentionally interfering with a batted ball to break up a double play' (Russell 1999: 29). So the other players remained in the game.
- *   ident* – in a 1983 game, 'a potentially game-winning home   disallowed . . . when it was discovered that pine tar resin had   over more than the bottom 18 inches of [the] bat' (Russell 1999:   50), contrary to the rules, even though it was agreed that this gave no advantage

In the first considerations of natural justice mean that tussling with the catcher is contrary to what should be allowed – and, indeed, the rules were later emended in this direction. But, as the rules then stood, Mack was not in contravention of the rule, although he *should* have been!

In the second case, like the first, the player gains an advantage by beha-viour not explicitly precluded under the rules as they then stood. Again, considerations of natural justice lead to a sensible outcome: the advantage cannot be permitted under any *reasonable* reading of the rules; and the umpire should have so ruled.

In the third case, the player is in clear contravention of a rule designed to prevent gaining an advantage – but, in this case, it was agreed on all sides to be no advantage (and possibly even a disadvantage). So there should not have been a penalty, despite the rules.

In all these cases, then, considerations of natural justice – of what seems fair and right, and in line with the spirit of the rules – conflicts with the letter of those rules. So, as these cases illustrate, and as Russell (1999: 30) notes, 'rules governing games cannot always be relied upon as definitive guides to the regulation of conduct'.

It might seem, at first glance, that all that is needed here are new rules, better rules: but (as we saw in Chapter 2 pp. 46–7) this is an illusion. For *any* set of rules, a case could arise like one of these, either where the rules as they stand are silent as to what to do – but the umpire must do something – or where what the rule prescribes or proscribes does not seem in line with considerations of natural justice or fairness. Here, appeal might be to

something like the *intentions* of those who first made the rules, as a way to determine what is in line with the *spirit* of those rules. But such a procedure is doomed, for three related reasons. First, we simply cannot know with any confidence what those rule-makers' intentions are/were; second, we cannot realistically expect that they *had* intentions to cover all the cases, especially in a changing world; third, the rule-makers are not a fount of all knowledge – they have given us the sport, to be developed as time (and technology) see fit; and this means that the sport's intentions may not be what they once were.

Principles and discretion

Instead, a more perceptive reading of the place of judges, referees and umpires recognizes that the application of rules, as of laws, *always* requires acts of discretion; and that such acts of discretion must be motivated. How might such an act of discretion be explained? A typical move is not to those rules themselves, but to the *spirit* of the rules, or to considerations of fair play, or some such. But how do these matters come to impinge on sport's performance? They stand to the rules of sport roughly as Ronald Dworkin's (legal) *principles* stand to his (legal) *rules*:[1] the *principle* that one should not benefit from one's crime prevents the grandfather-killer, Elmer, from inheriting his grandfather's wealth – there is no *rule* here (Dworkin 1978: 22–8, 71–80).[2] In just this way, the principles underlying a sport provide a *learned* background essential to appropriate participation in that sport. Hence, there is a context of principles here, to which any umpiring decision might appeal – at least, as the beginning of an argument.

So, faced with the need to exercise discretion (that is, where the explicit rules of the sport seem either silent or to have unclear or confusing application), a judge or referee draws on the principles underlying the sport. In the three cases above, appeal to the principles 'reads' the rules of baseball in line with considerations of natural justice. Then, in the first case (*Helping out at home*), it seems that the runner unfairly interferes with the catcher – he should be penalized, and the activities of other runners not be allowed to count. In the second case (*Hoak's sacrifice*), the batting side gained an unfair advantage: again, appeal to the principles means that the other player too should leave the game. In the third case (*Pine tar incident*), no advantage was gained: if anything, this was a disadvantage – as all sides agreed. It cannot be contrary to the spirit of the game (hence to its principles) to voluntarily disadvantage oneself: so the bat ought not to have been ruled illegal. In these ways, then, the discretion is grounded in appeal to the principles; it is not arbitrary. Any dispute about what *should* happen in a particular case is a debate either about what the relevant principles are or about how they apply in this case. So these are debates the knowledgeable about the sport could realistically have.

Moreover, these principles could never become (explicit) rules of the game. Or, more exactly, that it would not help to do so. For, in line with earlier points (Chapter 2 p. 47), even these new rules could not cover *all* cases – because there is no *all*, no finite totality of possible cases. Hence appeal to principles would still be needed even after these new rules were made.

In referring to the role for such principles, my point is not to emphasize the completeness or incompleteness of rules as represented by rule-formulations (the kind of thing better drafting might wrongly be thought to cure) – there is always an element of judgement in the application of a rule, and in 'knowing how to go on' (PI §151; §179) on the basis of a rule. Instead, such rules 'are not incomplete, like a book whose last page is missing, but abstract' (Dworkin 1978: 103). This means that they must be filled-in, *particularized* (Chapter 8 pp. 138–9), to a given context (exactly as earlier discussion predicted: Chapter 2 p. 51). And that immediately licences disputes about the appropriateness of the various cases offered.[3] For how exactly do the rules apply – and how should they be applied – in this (testing) case? There will always be room for dispute here, since no application of a rule is uniquely determined by the rule-formulation (Chapter 2 pp. 51–2).

We can see, then, to what an appeal to the principles actually appeals – we recognize how the training of judges, umpires, referees, is (or should be) partly a training in using the principles to decide cases where the rules are silent.

Nor should we think of this as an impossible burden on referees – their problems are primarily those considered earlier in the chapter (and Chapter 5 p. 99), concerning lack of knowledge, understanding or information, which are not the key ones here. One of Dworkin's own examples (1978: 102) to illustrate this point runs as follows:

> Suppose some rule of a chess tournament provides that the referee shall declare a game forfeit if one player 'unreasonably' annoys the other in the course of play. The language of the rule does not define what counts as 'unreasonable' annoyance . . .

His example could readily be replaced by one about sport: about cricket or soccer, for instance. And his point would be ours – that the rules do not circumscribe the exact behaviours they permit or prohibit.

Nor should we think such disputes rare: for they are driven by questions of principles. Rather, such principles are more pervasive than they might seem. As Dworkin (1978: 28) remarks, '[o]nce we identify legal principles as separate sorts of standards, different from legal rules, we are suddenly aware of them all around us'. For the normativity of such principles is visible in many of the social behaviours of human beings.[4]

Yet, when aiming to illustrate a human situation (especially a legal one) where there are rules but no principles, and (therefore?) one where such moral considerations do not apply, Dworkin (1978: 24)[5] uses a sporting

example, that of the rule in baseball 'that if a batter has had three strikes, he is out'. He claims that the decision to select *three* strikes (rather than, say, four) is arbitrary: if so, further justification would not be needed. But this is misleading once sport is viewed more realistically: moral(ish) principles do apply in at least some sports, as illuminated by the possibility of contravening the spirit of the rules. In Dworkin's example, for instance, one motivation for the rule must relate to a proposed or intended duration of a game – the rule '300 strikes and you are out' would make a typical game too long. But even here *some* consideration of fairness might be operative: that one strike did not give the batter a *fair* chance to display prowess, for example. So there is an implicit appeal to (principled) fairness. Saying this stresses the importance of the *possibility* of winning (and such like) where this means more than just the logical possibility. (In Chapter 7, I use the term 'spoiling' to roughly characterize behaviour that, while not contrary to the rules of a game/sport, is nonetheless not how one *ought* to play it: for participating in the game/match should mean participating in ways that respect one's opponents, showing due regard for them. Spoiling plays do not permit opponents the possibility of playing the game according to its spirit, a possibility one *must* grant to opponents taken seriously.)

A central thought here is that one learns at least *some* of the principles through learning how to '*construct* the game's character' (Dworkin 1978: 103) when we learn the rules. Dworkin's exposition takes the acquiring of principles as somehow prior to, and the basis for, such learning of rules: as he puts it, the principles provide a 'gravitational force' (Dworkin 1978: 115) operative within the rule. Certainly this process will be facilitated where we can build on established practices (better thought of as *customs*: see Chapter 4 pp. 78–9), as we might see arithmetic as built on drill; say, in matching diners to dinners. So the centre here might be our having learned *how to go on*. Rule-formulations then codify the customs and underlying principles as giving their content. But, in sporting cases, this cannot be quite right, since the sports will be constituted by those rules. Further, the interlock between the moral metaphors of justice – 'level playing field', 'fair play', and so on – and the specifics of sport mean that, in learning how to make sense of these ideas *as they apply in particular sports*, one is learning the general moral principles, by learning how to apply these key metaphors more exactly. (If this is true, it places a particular obligation on teachers of sport: they can be teaching the rules of a moral laboratory; Chapter 8 pp. 144–5.)

A crucial point here is hard to get *exactly* right: on the one hand, it must be acknowledged that no rule (or law) can deal with *all* cases. So one cannot – for instance – resolve *all* difficulties in a particular sport by making new rules for that sport (or new codes of professional ethics, for that matter: see McNamee 1995), rules which deal with every situation unequivocally. Now, one way to make *that* point would be to emphasize the role of judges (say, referees) in interpreting rules in real cases. Equally, and on the other hand, the kind of judicial discussion that determines *what the law is* can *look like* the making of law by judges (as Dworkin recognizes):[6] at the least, judges are not free to 'make the law' – say, in these 'hard cases'. One way to articulate this point would see judges as looking for the law. These two images of legal practice (and legal decision) *seem* to run in opposite directions. And what is true of law generally conceived is – by extension – true of the laws of particular sports. Some might ask, 'So what?'. Our reply is that we want (or perhaps need) to say both of these things, on different occasions: that the same form of words can be different questions in different mouths, with each being resolvable, taken case-by-case – yet without there being some *general* resolution! So there will be some occasions when the revealing answer will point in one direction, and other occasions when it will point in the other. As Baker and Hacker (1985a: 47 note) comment, of a similar difficulty, '[t]he question is misleading but the facts are clear'.

A parallel: the moral reading of the American Constitution?

It can be difficult to understand the idea that the *spirit* of a game (or sport) is held in place by principles (in Dworkin's sense) rather than simply by rules. But reflection on a parallel case may make that clearer: that case is the American Constitution, on the reading of Dworkin (1996). (Of course, if this *does* clarify the case at hand, it does not matter if Dworkin is actually mistaken about the Constitution.)

The central thought concerns those cases where – on the face of it – the constitution is silent: here, it seems to some that Supreme Court judges, in rendering judgements based on the Constitution, are actually making law. And, of course, judges are supposed only to interpret the law, not make it. (Notice that this objection parallels one levelled at our judges or referees in sport, above.)

For example, does the right to privacy, enshrined in the First Amendment, have a bearing on issues concerning abortion – as was argued in Roe v. Wade (1973: see Dworkin, 1996: 50–2)? Does the right to equality before the law, enshrined after the American Civil War in the Fourteenth Amendment, have any bearing on the rights of minorities defined *other than* by ethnicity (Dworkin 1996: 150)? We can be fairly sure that these issues were not in the minds of those who wrote these legal documents: so, on one idea of framers' intentions, they were not part of such intentions. That is to say, these connections were not reflected in the psychology of those particular men. But equally we can be pretty sure that the framers did not think about such issues, one way or the other. (If we had to come to a decision, we might begin to ask what they *would have* thought, if they had known more, and been asked.)

Dworkin argues that a plausible alternative is on offer, which he calls a 'moral reading' of the US Constitution: we should see principles at work in these laws – and then go on to debate the precise nature and extent of such principles. So it makes sense to urge that there is law already – prior to the action or decision of the judges – to the extent that the principles give a basis for deciding in cases. Then in applying the principles in these cases, as we will see, judges are really determining *what the law is*, rather than making new law.

So, with respect to the US Constitution, framers' intentions (properly understood) are determined by a mixture of history, (constitutional) integrity and practice (see Dworkin 1996: 10, 1986: 176–224). Then determining the intentions in the legal case is a matter of making the best fit; what is sometimes called *a matter of interpretation*. Yet, this is not conceptualized on a purely psychological model of intention – which is anyway incomplete (Dworkin 1996: 292–3), for there are different ways (even) these might be made out.[7] Instead, 'different hypotheses about the framers' mental states' (Dworkin 1996: 296) turn out to be 'different ways of structuring the same assumptions about what their mental states were' (Dworkin 1996: 296).

In speaking of intentions here, one might see oneself as attempting to determine the appropriate reading of a (philosophical) text (Baker and Morris 1996: 5–6) – there may be no absolutely decisive considerations here. Rather, such-and-such a reading seems to preserve integrity better than its competitors (Dworkin 1986: 217): this is an appeal to the *spirit* of what is meant, relying on general principles, and so on (typically moral or political principles and, for games at least, concerned with fairness and/or justice).

Then our more radical solution, in line with Dworkin's remarks, asks where the behaviour stands in terms of the 'real' rules – that is, the rules on their best interpretation, the interpretation that maintains the integrity (as Dworkin [1986: 94] puts it) of those rules. So, in legal disputes over the correct decision in a difficult case, the opposing judges are disagreeing about the correct interpretation of the law – over *what the law is* (Nagel 1995: 196). For instance, they might dispute 'how to construct the real statute in the circumstances of that case' (Dworkin 1986: 17). Again, in the case of Elmer (p. 105), who murdered his grandfather and was therefore unable to benefit from his will, Dworkin (1986: 17) comments, 'judges before whom a statute is laid need to construct the "real" statute – a statement of what difference the statute makes to the legal rights of various people – from the text in the statute book'.

As Dworkin (1986: 20) remarks, subsequent dispute among the judges would be 'about what the law was, about what the real statute the legislators enacted really said'. And, of course, were this also true of the statutes of our game, we might with justice argue that the rules of the game, its *real* rules, have a bearing here!

As Dworkin (1986: 217) says, one is here recognizing 'implicit standards between and beneath the explicit ones'. And these standards – enshrined in the principles – will typically be moral ones. Preserving integrity, in this sense, amounts to reading the rules of the practice so as to show that practice in its best light – thereby preserving its principles – in the light of what has gone before in that practice. Here, as Dworkin (1986: 227) records, '[h]istory matters because . . . [the] scheme of principles . . . must justify the standing as well as the content of . . . past decisions'. We need such integrity all the way up!

First, as Nagel (1995: 197) notes, integrity in this sense is 'an ambiguous virtue': construing the law and its purposes in this way 'makes decisions flow from a coherent set of principles, even when those principles are not your own'. So this idealized version offers an explanation of consistency requirements as well as a basis for disputes about what counts as consistently interpreting a rule of sport. Second, such a model of integrity fits practices like sport, where the rules (and even some of the principles) have explicit formulation, at least as well – and perhaps better – than it accords with Dworkin's preferred case, municipal legal systems. This is revealing since it cannot be far off the truth to say that the integrity being preserved is the integrity of the sport itself – and this accords with earlier talk of its *spirit*. Third, we know where to look for the interpretative acts here: namely, to the decisions of umpires and referees, as well as to appeals concerning those decisions. Here, a crucial difference is that, in contrast to typical judicial decisions, the decisions of umpires (etc.) will always be required in a fairly brief time span: the players (etc.) cannot wait for ever. This just places yet more importance on the umpires as *informed* judges: and hence places yet greater weight on their appropriate training.

In conclusion, then, the discussion highlights how considerations of natural justice (or of principles) must be invoked either when the rules seem silent or when, as most readily applied, they conflict with considerations of fairness. Here too some attention is given to the principled modification of rules, typically by rule-altering bodies: and once again one should reject the vision of a set of rules dealing appropriately with all cases, once and for all.

Dworkin (1986: 226) urges that legal rules, as regularly conceived, 'are not themselves programs *of* interpretation'. As Nagel (1995: 197) notes, this constitutes a *substantive* theory of law: and we could, of course, reject it.[8] But suppose, for the sake of argument, that we do not. What follows about the rules (the *laws*, as they are often rightly called) of sports?

This way of understanding the founder's intentions for the US Constitution can have a profound effect on what those intentions are taken to be; and hence on what the US Constitution is taken to licence or proscribe. We might expect a similar impact on our understanding of sport from adopting the corresponding view of the principles of sport: that much more is actually governed by the rules than might be thought – this will probably mean that some ideas downgraded to ethos will turn out, on this conception, to be genuine rules. So this view of rule-following has a revisionary potential: our view of how sporting rules apply may be transformed.

This sort of revisionism is, of course, not my usual way – we would need a good understanding of the nature of sport to do this. But we are really rebelling against how theorists have *told us* rules in sport (laws) operate: of course, that will be a suitable strategy to return us to a kind of reflective common sense – where we have thought through these cases (as they impinge on our problems), and returned to common sense with a refreshed conception of what it might imply.

7   Spoiling, cheating and playing the game

The previous chapter argued that the moral imperative sometimes (and rightly) located within sport is often not a direct consequence of the rules or laws of particular sports, a fact recognized when appeal is made, not to those rules themselves, but to the spirit of the rules, or to considerations of *fair play*, or some such. Yet how do these matters manage to impinge on sport's performance? There, I urged that such considerations stand to the rules of sport roughly as Dworkin's (legal) principles stand to his (legal) rules: the principles underlying a sport provide a learned background essential for appropriate participation in that sport.

In this chapter, the discussion of the place and nature of such principles is elaborated through a consideration of a form of 'legal' cheating, to be called *spoiling*. For their application is illuminated by the possibility of contravening the 'spirit of the rules'. Then the insights from this case are applied to the consideration of cheating more generally – thus discharging an obligation in connection with the 'logical incompatibility thesis' (Chapter 2 p. 35).

Spoiling – 'legal' cheating

As noted earlier (Chapter 5 p. 107), saying that the batter in cricket should be given a *fair* chance to display prowess stresses the importance of the *possibility* of winning (etc.) where this means more than just the logical possibility. So it highlights that constraints on how one ought to play extend further than simply those enshrined in explicit rules. To plot the contours of such constraints, consider a complex idea I call *spoiling*. The term *spoiling* is here used to roughly characterize behaviour that, while not contrary to the rules of a game/sport, is nonetheless not how one *ought* to play it: for participating in the game or match should mean participating in ways that respect one's opponents, showing due regard for them. Spoiling plays do not permit opponents the possibility of playing the game according to its spirit, a possibility one *must* grant to opponents taken seriously. Although permitted by the rules, such plays are recognized – at least by knowledgeable audiences – as inappropriate ways to play the game/sport: an arena where players who 'spoil' may legitimately be criticized by the audience, team-mates and the media, but not by referees.

A consideration of spoiling plays will defend and elaborate the thesis that (properly understood) such principles offer essential moral constraints on (some) sports. Key differences between principles of this kind and typical rules constitutive of sport highlight the framework character of those principles. And, since the principles regulate human interactions (in the sense of headlining what one ought or ought not to do), it cannot be far off the mark to call them 'moral'.

Can we acquire *moral* principles through learning in *sporting* situations? Arguments for particularism in morality (Chapter 8 p. 139) emphasize the sporting character of these situations. But a more realistic account of the relation of the particular to the abstract resolves this tension.

Sketching such an account of the constraint of sport by (moral) principles supports the idea that, *for this reason*, some sports have the capacity to provide examples of those concrete particulars that alone permit the learning, and learning to apply, of moral concepts: in short, that some sport can function as a *moral laboratory*, in which moral concepts are acquired, but with less risked than in genuine moral confrontations. And this idea will be further elaborated later (Chapter 8 pp. 129–30).

The spoiling example

Before returning to abstract considerations, a concrete example is useful. As my central example is from cricket, I will spell it out at some length, drawing rough parallels to baseball. It is the end of a limited-over cricket match: there is one delivery (one ball) to go and the batting-side needs *six runs* to win. In principle, six runs might be scored in a number of ways from one delivery; in practice, these runs can only be scored by the batsman hitting the ball over the boundary rope without its bouncing – 'on the fly', as people say. Typically the bowler in cricket delivers the ball overarm, where it bounces *roughly* in front of the batsman: such a delivery might be hit for six, hit over the boundary rope on the fly: and this is especially likely given that the relevant batsman is a *good* hitter of sixes.

To give (fictional) names to the players, let us call the bowler 'Trevor Chappell'. What he does – following the instructions of his captain (whom we will call 'Greg Chappell', and designate to be his brother) – is to bowl underarm, along the ground. This facilitates the batsman's *hitting* the ball, but effectively precludes his hitting it 'for six'. As a result, Chappell's side wins the match.

Now, one is permitted to bowl underarm in cricket: there is no rule precluding it. Further, one is permitted to bowl along the ground; again, there is no rule prohibiting it. But the net effect of the action is to win the match with a technique which – as people say – 'is not cricket': it is a *spoiling* gesture.

A subsequent rule change, arguably as a result of the events described, simply made a different (and more complex) way of spoiling possible. For, as we have seen (Chapter 2 p. 47), sets of rules can never handle *all* cases because there is no such finite totality: a boys' comic when I was a child included a cartoon strip, interestingly called 'Is it cricket?', about a player who could bowl high in the air, so that the ball descended onto the wicket. Since this is not a practical possibility that (as far as I know) cricket's rule-makers have considered, it is presumably legal to do this: but is it cricket?

To return to our cases, notice that bowling the last delivery of a limited-overs match underarm, along the ground, is not a technique one could always use. First, it would not always be necessary: it is effective in this case partly because here one is trying to preclude (exactly) *six* runs, and would be quite happy to concede, say, *four* runs – that would still leave the Chappell team winners! Second, it would be counter-productive if all teams used it, either throughout the game (which would destroy much of the excitement) or at the end, where its predictability would make it useless as a match-winner – everyone would be doing it!

This example is powerful partly because cricket is regularly offered as a model of fair play;[1] although today's high-class game, with its 'sledging'[2] is often far from that.

It is granted on all sides that this behaviour is permitted by the rules of the sport. But if this spoiling behaviour really were OK, why not do it *all* the time? Only using it on this (strange) occasion is tacit acknowledgement that it is not OK. (Also, as noted above, there are practical issues about the effectiveness of it as a long-term strategy, one to then be adopted by one's opponents, say.)

This is an example of spoiling because bowling in that fashion at that point in the game does not give the opposing side a fair chance. . . . So spoiling has a direct connection to the 'spirit of the game' idea – to the *essence* of a sporting contest, as we might put it. But that puns on the term 'sporting', both to mean conforming to the rules of the game (and hence part of that sport) and to mean played appropriately!

Spoiling comes about when there is a conflict between the letter of the rules (the written rule or statute) and the spirit of the rules – that is, the principles (for instance, of fairness) on which the rules rest.

In determining the relevant principles here, notice the (*conceptual*) importance, within cricket, of the idea of a 'wide': a delivery beyond where the batsman can plausibly hit the ball. Here we see the commitment, within cricket, to the bowling of deliveries from which the batsman *can* score, if he is sufficiently skilled. That its rules allow the concept of a *wide* therefore indicates something about the principles underlying cricket. Further, the penalty for bowling a *wide* is twofold: first, the bowling side automatically gains one run for the wide; second, the ball is delivered again. In this way, the bowling side simply loses one run and still has to bowl that delivery. Its importance here, though, lies in making visible the connection of sport's rules to its principles – as the case of spoiling identifies. In recognizing the place of (effectively) moral principles here – and of the preservation of the integrity of the sport thereby – we begin to see how the hoped-for connection of sport to the moral might be defended. (Notice, though, that this concerns what sport can do, not what it must, or inevitably will, do.)

The issue of generality

But need there be *one* account here for sport in general? Suppose that we resolve this case: to what degree are there *precedents* being set here? Moral notions central to our lives (also?) have a role in sport, a role recognized in the moral metaphors from which this chapter began. But those ideas are either *not* metaphorical or are *less* metaphorical in the sporting context, where there really can be fair playing and the levelness of actual playing fields. Seeing how these ideas interact with the rules (and spirit) of sport can show how such notions might *apply* – and hence how they might be applied more generally. This acknowledges a kind of generality of application which is very different from simply generalizing: as we might put it, it is the generalizability of the particularist. For it grants that we may formulate principles, but that their application in new cases will always be problematic. That is one reason why one cannot (usefully) write down such principles. Or, we can write them down, but not helpfully: the principle against spoiling might be, 'Play the game'; or, more exactly, 'Do not act so as to impede your opponent's playing to the spirit of the rules.'

Of course, one is here formulating in the abstract the objection to spoiling: but this simply reflects the contours of the relevant principle – it certainly would not be exceptionless. So that rendering the principle against spoiling as 'Play the game' does not give useful guidance as to what to *do* in a particular situation; nor how to judge what someone else does. This is especially true when the principle applies to more than one sport, as well as to different situations *within* a sport. But being told 'play the game' may be informative for an experienced cricketer, highlighting ways in which my behaviour to date was less than exemplary. Even more revealing is when I am told, say by my captain and elder brother, to *not* 'play the game': I might know what to do *then* just because I *do* know 'how to go on' without contravening this principle – although on this occasion I do not do so.

Formulating the abstract principle is doubly unhelpful. Of course, like any rule-formulation, the application of my principle-formulation is always a matter of judgement. But, more crucially, the application here is circumscribed by the specific nature of the sport itself. Unsurprisingly, this conclusion reinforces the particularism (explicitly) assumed earlier.

Thus we recognize the importance of principles: they can give us a basis for deciding in places where – at first blush – the rules seem silent. But a good question here will be: how do we (typically) learn sporting principles?

My most general answer is that this happens in *appropriate* teaching of the sporting activity. So what one learns is not – and could not be – just a formulation of the principle (a principle-formulation) but rather how to *behave* in accordance with the principle: for instance, how to manifest 'fair play' (which is, of course, no guarantee that one will then actually play fairly). In effect, then, my thought is that principles are taught when rules are properly taught – where the term 'properly' makes just that point!

In this one case at least, we see very clearly the principle at work: that is, we see the basis for arguing that this activity is inappropriate despite its being legal – in conflict *only* with the principles, not with the rules (too). Of course, such cases are few and far between: most cases will conflict with rules too. Moreover, it may only be possible to have spoiling (in this sense) in some sporting activities, not all. Perhaps cricket lends itself especially well here: we want to say, of the spoiling, 'It is not cricket!', in spite of the fact that – since it was within the rules – it precisely *was* cricket.

In teaching the rules of a game (for example, cricket), a teacher sensitive to the principles might inculcate those principles too: indeed, those of us who were well-taught can remember this process. So, if we cannot *say* how to teach these principles, we do at least know. But now a further issue intrudes. How, given the teaching and learning of sporting principles, does this apply to morality? On this model, an abstract principle is learned from (and in) concrete instances in sport. We might then also formulate – perhaps for theoretical reasons – abstract moral principles. But, if we did so, their application in new situations would still be contentious. Principles of (roughly) rule-application are moral. For instance, there is a moral obligation to mean what one says, in two senses (see Cavell 1969: 32): that one *does* mean what one says, because (other things being equal) one means what one's words mean, to put it roughly: and because the alternatives are lying or frivolity (or self-deception) – that is, moral failings. So we can move from these 'principles' by then applying them to concrete moral situations.

Of course, a limitation of my argument must be acknowledged here: spoiling is at best *one* such index of moral connection; moreover, it is for some sports only.[3] But it is not for that reason a useless or trivial index. For these cases illustrate why someone might misconceive the relation of sport to moral development as well as offering some fixed points for many discussions (although not all). As we might say, they point to answers to *particular* perplexities – there are no wholly general problems here.

Finding the *real* rules?

As noted above, there is something fishy about spoiling procedures: otherwise, only tactical considerations would preclude their being used throughout the game – and this is not so. Might we make some more of this, by asking whether such a procedure is as obviously within the rules of the game as it appears?

At first sight, this behaviour is certainly permitted by the rules of the sport – it is not explicitly excluded. But, as suggested in Chapter 6, a more radical solution might ask whether the behaviour is excluded by the 'real' rules – that is, the rules on their best interpretation. For Dworkin (1986: 94), this will be the interpretation that maintains the integrity of those rules, the principles underlying them (typically, for games and sports at least, concerned with fairness or justice).

Faced with this insight, we can clarify our task. First, we should rephrase our account of spoiling – it may be contrary to the rules on their *real* interpretation (that is, roughly, with the principles imported) although not on a more conservative or literalist interpretation.

Second, and more important, Dworkin is here offering a different perspective on the fact that any *written* statute requires 'interpretation' (that is, understanding) for its implementation in *this* case. But it invites us to see this as an *essential*, and as a *productive*, feature of such law. We have already noted that – on pain of regress – the applications of rules cannot themselves be a matter of rules. Here we see its weirder sister: that what is and what is not a *real* rule is an essentially interpretive process, such that pointing to the wording of some statute cannot (typically) decide the matter. And if this were true of the statutes of a legal system (*any* legal system, as a matter of logic), how much more likely that these points apply (in spades) to the rules of sports?

This, then, addresses two points: first, one cannot resolve *all* of the moral problems (potentially) occurring in a particular sporting situation by tinkering with the sport's rules: second, the pressure here genuinely is pressure from the principles (in Dworkin's sense) which drive those rules – and that is a way of asserting that these genuinely are moral concerns.

In illustrating the place of (roughly) principles in sport, spoiling illuminates some of the ways sport might be thought generally valuable.

Some other cases

A key question (one that readers may have been asking for some time) is: *can one spoil in sports other than cricket?* The crucial characteristics of spoiling, as characterized here, might make one doubt this. The spoiling behaviour must be *within* the rules of the sport (so attracting no penalty, nor gaining censure from the governing body) yet contrary to the that sport's spirit: this will mean, roughly, contrary to how it *is* played (its ethos), rather than to how it *might* be. And the activity must give the perpetrators an advantage – at least in that context. I do not know enough about *all* sport to guarantee whether it applies elsewhere. Nor can we produce some transcendental argument to determine the matter once and for all.

Consider some cases which are *not* spoiling. If I waste time in soccer (say, by kicking the ball away prior to a free kick), I may be penalized; at the least, a competent referee simply adds on the time wasted. So nothing is gained. Thus what I do *is* contrary to the rules; and recognized as such. Therefore this is not spoiling as I have explained it, since this is contrary to the letter of the law. (Still, given that there was no penalty . . . well, there is *really* no advantage either, if the referee is 'on the ball'.) Correspondingly, a quarterback who 'throws the ball away' to avoid being sacked is not spoiling because his behaviour is *not* censured (by players or officials); while a basketball player who fouls an opponent in the act of shooting is doing something both *expected* of him and (as the rules are read by referees) not contrary to the rules – as the imposition of fixed penalties for this behaviour is taken to illustrate. Far from being a behaviour censured, it is behaviour applauded (or at least required) within the contemporary playing of the game.

One might think of intentionally 'walking' a batter in baseball as akin to spoiling. As Haugeland (1998: 162 note 1) explains:

> Generally, the opposing pitcher . . . would try to avoid giving a batter a free 'balls on base' (also called a 'walk'); but in certain threatening situations, especially when the current batter is on a 'hot streak', then that batter is 'walked' intentionally.

This activity, which might upset fans, is clearly perfectly legal – and no doubt strategic. Moreover, the pitching side *might* get an advantage from it. (But not always: in one baseball game in 2002, the Anaheim Angels [winners of the World Series that year] walked one batter, only to have the very next 'at bat' hit a home run!) This cannot be a central case of spoiling, though, as another batter always gets the chance to win the game; the advantage is nowhere near as final (or as obvious) as in the original example of spoiling.

We learn, by attending to the contemporary version, that sport retains the possibility of an engagement with morality: the spoiling cases both show this to us and give us insight into its basis in what, following Dworkin, have been called principles – a moral underpinning not divorced from contexts of realization in sports practice.

Cheating and rule-following

Earlier, spoiling was classified as a kind of 'legal' cheating; not in contravention of the rules, but was contrary to the spirit of the game or sport. Such an appeal to the spirit of the sport received its 'cash value' from (moral) principles – in Dworkin's sense – underlying the rules of the sport. But what exactly *is* cheating? Leaman (1995: 195) recognizes the difficulty of an exceptionless account of cheating to cover all cases: 'It is not a simple matter to determine when the rules of a game are being kept.'

We can briefly explore the concept of cheating, drawing on what we have learned from the case of spoiling. Doing so involves rehearsing standard objections to standard accounts. For it might seem that cheating in sport centrally involves activities (a) with the intention to deceive (at least, to deceive the referee or umpire), where (b) some rule is intentionally broken, to (c) the benefit of one side. These will be characteristics of very many cases of cheating: for instance, when I trip an opponent, I hope that the referee will not notice, in line with (a) above; I know that such tripping is contrary to the rules, in line with (b); and I hope to gain thereby, in line with (c) – perhaps by my team going on to score. Yet are these the contours of *all* cheating in sport?

Does cheating always involve the intention to deceive? Of course, many cases of cheating *will* have this character: for instance, when it was discovered that Boris Onischenko (a modern pentathlete from the USSR, during the team competition at the 1976 Olympics in Montreal) 'had wired his sword with a well-hidden circuit-breaker which enabled him to register a hit whenever he wanted' (Wallechinsky 1988: 373), the intention to deceive was pretty clear. For this is not how the épée discipline was conceived! And the marked improvement in Onischenko's scores with the épée since 1970 suggest that this was not an isolated incident. But this degree of intendedness to deceive does not apply in *all* cases: for instance, we can imagine cases where a professional foul is committed (say, in soccer where an opposition striker is brought down in front of the goalmouth) despite being in clear view of the referee or umpire. So this condition is not essential, contrary to (a) above.

What about the intention to break rules? Is this always present? Three kinds of cases suggest not. First, the intention here need not be a *rule-breaking* one. For instance, if you have already been booked (in soccer) or have four personal fouls (in basketball), you are in a vulnerable position, as even a minor rule violation might see you excluded from the game. Then I might 'pick on you' – put you under additional pressure within the rules or even foul you (in a mild way) in the hope that you will be sent off. (Even if I am censured too, in the case as imagined, *yours* – and hence your side's – will be the greater penalty.) Typically, rules of sports do not explicitly preclude this kind of 'picking on' – of course, there will be general prohibitions against, say, my fouling you, but no specific rules against actions of *this* specific sort. Yet the action here will not be fully characterized unless its picking-on character is mentioned. So this is inappropriate behaviour; arguably, it does constitute cheating (I am seeking to gain an advantage outside of the rules), and it is intended. But it cannot be classified as intentionally breaking *the rules*. Indeed, it is more like gamesmanship (see below).[4] Here, then, even when an explicit rule is not broken, it seems possible to cheat within the rules – but this would, at the least, require the intention to cheat.

Second, the mere fact of doing such-and-such may constitute fouling (and hence may amount to cheating if it goes unpenalized). That is, we do not need to explore the player's psychology to recognize handball as contrary to the rules of soccer (hence, if unnoticed, as cheating): finding that it was not *intended* would be beside the point. To have done it and not turned yourself in to the referee will be cheating. Of course, sometimes, merely contravening the rules *may* be put aside as a mistake or accident, at least in some cases. So that, for example, if the ball hits the arm of a soccer player, but this is clearly accidental on his part, behaviour which is in contravention of the rules might still be permitted: the referee might decide that this did not, after all, constitute handball (even though the very same kind of contact would constitute handball if deliberate).

Third, a player can gain an unfair advantage through ignorance of the relevant ethos (we have already mentioned such a case: Chapter 3 p. 57): here, a player gained an advantage by not recognizing the (unofficial) conventions in place in (for this example) Premiership soccer in England, in a match between Arsenal and Sheffield Wednesday. Since the ball was kicked out of play following an injury, the convention was that the ball should be returned to the side in possession at the time of the incident: and considerations of fairness support such a policy. When this convention was ignored and the winning goal scored, it struck some as *cheating*. In this case, the manager of the winning side clearly felt that 'justice had not been done' and (uncharacteristically) offered to replay the match. This seems intention-less: the moral here is that the *advantage gained* from this behaviour is what makes it suspect. Had the ball gone wide of the net, there would have been no suggestion of replays. So the advantage seems germane. And this will in general be the outcome of *advantage* rules in many sports: that if a player or side which has been fouled is thereby advantaged, no penalty *need* be exacted on the other side (or player). As we will see (below), this highlights a connection between cheating and one's side benefiting.

We have recognized [in (c) above] that the intention of benefiting oneself or one's side is crucial here, although rule-breaking (or cheating) may not always achieve this advantage. The insight here is that giving one's opponent an advantage is *not* cheating – so the demand for fairness is against selfishness: we will not be *cheating* if our rule-breaking behaviour benefits our opponents, whatever else we may be doing. Thus, when the English bridge team at the 1965 Bermuda Bowl were accused of cheating, a satisfactory response to the accusations would have been that, on the hands where the cheating was supposed to have occurred, the English did rather worse than other teams (see Flint and North 1970). So, if there was rule-breaking, it disadvantaged the breakers!

What of 'gamesmanship': is it cheating? Suppose, as a fielder in cricket, I do my best to put off the batsman (the practice is called 'sledging'). This too is reprehensible, partly for the same reason as the spoiling gestures; namely, that it does not afford the batsman the opportunity to display his or her prowess. (It cannot be an accident that Australian cricketers are prime purveyors of both practices.) Again, the tennis player who attempts to disrupt the opponents rhythm by, say, taking as long as is permissible between points is not so very different from the one whose shoe laces become mysteriously untied, and therefore more time is taken – more, that is, than would be possible under the rules.

The strategy deployed above seems to involve searching for counter-cases (or counter-examples) to the theses of theorists of *fairness* (or cheating). But, in reality, here it simply attempts to use insights from those theorists to plot some of the contours of different concrete cases. Of course, *if* one thought of the project of philosophy (of sport) in this all-or-nothing way, these would count as counter-cases; and hence highlight reasons why – on *that* understanding – the insights cannot simply be combined.

The main point: there can be no exceptionless account of cheating for even one sport, much less for *Sport*; but why should we think such an exceptionless account *was* possible? This assumption manifests again that commitment to determinacy which has been one target throughout this text, in combination – as here – with a misconception about the determinacy (or closed-ness) of rules.

What is wrong with cheating?

Instead of merely asking what cheating is, we can follow Leaman (1995: 195) by asking what is so bad about cheating. As we will see, the answer reinforces our (essentially moral) account of the nature of sporting value. In this way, we better understand the temptations behind the logical incompatibility thesis.

Is cheating wrong because it is against 'central purpose of the game' (see Morgan 1995: 54)? The thought here is that joining in the game at all is committing oneself to playing the game in a non-cheating way. This insight, like our comments above, recognizes principles (of a roughly moral kind) underlying sporting practice, and going beyond the rules. However, the precise formulation – in terms of a 'central purpose of the game' – seems suspect: is there one purpose, to be read-off from rules? It seems not. Indeed, this would reinstate assumptions about determinacy here – that there *must be* some such purpose! But why *must* there be? In particular, why must such a purpose (were there one) be accessible from the *rules*? Of course, the connection of cheating to rule-breaking is relevant here, but it is not the only factor.

Compare cheating in sport with lying (a widely used example: see Leaman 1995: 195). Then cheating is bad for the same kind of reason lying is bad. This seems plausible just because lying can seem to undermine the whole possibility of communication between us: if I do not know whether you are lying, I cannot take you at your word. For I do not know what your *word* is. Therefore, like lying, cheating is morally reprehensible because . . . ? Well, this suggests that fundamental to what is bad about lying is the (negative) connection to *assertion*: that saying such-and-such (for instance, that it is raining) is normally taken as asserting such-and-such, and hence as offering one's warrant for the truth of such-and-such. Then lying is reprehensible because it undermines the implication of our meaning what we say. And we must *mean* what we say because the alternatives (lying, frivolity, self-deception) undermine the idea of *asserting* – of actually *saying* anything (if taken to logical conclusion).

So, it might seem that cheating undermined the game or sport in the same way as lying undermines assertion – we agreed to play *this* game; thereby agreed to abide by its rules in both their regulative and constitutive uses. Further, we have accepted its principles. This explanation of what is bad about cheating is attractive both in offering a morally relevant account, and in accounting for the idea of cheating as undermining the 'central purpose of the game' – as lying undermines the central (communicative) purpose of language. Or so it seems.

Fuller discussion of the account of lying can be deferred indefinitely; in particular, the assumption (imported above) that the central purpose of language was communicative seems obviously misplaced.[5] These are not our topics here.

But in general, contrary to the account, cheating is not like this. First, there is not, *in principle*, the same problem with *knowing* whether someone is cheating – however difficult in practice. So the mere possibility of cheating has no destructive force. Second, one could not cheat all the time, anymore than we could lie *all* (or most) of the time. Were we to do so, this would change the game (at least at the level of *ethos*; Chapter 3 p. 56).

Moreover, cheating is correctly, and insightfully, connected to the gaining of *unfair advantage*. But, again, this cannot be right in its full generality, since it is still cheating if both sides do it (that is, where there is no advantage – hence no *unfair* advantage).

We know that breaking just any formal rule of a game does not invalidate that game. (Compare the logical incompatibility thesis: Chapter 2 p. 35.) Imagining that absolutely *any* rule-breaking means one is not playing the game confuses constitutive *uses* of rules with the regulative ones (Chapter 2 pp. 35–7): some rule-breaking is expected – that is why there are umpires, referees and the like. The role of the umpire or referee (and so on) as an *authority* enshrines rule-breaking, and even cheating, into the structure of the game (Leaman 1995: 197).

Why obey rules?

Given some contrast of *broadly* the regulative/constitutive kind, the question 'Why should I obey rules of a sport?' becomes:

- Why should I obey *regulative* rules? (Answer: if I do not, I will be penalized.)
- Why should I obey *constitutive* rules? (Answer: if I do not, then I am not playing the game.)

And even if (also) some constitutive rules invoke penalties, that simply seems to offer a mixture of these two answers. Both answers seem broadly right: regulative rules impinge on me while I am playing (and there may be a slight spillover here – say, my 'bringing the game into disrepute'). Further, breaking constitutive rules does seem inconsistent with playing the game. But, as noted (Chapter 2 p. 43), my position maintains the regulative/constitutive distinction (roughly), but for *uses* of rules, not the rules themselves. Thus, fluctuations here (similar to the fluctuation between criteria and symptoms: PI §354) have rules *used* as regulative on one occasion and constitutive on another, without any damaging consequences. Thus my suggestion turns these questions upside down: we ask about a regulative use of the rule when the context primarily concerns penalties, and a constitutive use when that context addresses the nature of the actions performed.

Here, we can usefully reconsider the place of 'gamesmanship' (Leaman 1995: 196), in particular in connection to 'lusory attitude' (Suits 1995a: 10–11). The insight behind the lusory attitude (Chapter 1 p. 18) was the need to see oneself as game-playing, as joining in with the game – is this 'part of the game'? Yes, because only when we recognize something like this do we see what playing the game involves. But can one indulge in gamesmanship consistently? It might seem that doing so is engaging in self-deception. In fact, one can accept certain rules in the constitutive uses (that is, as permitting the action of, say, goal-scoring) and still see that breaking them (or bending them) is consistent with this acceptance, especially if those rules also have a regulative use. For I might decide to gain an (unfair-ish) advantage if I can, while still recognizing it as sharp practice.

Yet one does not have to participate in the game – it is voluntary (or participation is arbitrary) in just this sense. First, that one can cheat at all, and especially that one can *decide* to cheat, shows that entry into the game – adopting the 'lusory attitude', if you like – involves a *normative* commitment taken on, rather than being (for example) a *causal* consequence of drives, desires, and such like;[6] this is not something *natural*, if that implies that animals might share it. And formalists and their opponents agree that the case of cheating shows something fundamental about the moral dimension of sport – and especially its connection to fairness, justice, and so on. Yet, second, the obligation to abide by the rules (once one is in the game) is a *moral* obligation undertaken in joining the game; roughly akin to keeping one's promises.[7] We (voluntarily) buy into the extant *practice*, where that practice underlies the normativity of both rules and *ethoi*, rather than providing that normativity (Chapter 4 pp. 81–2) – the game functions as a kind of (informal) *contract*. Then the obligation is roughly as sketched above: to play by the constitutive rules, and to abide by the regulative rules . . . or to accept the penalties for not so doing.

A standard objection to the contractual view of sporting obligation is often raised when this view is deployed to explain fair play – where appeal to the contractual is common (for instance, Loland 1998: 93).[8] A recent incarnation considers the case of racquetless Josie:

your opponent in an important [squash] match . . . [who] has arrived (not to her fault) without a racquet. She will forfeit the game. You use the same kind of racquet and grip as she, and you have a back-up racquet . . . without her, you would almost certainly win the championship. The game against her will be tough . . .

(Butcher and Schneider 2003: 157)

Should you lend her your racquet? Certainly, you are not obliged to do so. As Butcher and Schneider (2003: 157) note: 'Respect for the rules does not help. You break no rules in declining to lend Josie your racquet.' Still, it seems the *fair* thing to do. Yet this is supposed to be inexplicable from the kind of contractualist viewpoint sketched here. For Butcher and Schneider (2003: 159):

> fair play cannot be reduced entirely to keeping an agreement . . . [because] . . . [y]ou break no rule, and hence break no promise, by declining to lend her your racquet . . . [since] . . . [y]our contractual agreement with Josie is to play fairly, to keep to the rules of the game. (my order)

Yet the *range* of obligation must be recognized here: *of course*, I am not obliged to lend Josie my racquet by considerations of fair play – we haven't even started playing yet! But considerations of fairness in sport apply elsewhere: here, that we begin on roughly equal terms – the idea of a *level playing field*. That will be missing if Josie remains racquetless. So there *is* a fairness consideration here; and it is part of my contractual commitment, even though the aspects of that commitment mentioned earlier have mostly concerned what follows from my joining in. And, as with my joining in, there is a voluntary element here: it is not that I *must* lend my racquet, but only that I *should* do so.

This objection also results from an unsophisticated understanding of contracts. In particular, all contracts are *defeasible* (McFee 1992: 61–3): calling the obligation here a *contract* implies that it could be defeated by 'recognized heads of exception'; for instance, legal contracts must be 'true, full and free' (McFee 1992: 62). So noting a contract between us does not amount to some exceptionless generalization, or some all-or-nothing relation (of the kind admired by, say, formalists).

Is cheating 'breaking one's [implicit] contract' to play the game? The answer is 'yes'; but that 'contract' involves a commitment to both constitutive and regulative uses of rules; and to the defeasibility of contracts. Of course, one cannot break *all* of the rules and still be playing the game, because doing so involves giving up the rules on their constitutive understanding (or in their constitutive use). Further, certain forms of cheating and such like becoming widespread *would* affect the game, by counting against such a commitment to the constitutive recognition on the part of players. If forward-passing became widespread in rugby, for instance, observers would doubt that the game was one in which, say, *tries* could be scored, since part of the action of try-scoring implies that the ball arrives over the line (and is touched down) without a forward pass. Rejecting the rules undermines the possibility of performing precisely those actions. Then joining the game is adopting the rules in their constitutive uses.

This implicitly recognizes that the obligation to abide by rules is accepted in joining the game, just as the obligation to speak the truth is implicit in (some kinds of) conversation: the comparison of cheating with lying gets that right. But there are *two* obligations here, in both cases: first, one must mean what one says because the alternatives are lying, self-deception and frivolousness (see p. 116) – this moral obligation is implicit in joining the conversation. In a parallel way, one must abide by the rules if one is to play the game: if this too is a moral obligation, we are thinking of the rules primarily in their regulative uses. Yet one must mean what one says also because, roughly, what one says *is* what one means, other things being equal – this is a constitutive implication of language-using. Similarly, the constitutive force of the rules of sport imports what, above, I called a *contract*: the logical obligation to abide by the rules if one is playing the game – and this logical obligation is the insight behind the logical incompatibility thesis. But that thesis is confused because it fails to recognize the dual uses of rules – and hence the dual nature of the obligations.

We now see what is right in the idea that cheating makes nonsense of the *purpose* in playing the game. For that really says that the aim of the game – the purpose in this sense – must be respected; and such a commitment can be undermined by cheating. Of course, we acknowledge the variety of purposes for which people play games – but the purpose of the *players* is different from the purposes *within* the game (the first is of interest to psychology and sociology). Recall here (Chapter 1 p. 18), Suits's (1995: 8) three aims or goals, which highlight such purposes:

1   Pre-lusory goal – simple version of, say, crossing the line first: 'specifiable state of affairs' (Suits 1995: 9);
2   Lusory goal – achieve pre-lusory goal but within rules;
3   Aim in participating: for example, enjoyment, etc.

This third goal may explain why players participate – why they do it – but it is not a goal *of the game* or sport, since sport could be performed either for other reasons or for no reasons. Since *this* kind of purpose is extrinsic to sport, one cannot make nonsense of it by cheating. Then either the claim about cheating making nonsense of the purpose in playing the game either is wrong because it relates to goals like those of Suits's third type; or is just a restatement of the earlier point about aim of the game. So there is nothing special in the reference to *purpose* here; although the importance of cheating does emphasize moral dimensions within sports playing.

Conclusion to Part II: the moral imperative is intrinsic

This chapter has highlighted, once again, the moral imperative at the heart of sport: as our spoiling case showed, obligations to the spirit of a sport are moral obligations. Further, these obligations are undertaken – as a (weak) contract – in entering a game or sport, since doing so grants the rules of the activity in their constitutive uses. Indeed, not doing so would preclude in principle performing the actions of which the sport is composed; in particular, those central to scoring in that sport.

A key point here is that this moral connection is not extrinsic: it does not relate to a use of sport (say, by the state). So it cannot be added to or subtracted from sport.

This idea provides one element of the overall conclusion to Part II, stressing an essential connection between sport and morality (broadly conceived). But the connection is fairly weak: Part III offers a stronger connection, at least for some sport, sufficient to explain the value of (at least some) sport. Other elements of Part II have resulted from applying insights concerning rule-following and definiteness to another context within the understanding of sport: namely, the understanding of its judging. Again, the theoretical points have shown how, if well done, the judging of sport is reliable – but without drawing on a mechanical application of rules that are both clear and exceptionless.

Part III
Rules in valuing sport

8 The project of a moral laboratory; and particularism

The moral imperative sometimes (and, I would claim, rightly) located within sport is often not a *direct* consequence of the rules or laws of particular sports: this fact is recognized when appeal is made, not to those rules themselves, but to the *spirit* of the rules, or to considerations of fair play, or some such. As we saw in Chapter 6 p. 107, the acquiring of principles is prior to, and the basis for, (appropriate) learning of rules. As Dworkin (1978: 115) puts it, the principles provide a 'gravitational force' operative within the rule. Discussion there put due weight on the moral metaphors of justice – 'level playing field', 'fair play' and such like – in their use in the specifics of sport. This chapter will say a little more – still sketchily – concerning two of the most important moral notions here, notions used to ground *moral metaphors* in general use: *fair play* and *level playing-field*. Doing so will offer a stronger version of our connection of sport to the moral.

There is a weaker and a stronger thesis here. By the weaker, the kinds of moral engagement required of rule-following (Chapter 7 p. 125) – understood in our particularist fashion (see p. 139) – indicate a moral imperative for sport sufficient to justify a weak version of the *moral laboratory*: rule-observance takes place in sport when rule-observance as such is, at bottom, a moral injunction on those engaged in the relevant activities. The constraints here were met simply when appeal to underlying principles was seen as *moral* appeal to *moral* principles: the moral dimension integral to sport was visible when the principles guiding the discretionary judgements of umpires or referees were recognized as moral principles.

But by the stronger thesis, deployed here, the *content* of sporting rules also has a moral dimension, visible in the moral use of sporting metaphors: in particular, *fair play* and *level playing-field*. Then learning to deploy the principles, and the moral metaphors they support, might offer a picture of the value of sport. For, in learning the exact application of these key metaphors, by learning how to make sense of these ideas *as they apply in particular sports*, one is at the same time learning the general moral principles. Positively, these notions indicate two major constraints on justice: namely, the ideas of equal treatment and of equality of initial condition. But, negatively, *all* sports cannot realistically be treated in such justice-related terms: those notions will be central to the mastery of only *some* sports at *some* levels.

Hence, they will be learned in learning 'how to go on' rule-followingly – and to abide by the principles (in Dworkin's sense: Chapter 6 p. 105) – only in those sports. Or so I shall urge. So this reading of the moral imperative of sport will support ascription to the moral laboratory of only some sport on some occasions.

However, both readings of the moral imperative idea share a problem: how to relate the general (the rule) to the particular (the action learnt or performed) – since '[t]he general cannot take the place of the particular' (Ms 180 (a) p. 35r). Or, more perspicuously, how the general notions of *morality* can grow from the particular events (and notions) of *sport*.

In thus drawing on moral possibilities of sport (in both these ways), Part III is well-placed to offer a moral reply to questions about sporting value. For the value of sport must be importantly different from that ascribed to, say, soap operas – which, while informative as a 'cultural lens' (Beckles 1995: 1) for society, are of no redeeming value intrinsically. The argument is in four main parts:

- First, it presents an abstract account of what would be needed for a *moral* picture of the intrinsic value of sport (compare McFee 2000c). One virtue of this procedure is that – once again – there is a formal argument to be considered: here, the student can attempt to deploy arguments in favour of each premise (or against them), reconsider the *logic* of the argument (and how, if at all, it might be augmented), and consider what should follow from the argument. (Formalizations make these processes easier for the [relative] beginner.)
- Second, the argument elaborates a picture of moral judgement and moral reasoning (a particularist or contextualist one) on which to defend an account of sport such as that sketched above.
- Third, it develops that account as it applies within sport, showing moral issues made *concrete* by sporting situations.
- Fourth, and finally, it asks what might be said of the value of (any) sport not justified in this way. Certainly the earlier explanations could not apply to any such sport. Central here (once again) is the contrast between intrinsic and extrinsic justifications of sport – or intrinsic and extrinsic attributions of the *value* of sport.

The argument concludes both that extrinsic justifications leave a 'sport-shaped hole' in one's theory – an accusation that might be levelled against much sociology of sport (especially the sociology of sporting consumption), and that an account of the intrinsic value of sport is sustainable.

Sport's moral dimension?

A moral imperative within sport might be identified in many ways. But, if our aim here is to explore the stronger thesis identified above, we must make sense of sport as intrinsically valuable. How? Part of the motivation of the Olympic Games – in the rhetoric of Pierre de Coubertin at least – turned on just such *moral* possibilities of sport: that participation in sport was (potentially) morally educative. So this might offer a model. For example, De Coubertin (2000: 537) writes that:

> wise and peaceful internationalism will make . . . [its] way into the new stadium. There . . . [it] will glorify the honour and selflessness that will enable athletics to carry out its task of moral betterment and social peace . . .

This idea of sport as morally educative had, of course, a developed history, to which De Coubertin appealed, in the athleticist rhetoric of the English public schools – with two fundamental theses emphasizing the (supposed) moral benefits of participation in sport. As expressed by Peter McIntosh (1979: 27): '[t]he first was that competitive sport . . . had an ethical basis, and the second was that training in moral behaviour on the playing field was transferable to the world beyond'.

If correct, such a position has the *potential* to justify a quite widespread concern with sport, for it claims to identify a valued characteristic intrinsic to sport. I am drawn to such a *general* idea of sport as having some such morally educative potential – indeed, I do not see how else some general (intrinsic) value might be ascribed to sport.

But is such moral justification for sport needed? Does its place (its social role) as a leisure activity not provide all the justification that is required? This is no justification at all, because it is no intrinsic justification. If one wants to justify *sport*, that justification must rely on features of sport as such – hence on intrinsic features – rather than on features which, while explaining concern (say, 'I do it for the money'), fail to explain that concern in terms of sport's features: features *extrinsic* to sport could be in place for something entirely without merit – as one might regard soap operas as entirely without merit and yet not deny their importance viewed as commodities. Moreover, those who regard sport as 'our most sophisticated and sensitive cultural lens' (Beckles 1995: 1) use sport to investigate society – as this lens metaphor makes plain. Although both legitimate and rewarding, this is not the only interest that one might have in, say, cricket (Beckles's example), or in sport more generally.

This discussion identifies *a sport-shaped hole* in those social theories which take sport as, say, opiate of the masses, prison of measured time, force in the civilizing process. . . . The sociology of sports consumption can tell us everything about sport *except* what makes it sport – for the terms of the (sociological) discussion apply as well to activities other than sport as they do to sporting activities.

Suppose we characterize sport in Britain as John Hargreaves (1986: 209) does, as 'implicated in the achievement, maintenance and development of

bourgeois hegemony in British society during the last century and a half'
(Sugden and Bairner 1993: 133).

Then we use terms in respect of sporting events which also have application outside of sport. Or, again, Paul Willis (1973), writing about women's
place in sport, simply applies insights which – were they sound – would
apply equally to women's place in the world of work (from where, in fact,
Willis developed them). Broadly sociological concerns of this sort are extrinsic to sport: they can (at best) explain human motivations in these
general ways. But none of these remarks bears on the *distinctive* nature or
role of sports (or games).To see this, we need only recognize that a related
but non-game ritual activity (a) might be *mistaken* for sport, and (b) would
be explained in this way as adequately as sport was.[1] So this mode of explanation is extrinsic to sport itself: the features it mentions are not features
essential to sport. For we have seen (Chapter 3 pp. 64–6; Chapter 7 p. 125)
the best that can be made of a 'purpose within the game': and that was
intrinsic. Thus, if we compare these kinds of explanation with an (imaginary) theory which had an intrinsic connection to the world of sport, we
could see clearly what the expression 'sport-shaped hole in one's theory'
amounts to here (compare 'art-shaped hole' [McFee 1992: 294–7]).

Yet the first athleticist thesis – that competitive sport had an ethical basis
– seems just false: sport neither necessarily promotes ethical performance
on the field nor necessarily teaches ethical principles. Even those formalists who take merely playing sport according to the rules to be ethically
approvable behaviour should admit that the rules must be actualized in
practice. Yet the behaviour must depend on the rules, not simply conform
to them. And no rule uniquely circumscribes the behaviour it requires or
prohibits, as we acknowledged (Chapter 2 p. 52): rather, any rule's application to behaviour involves an exercise of judgement, of a kind a referee or
umpire might make (Chapter 6 pp. 105–6). Practical sense must be made of
these (formal) rules. For any activity, appeal to rules *alone* cannot be sufficient. There remains a gap between sporting activity and the moral (McFee
2000b: 173–4): merely participating in sport might or might not actualize
the rules in a morally-relevant way. But one need not (indeed, if I am right,
cannot) claim that sport *always* has this impact: rather, it might in certain
cases. Even *that* connection of sport to the moral sphere is sufficient to
warrant taking sport seriously.

But how might this educational potential for sport be argued for? In
reply, I will present a research agenda of mine – motivating both the general
agenda and its specific premises.

Explanations and qualifications

It is worth entering three notes of caution and a fourth in explanation.

First, my reference to *the moral* must be understood as to the *sphere* of
morality, rather than simply to what is (morally) good. Nevertheless, such a

connection to the sphere of morality could only be sustained if, at least *some* of the time, the outcome was right-thinking or right-action. For we only recognize concerns as moral – rather than, say, prudential[2] – by exploring obligations, and the like, investigating how they are (appropriately) explained; and finding morally-relevant explanations must, in some cases, mark-out at least right-thinking. Still, there is no suggestion here that *all* connections with sport will *always* have a *positive* moral impact.

Second, morality has a complex relation to questions of human harm – better, to explaining some of the ways humans can *be* harmed (see Parry [1998] for some connection to sport). Here, I simply put that issue to one side, accepting Konrad Lorenz's view that human sports aim 'to ascertain which . . . [team] . . . is the stronger, *without hurting the weaker*' (Lorenz 1966: 94; orginal emphasis). For this locates *our* issue – although we might still want to highlight the degree of ear-biting and cheek-breaking in the sporting world that is thereby put aside!

Third, potentials are not always achieved: suppose some IOC members are scoundrels, self-serving and corrupt (Jennings 1996: 301–4). We should not conclude that the Olympic Ideal therefore does not exist – although we might wonder about its realizability! Here, the *execution* of the project is flawed, not the project itself. So the view explored here accepts a morally educative potential for sport, even if that is neither inevitable, in ways De Coubertin seems to have thought, nor to be understood as generalizing quite as sometimes hoped (or idealized).

In this context, corruption in sport's practice intersects with our concerns; here, exemplified via the Olympic movement. Suppose that the process of selection of a host city for the Games has been corrupt, at least in the last few years – with Salt Lake City a clear example (Jennings and Sambrook 2000: 19–48). Still, did this really disadvantage the athletes/competitors? If it did not, perhaps the values of the sporting event itself were not (much) compromised. Salt Lake City might offer facilities at least as good as those of its rivals. Then, no damage was done to the sport itself – the damage was to the context, not to the competition! This sort of corruption is regrettable (and, ideally, should be eliminated). But it does not tarnish the Olympic *values* as such, merely their implementation in practice.

The other extreme might be exemplified by the boxing finals in Seoul (already mentioned: see Chapter 5 p. 93): if even half of what Andrew Jennings (1996: 79–92; Jennings and Sambrook 2000: 205–8, 212–16) describes is correct, these events involved unfair judging. Here the corruption operates in the sporting practices themselves. Again, the corruption is to be regretted (and, ideally, eliminated) but now the task is more pressing: any virtues that accrue to *sporting* contests cannot accrue to these – they are *not* sporting (in the other sense of the word) because not fair. (This case is of systematic and deliberate lack of fairness, not merely occasional error.)

The issue of drug-taking might be somewhat intermediate. In part, and like the initial case, Olympic rhetoric does not match practice: former IOC

President Samaranch says that, 'The message is very clear. This is a new fight against doping' (quoted Sullivan 2000: 55), but proscribed drugs *are* taken at the Olympics. An Olympic movement genuinely committed to the elimination of such activities would not act as this one has (Jennings 1996: 232–49, 298–9; Jennings and Sambrook 2000: 290–306): but, again, that is corrupt practice only. But (like our other case) there is an unfairness here too: some athletes will be punished for drug-taking while, for others, the documents necessary to identify their 'B' samples will have been shredded in error – in Seoul 1988 (Jennings 1996: 241–3) and, perhaps, Atlanta 1996 (Mackay 1996: 2)! If these athletes *were* guilty (and, after all, their 'A' samples were ruled positive), they 'got away with it'. Here too, though, the IOC should be more vigilant, and perhaps differently motivated.[3]

Whatever their detail, such cases indicate different obligations which (one might think) have not been met. But every case suggests something *remediable* by a more scrupulous Committee, more consistent in the understanding and application of its own rules, and more attentive to the demands of natural justice.

The fourth element returns us to our starting point in connecting sport to the moral sphere. The rhetoric of sport is replete with metaphors employed in general ethical discussion – our examples: the idea of fair play and of a level playing field. These reflect ethical concerns *within* sport. And De Coubertin's amateurism (whatever its faults in theory or practice) was fuelled by concerns with sport done 'for its own sake', and with fairness: with behaving fairly (appropriately, justly) towards others . . . here, in the sporting context.

Yet what exactly do these two metaphors – 'fair play' and 'level playing field' – offer to sports-practice: what precisely do they suggest or proscribe? Also, what does some root metaphor tell us about moral situations more generally – what would it be to require fair play or a level playing field in one's business dealings, say, or one's interactions with others?

Our initial concerns are with the sporting case. So let us briefly consider each of these examples:

- *Fair play*: not fairness, notice, which might relate to the starting point of the contest (and is picked up in the other metaphor) but with the manner of the contest, having implications for how to interpret the rules as they relate to the manner of playing. For example, if there is no rule specifically against taking a knife into the rugby scrum, but there are rules about what it *is* permissible to take onto the field, then other questions are raised. Here, a principle on which to base, say, refereeing decisions is more helpful than list of what is permitted, since it offers help with as-yet unconfronted cases.
- *Level playing field*: we roughly understand the root metaphor, and the reason for it: that neither side should be unfairly advantaged initially

– this is also the basis for, say, the practice of changing ends at half-time: that inbuilt advantage be equalized.

So, as suggested, the primary concern of each is with considerations of justice: with getting one's just deserts (on the day!).

At the level of *principles* (Chapter 6 p. 105) here, one thinks first of equality, and of fair treatment. But I am drawn to the idea that, in practice, *fairness* (in this sense) is a 'trouser-concept' (Austin 1962: 70) – that *unfair* 'wears the trousers'. That is, we do not really decide that such-and-such is fair; rather, we conclude that it is *not unfair*. That is to say, the *content* of fairness in a particular sporting context is wholly given by what is proscribed, explicitly or implicitly. Then arguments will always turn on whether or not such-and-such is unfair, in relation to the specific rules of *this* sport, or some more general context of principles or *ethoi*. As with *complete* (Baker and Hacker 1980: 79–81; Chapter 2 p. 52), we arrive at what is fair by contrast. So really no sharp account of *fair play* is possible. Rather, what is not unfair is thereby acknowledged as fair. And even when we formulate the issue differently – that is, we ask, 'Is doing such-and-such *fair*?' – that question is given content by the idea of the unfairness of behaving differently.

The relevant comparison (Austin 1962: 62–77) is with the term 'real': we know what the *real* colour of her hair is only by recognizing (and contrasting) the ways its colour might not be *real*: say, by being dyed, by being in such-and-such light, by now reflecting the ravages of age. Any of these applies differently from, say, the real colour of a curtain or the real shape of a cat. All in all, no neat account can be offered here: the matter is contextual.

We can sketch some broad contours: (a) the rules determine what is and what is not unfair, by articulating the kinds of (un)fairness involved; (b) this relation to the rules (and to rule-following) precludes there being a full-stop here, since there is no set of behaviours *absolutely* ruled out;[4] no sense of *all* here (Chapter 2 p. 47); (c) the principles we can extract from the cases we confront, or which we learn in learning the sport, allow us to make sense of – and perhaps adjudicate on – future cases.

So, when we ask if such-and-such is fair, we are really asking whether it is not unfair (see above). But this is another way to recognize that a definition of fair play, accurate for all past occasions, could never be useful here.[5] And neither would a parallel account of fairness.

A good example here: the regulations for 'permitted' drugs – are they fair? What is needed is equal treatment, in a respect where – at present – that treatment is not equal. For instance, those competitors who abide by a sports federation's regulations, when (say) the Olympic ones are more lax, will effectively be penalized – this occurred for Valium and Librium in the modern pentathlon at the 1976 Olympic Games: the drugs (agreed to be advantageous in the shooting phase of the discipline) were used by *some* competitors and, since they were permitted by Olympics regulations (at the time), such competitors gained an advantage over those who stuck to the regulations of the International Modern Pentathlon Union, which had banned the use of these drugs (Wallechinsky 1988: 368). Equally abiding by the more stringent rules of FIFA (the International Soccer Federation) for the use of ephedrine (a common component of medication for colds) would at one time have disadvantaged players in the NBA, where this substance was not forbidden (Tamburrini 2000: 36). So the various athletes were not starting on equal terms. Still, at least we see fairness if all the competitors from a particular sport are constrained in the *same* way during a particular competition.

We have seen how the various sports should be regarded as underpinned by various principles (especially those concerning fairness, in both the ways discussed above). But what inequalities do not contradict these principles, and the concern with fairness they embody?

Real equality is not to be expected: this point is made eloquently in an advertisement, featuring John McEnroe as a commentator, of an 'endless' tennis match between Pete Sampras and Andre Agassi, because both are evenly matched. One point continues for months, McEnroe grows a beard . . . and finally the point is a let: it must be replayed! Here, you might think: they were *too* equal. We go by: 'May the best man win' – that is, there is deemed to be a *better man*, on the day.

Rather, *equality of opportunity* is taken as meaning that certain specific 'advantages' have been ruled out (in principle): for example, certain kinds of performance-enhancing drugs (and, if we cannot make some analysis stick, there is no reason for, nor principle behind, such an exclusion). Why, therefore, are they excluded? Without answering this difficult question, consider two specific issues:

1 'Natural inequalities' – consider, as an analogy, a mathematics test: I find myself up against Isaac Newton – neither of us is advantaged, beyond Newton's natural advantage. Isn't this just like, for instance, boxers of different weights being separated? How *far* should we take this idea? What about limiting matches between basketball teams of different (average) heights? Or, perhaps, basketball teams of different skills?
2 Inequalities of resource – you have the fine shoes, and I do not: or the fine training regime, or the funding to not have to work full time, or the funding to not have to work . . . etc. etc. – lots of (different?) issues.

So even the *detail* of these metaphors is not clear. Still, their motivation is; and that is enough – we cannot expect any fuller account. Any answer would need to be contextualized. Of course, many issues concerning the nature of fairness are not explored here, although some are helpfully discussed in Loland (2002: 71–6 especially). But these remarks should be seen as offering helpful hints and reminders for particular discussions, were we to consider them.

Finally, throughout this chapter, the focus is on *competitive sports*. But what about non-competitive sports (including my own favourite, sub-aqua)? Given my starting point in this chapter and the fact that they are not in the Olympics, they can be ignored. Further, they do not provide opportunities for fair play or the requirement for a level playing field – although they may well offer other moral opportunities, not considered here. So such sports can be excluded from this consideration, as being unsuitable.

In summary, these two metaphors – of fair play and level playing field – are (among) the things ethics gets from sport: I suggest that *a* value in sport resides precisely here – the metaphors or slogans available in sporting contexts, and sport provides concrete instantiations of relevant principles. Moreover, this possibility offers some detail to *an* account of sport's value.

The argument

In summary, and presented hypothetically, the argument is this:

1   *If* sport is valuable, of its nature or intrinsically;
2   *If* such value has some connection to the moral (as it must, for Olympism);
3   *If* moral judgements are essentially *particular*;
4   *If* sport can present the particularization of (moral?) cases; and
5   *If* such cases concretize moral metaphors, such as 'fair play', 'level playing field'; then
6   Sport might function as a moral laboratory.

In explaining *how* sport might function in the moral sphere, I offer both *reason* to think that it does and a *basis* for investigation.

Now, any argument may be contested only either by contesting the premises or by disputing that the conclusion follows from those premises – that is, by disputing the logic. Those who find this conclusion uncongenial, or even those who think it wrong, must show what is amiss with the argument that leads to that conclusion, in one of these ways.

As to the logic of the argument – that the conclusion follows from those premises – it is easy to see how that conclusion depends on those premises. Even if the argument is not formally valid, it should be accepted as compelling. Making the formulation impeccable would make it both a lot longer and considerably more complex. But surely this argument is sufficiently transparent at present, as we can see if we make the assumptions that the premises articulate.

From the identification, in the first premise, of a *value* for sport, we recognize that value as moral (second premise) and then characterize moral value as particular (third premise). Once these premises are granted, it follows that sport *has* a moral value of a particularized kind (like other moral value). Now premises four and five contribute the idea that this (particularized) value might be exemplified in sporting situations, and hence might be learned from them. And this suggests how sport might function as a site of moral exploration, investigation and education. So granting the truth of the premises *does* (at first blush) guarantee the conclusion's truth; or, at least, give us reason to adopt it.

However, before saying something in explanation – and in justification – of each premise in turn, notice that finding my argument flawed is not equivalent to finding my conclusion flawed: that other arguments might yet be offered. But in that situation one has no *reason* to accept my conclusion – as one would have if the argument were sound; further, I would not be considering *this* argument if another were obvious.

Investigation of the premises

We now turn to the question of whether the truth of the premises should indeed be granted. Here I urge simply that we have reason to adopt each. Indeed, in part, this is a research agenda precisely because the truth of each premise requires investigation. Were the conditional importance of the argument granted, such investigation becomes justified.

Let us, therefore, consider each premise, reminding ourselves what it contributes to the argument, and asking if it seems plausible.

The first two premises: sport as morally valuable

The first premise picks out a condition to be met if sport deserves the importance I, and others, claim attaches to it. Moreover, were this premise denied, some other starting point for the value of sport must be offered: but if, as I have urged, such a justification must be an *intrinsic* one, it will come to roughly this one. For value attaching to the interpersonal is typically moral, at least in the most generous sense. That is what the second premise asserts, in taking the value at issue to be a *moral* value. Since central moral principles concern fairness (and therefore justice), if the potential value of sport is moral value, considering sport here is indeed considering a sense of justice as inculcated. And, of course, the arguments of Chapters 6 and 7 highlight a moral imperative at the heart of sport. Although the truth of these premises is not *demonstrated*, I have done enough to make them more plausible than their respective denials.

Premise three: moral judgement as essentially particular

My main point here will be served if it is granted that we learn moral concepts in particular cases: learn what lying is, and what is wrong with it, by considering cases of lying, in the real world or in fictions; and that even if we are sometimes presented with general abstract rules ('thou shalt not kill'), we must make sense of them in concrete contexts, applying them to the situations in which we find ourselves (see p. 142).

Yet how does one *learn* moral concepts, learn to *use* them and to *understand* them? The insight of particularism is that, in learning morality, one does not learn a set of principles (only?), much less a set of rules – rather, one learns to make moral judgements; and one learns that first in specific contexts (Dancy 1993: 56–7). Since any such learning must take place in *some* particular situation, one might hope for learning-situations, *not* ones of maximum risk to life, limb, sanity or world peace.

The cases here give us an initial reason to adopt this particularist conception of moral judgement: give it the balance of probabilities. (We will come to a fuller articulation and defence: see pp. 141–4.) Two misconceptions might seem to speak against it: first, the view of morality as a system of *rules* – we have highlighted the mistakes here, namely that the application of rules cannot itself be a matter of rules. So something other than rules is required. Second, the assumption of a tension between particularism and moral principles; but, as we will see (p. 142), particularism is only opposed to *substantive* moral principles, not to moral principles *as such*. For such substantive moral principles are of precisely the kind claimed to apply clear in one situation because applying in another. On the contrary, for particularists, 'no set of [substantive] principles will succeed in generating answers to questions about what to do in particular cases' (Dancy 1993: 56).

Our discussion of 'thou shalt not kill' highlighted the difficulties here. The insight is 'that the moral relevance of a property in a new case cannot be predicted from its relevance elsewhere' (Dancy 1993: 57). Here 'predicted' is the key term: for, of course, we will agree – once the plan of action is decided upon – that this case *instantiates* the principle. But we could not know this before the fact.

Suppose such a particularized character is granted for sporting value (it will be discussed in some more detail, if still briefly, on p. 141). But, then, how is that value to be learned, or explored?

Premises four and five: particularization through cases exemplifying sporting situations

Premises four and five together sketch our solution. Crucial here is the central moral role of *justice*. Dworkin (1985: 219) rightly calls 'the practice of worrying about what justice really is . . . the single most important social practice we have' (my order). And that is just what is happening here. To begin with premise five, the metaphors of fair play and level playing field give only the abstract form of, say, the complaint against unfairness, or the requirement for equal consideration: sporting situations make these considerations concrete (in line with the particularism of premise three).

Sporting contests always admit the possibility of someone not participating fairly (that is, contravening the fair play condition) or of participation from a position of unfair initial disadvantage (that is, contravening the level playing field condition) – this seems built in to the possibility of competitive activity. So a framework for any practice worthy of the name 'sport' may support these two metaphors. That the contextualizations here are indeed moral is suggested both by the prevalence of the sporting metaphors in moral contexts and by reflection on the (typical) experience of learning sporting principles. This usually happens in *appropriate* teaching of the sporting activity: what one learns is not – and could not be – just a formulation of the principle (a principle-formulation) but how to *behave* in accordance with the principle: for instance, how to manifest fair play (which is, of course, no guarantee that one will then actually play fairly). In effect, then, principles are taught when rules are properly taught – where the term 'properly' makes just that point! In teaching the rules of a game (for example, cricket), a teacher sensitive to the principles might inculcate those principles too. As we recognized (Chapter 6 p. 116), we at least *know* how to teach such principles, even if we cannot *say* how. For we learnt them in this way. Thus the model is of abstract principles learned from (and in) concrete instances in sport, then applied to concrete moral situations. Taken together, these warrant my commitment to the moral possibilities of sport.

The argument's conclusion: the moral laboratory

Sport, then, has the possibility of providing us with just such concrete cases where we can behave fairly (or justly) – examples of fair play – and also cases where inappropriate initial advantage can be taken (cases where there *isn't* a level playing field): hence, sport offers people a chance to operate with these concepts, and to act on them; to use them in discussion and to have others offer them. It also offers opportunities to confront others *not* acting on them – and, even, to fail to act on them oneself. In this way, one can explore the contours of morally-relevant possibilities. This is what I mean in speaking of sport as a *moral laboratory*.[6]

Moreover, sport has – typically – at least two main advantages as a learning site over encountering moral problems in one's life more generally. Both relate to the essential nature of sport. First, sport typically has a set of *codified* rules: in this way, the rules (and the manner both of implementing and of changing them) are more straightforward than (other?) moral rules – which is not to say, of course, that their implementation is straightforward: judgement is still required. Second, the consequences of *failing* to behave in line with the rules (etc.) are typically much less severe: no-one ends up dead or maimed, for example – even if this does happen sometimes. So sport offers the possibility of learning judgement with less (than usual) consequences, less risked.

Suppose these ideas are accepted: do they achieve what is required? The original De Coubertin position, drawn from athleticism, urged both the moral character of sport and the transferability of that morality to the rest of one's life. Our particularist account of morality might accord *a* place within sporting situations for (the possibility of) moral choice – not the kind of *essential* moral education De Coubertin believed in, but more plausible for that. So we have a limited defence of this thesis.

Yet its very particularism might seem to undermine the usefulness of such a conclusion: for in the moral laboratory crucially I learn *sport-morality*, rather than something which automatically generalizes. Yet Olympism's justification lay in the possibility of a quite *general* good – one not circumscribed by sport. But, as we shall see, our particularism is not a kind of 'no-transfer' thesis. For, if in learning moral judgement one learns 'how to go on' (PI §151), one is *automatically* learning notions which might, in principle, have application elsewhere; and, since every later application will typically be *different* (from a particularist perspective), learning the concepts at all amounts to the first steps in learning to apply them *outside* familiar cases.

Particularism and moral judgement

It is worth saying a little more about a particularist account of moral judgement, and the connection of particularism both to morality (on the one hand), and to the generality of rules and principles in Dworkin's sense (on the other).

Then, the general thesis of *particularism* has two aspects: first, the particularity of moral judgement, noted above (p. 139), where 'the moral relevance of a property in a new case cannot be predicted from its relevance elsewhere' (Dancy 1993: 57).

As we recognized, particularism is opposed to *substantial* moral principles, not to moral principles *as such*. The point is just that we could not know this principle (in its application *here*) before the fact. More recently, Dancy (2000a: 132) has made the point explicit in terms of two principles:

- That what is a reason in one situation may alter or lose its polarity in another;
- The way in which the reasons here presently combine with each other is not necessarily determinable in any simply additive way.

So that one cannot infer from the fact that such-and-such was a reason for so-and-so judgement in *this* case that it will be in *that* case.

A second, related aspect of particularism is that general rules (exemplified by, say, the Ten Commandments) cannot be efficacious, since there is room for a decision or choice as to what behaviour the rule prescribes or proscribes in this situation. Here, Martha Nussbaum (1990: 38) rightly highlights the priority of 'particular perception . . . over fixed rules'. Even general abstract rules ('thou shalt not kill') must be made sense of in concrete contexts, applying them to the situations in which we find ourselves.

This can be difficult. A young soldier who thinks that, say, this general rule against killing might be rendered inapplicable by, for instance, his duty to his country in a just war or an order from his commanding officer, might revise that conclusion, faced with a real, live enemy soldier. Equally, he might not! Clearly, one would have liked (and hoped) to resolve such a question before one was in front of the enemy's bayonet. How might moral judgements be learned with less risked?

One cannot simply appeal to one's rule ('thou shalt not kill'): for what does that rule amount to in *this* situation? Knowing the rule alone does not look promising here: that is just a *formalization*, to be applied (where possible) in the new situations faced. Is killing still as *absolutely* prohibited in this new context? Or was the prohibition never *that* absolute? The rule alone cannot decide. Equally, further rules will not help – on pain of the regress. And this was part of our earlier rejection of formalism. As we put it before, the insight of particularism is that, in learning morality, one does not learn a set of principles (only?), much less a set of rules – rather, one learns to make moral judgements; and one learns that first in specific contexts.

The particularism here stresses the specificity of questions and answers; differing little in upshot to the previous contextualist ideas. Dancy (1993: 64) offers a version of this sort of particularist picture:

> our account of the person on whom we can rely to make sound moral judgements is not very long. Such a person is someone who gets it right case by case. To be so consistently successful, we need a broad range of sensitivities, so that no relevant feature escapes us, and we do not mistake its relevance either. But that is all there is to say on the matter. To have the relevant sensitivities just is to be able to get things right case by case. The only remaining question is how we get into this enviable state. And the answer is that for us it is probably too late. . . . moral education is the key; for those who are past educating, there is no real remedy.

The counter-thought might be that this view lacks a prior appeal to moral psychology. For me, the absence of a moral psychology is a virtue of the position: 'In the beginning was the deed' (OC §402).

Nor should we see particularism as closing the book on all generality. After all, what is the point of consideration of what others ought to do *here* and *now*? The issue is raised in an amusing way by Allan Gibbard (2002: 52), in terms of the 'Jack and Jill' nursery rhyme:

> Jack and Jill need water . . . but the hill is slippery. I say that Jack ought not to go up the hill, but you disagree. What's the issue between

us? . . . It's not an issue of what to do in your case or in mine, but somehow in Jack's, in Jack's shoes.

Still, the issue is not simply one of the here and now. If it were, there would be no point in any speculation as to what he *should* have done, by us – or even by Jack: 'Why . . . should Jack rethink his decision, when the moving finger has writ and he can't unbreak his crown?' (Gibbard 2002: 52). Gibbard's answer seems the right one for Jack; and, in that way, explains both that present reflection bears on future cases but that it does not do so by creating an immutable rule:

> Jack reconsiders after the fact because he will face such choices again; he is engaged in a kind of rehearsal for future choices. . . . Jack's exact circumstances include everything about him, and our question is what to do if one is he – and thus like him in every respect in which we differ.
> (Gibbard 2002: 52–3)

But we will never be in precisely that situation: nor could we be – we are not Jack. Yet neither can Jack himself, at least if he has the capacity to remember (and perhaps profit from) his past. So the argument suggests that what is learned from thinking about Jack's case, and his decisions, may be brought to bear on our (rather different) cases, and our decisions. But, since the cases are different, what is learned will need to be *applied* in this new situation. That cannot simply amount to the mechanical application of a rule. Or, perhaps better, if we think of it as *the application of a rule*, that will be because we recognize (Chapter 2 p. 46) that all rules require such application – that it is never purely mechanical.

This particularist conception of moral judgement is both a specific thesis in philosophy and highly contentious. Still, the cases here make it attractive. So this position is at least arguable. Here, Nussbaum offers considerations against generality, commenting on 'the need for fine-tuned *concreteness* in ethical attention and judgement' (Nussbaum 1990: 38), and sketching key elements of 'the priority of the particular' (Nussbaum 1990: 37). Three aspects making problematic any general account, 'fixed in advance of the particular case' (Nussbaum 1990: 38), are:

- New and unexpected features;
- The context-embeddedness of relevant features;
- Ethical relevance of particular persons and relationships.

The first two are familiar from our discussion of particularity in relation to rules (Chapter 2 pp. 47–52). Moreover, the second, and perhaps the third, are characteristics of my general account of understanding (see Chapter 1 pp. 28–31; Chapter 2 pp. 47–52), while recognizing the first is part of its motivation. For why is greater generality either desirable or attainable?

Indeed, the priority of argumentative strategies wherein we look (or hope) for persons in exactly similar circumstances is disputed, as in our hypothetical case above (from Gibbard). Of course, in one sense, it is trivially true that *if* I am in exactly the same circumstances as another person, and like them in all the other ways, I *should* act as that person should have – this is trivialized by taking 'exactly the same circumstances' in this powerful fashion. In reality, the difficulty lies in what might be relevantly similar here. To reuse an example (see McFee 2000a: 125), the Meryl Streep character in the film *Sophie's Choice* (1982) has to choose which of her two children will be adopted by a Nazi family (and therefore be likely to survive), which child goes to the concentration camp and likely death. In the film, the choice Sophie makes is *explicable* – we see the predicament of a Jewish woman and her children, during the Second World War, in Hitler's Europe, and so on. We recognize the pressures that require her to choose in this ghastly situation. Yet is Sophie's actual choice *inevitable*? Might we have chosen differently? That question has a point only for someone in a relevantly similar situation. But which are the *relevant* similarities? What is the weight of the woman's being, say, Jewish, given that Hitler's Europe was horrible for gypsies also? What is the weight of its being the *mother* who faces the terrible choice rather than, for instance, (two different cases) the father or an aunt? (And so on, for various aspects of the case.) There are no clear answers here – we might understand what 'caused' *this* woman in *this* situation to make *this* choice; but have we a basis for moving beyond such specificities? Suppose that, discussing of the film, I say, 'In her position, I would have done the same.' This is plausibly true, as long as I am being honest, and so on. Yet, at best, this is made true by the way the explanation is constructed: were I roughly in her position, and yet chose differently, that would show that I was not in her *precise* position. Surely we have reason to suppose that *her* choice is necessarily specific: there is no hope of producing a 'law' that could then be used in *other* cases – for example, in *my* case. But that must make us give up the longing for a wholly general principle. And this will support the particularism which, I have urged, is central to my conception of the moral laboratory.

Thinking about the moral laboratory

An overriding concern of the *moral laboratory*[7] is with fairness: rules in sport are sometimes changed to facilitate just performance (fair play). For example, the introduction of the idea of a professional foul into soccer: that is, a foul which would be penalized sufficiently to equalize the situation. And this is regularly offered as an explanation of proposed rule changes.

Of course, this is a silly method, given the need for judgement in the application of *all* rules (that is, the impossibility of sealing off all possible [mis-] interpretations). The arguments of Chapter 2 show us that the hope for definiteness here – sealing off all possibilities – is vain. One cannot expect any rule change to necessarily succeed in imposing fairness, no matter how well drafted. However carefully one builds-in details of this situation only, other 'readings' of it – and hence other ways of treating it – are always possible: indeed, this is a quite general thesis from the philosophy of language, the thesis of occasion-sensitivity (Chapter 2 pp. 49–52).

So the hope for rules which in and of themselves 'improve' fairness in a particular sport is vain – if we cannot find such exceptionless rules elsewhere, we should not expect them for sport. Yet, nevertheless, this does represent one rationale! The proposed rule change would indeed be justified to the extent that it really enhanced fairness or fair play. To that degree, this aspiration is consonant with, and exemplifies, the moral character of sport. That it fails in *practice* might just be taken to reinforce that point.

This chapter began from the interpenetration of moral notions with our lives – the moral metaphors from sport recognize that these notions (also?) have a role in sport. But, as noted, those ideas are either *not* metaphorical or are *less* metaphorical in the sporting context – there really can be fair playing and the levelness of actual playing fields! Seeing how these ideas interact with the rules and principles (and spirit) of sport can show us how such notions might *apply* – and hence, perhaps, how they might be applied more generally. So the moral laboratory is only teaching morality in sport (if it is), but that itself might have the possibility to achieve more: that is, to teach one to be a better human – perhaps, in learning to take *fragments* of one's life seriously, one learns to take life seriously.

This parallel also makes plain a limitation of the moral laboratory, a problem for the practice, not the theory. Just as someone might be a master of pure mathematics but unable to manage elementary applied maths (say, unable quickly to check one's change after buying a round of drinks), so a master of the moral concepts in the sporting context might be unable to apply them outside the laboratory. There is no theoretical safeguard here, no guarantee that generalizability won't be thwarted (*pace* de Coubertin) – although eternal vigilance might work against this being a regular occurrence; and valuing sport partly as a moral laboratory might make such vigilance easier to organize!

As moral laboratory, sport is not a site for *trying out* morality: rather, it concerns learning to play within rules . . . to circumscribe one's conduct within explicit rules: later, such 'rules' will not (typically) be (so) explicit. So having learned *principles* will be more important.

Its possibilities as a moral laboratory are *intrinsic* to sport – they derive from its being rule-governed, involving human interactions where both fairness and harm are possible, and where the risk is not too great (perhaps there are other characteristics too). But this possibility is not *unique* to sport – although it is hard to think of plausible candidates.

Problem: the moral nature of sport?

But is sport as I have described it? If it is not, this project is misconceived.

Certainly, not all uncontentious sport *conforms* to this description – a fact not *that* important, if most sport did. It might seem, then, that one must determine whether or not the *majority* of sports are like this. But it also seems inappropriate to be counting heads here, to determine what *most* sports do (in theory and in practice). Even if there are exceptions, sports not fitting the model sketched above, that model would still be useful if it offered us insight into *some* sports. Yet it does seem important to plot the scope and limits of any such model. For clearly, not all sport operates by emphasizing fairness and suchlike (the rules of basketball [as interpreted] require players to foul) – a horrible possibility here is the morally harmful side of sport. That is, the *moral* force in some sports might be towards *immoral* action. For if the connection is just to moral *issues*, then first there is no guarantee that contact with sport will be *positively* educative in respect of morality *and* second it is not clear that sport is *always* committed to the educative matters; or, better, that *all* sport is.

Of course, the connection to rule-breaking activity might still be seen under the aspect of rule-related activity – and, as such, enjoys the moral commitment to the rules in their constitutive understanding (Chapter 7 pp. 122–5). But this is a much weaker requirement than the more explicit concerns with justice, fairness and the like which have grounded this chapter.

It is difficult to move on from here in the abstract: some concrete cases are needed. Yet sport operates for many purposes, and at many levels of performance and spectatorship. Which should be selected? Having begun the chapter from De Coubertin (and in line with my interests), the examples come from high-level performance: namely, from Olympic sport. But the substance of these points could be restructured for other cases. (For example, with playground activities where considerations of fair play had *no* place, one can readily imagine disputes about the sport status of the activity.)

One way forward from these recognitions – especially for Olympism – would be the road of exclusion. Only some sports are appropriate to the moral laboratory, which is not to deny the interest of others, but just to deny them *this* interest. Take this to supply *appropriate* sports (for Olympism) as a basis for including/excluding 'candidate' Olympic events, given the need to reduce the size of the Games.

Let us briefly consider some candidates, to show *some* of the relevant considerations:

- Boxing – the essential violence of the sport, the essential damage to others, precludes it from sensible consideration for the moral laboratory. Whatever the redeeming social values of, say, fighting for the Holy Family,[8] little of *moral* worth is to be found in boxing itself, even in its amateur incarnation (that is, before we turn to biting chunks from the opponent's ear). Were I wrong, advocates of boxing would show that it has *indeed* a place in the moral laboratory – that is, conduct the argument in my terms, so that (at worst) I am wrong only about empirical details.

- Synchronized swimming – this activity does not conduce to inappropriate moral values (as one might urge for boxing) so much as have no bearing on morality one way or another. Again, were this clear, its place could then be argued against. If a retort emphasizes its competitive nature, our counterblast should stress the difficulty of integrating such competitiveness into essentially aesthetic activities. (And then we should also look hard at gymnastic vaulting, for instance.)

  Of course, its (weaker) connection to morality, though the moral imperative of the 'contract' to deploy constitutive rules, might be enough here. That would grant that sport *as such* had some place in our moral laboratory. Still, one would still contrast this case (and similar ones) with sports where the stronger connection to justice and fairness was apparent.

- Basketball – basketball was initially a non-contact sport (Chapter 2 p. 37): under one of its original thirteen rules,[9] 'shouldering, holding, pushing, tripping or striking an opponent was not allowed'. Equally, these rules are now interpreted so as to require of players foul play (rule-breaking in precisely this aspect). For instance, as Wilkes (1994: 96) notes, 'Though basketball is sometimes referred to as a noncontact sport, it is far from that – aggressive play with bodily contact is the rule rather than the exception.'

Moreover, such behaviour is expected by both coaches and referees. So that there is certainly a conflict here between the spirit of one rule and the interpretation of others.

The issue for basketball is *not* just that of players seeing what they can get away with – what the referee will not notice, for example; or will not penalize. So the situation differs from that in some other sports.

Specific penalties for rule-breaking *within* the rules of the game do not exclude the player from the game permanently, do not result in automatic advantage to the other side in terms of the score (although giving a high probability of the other side scoring). An initial rationale for such rules was to equalize a situation where a player makes *accidental* contact with another (say, through over-enthusiasm), and where this would advantage his team. Moreover, the fixing of some permitted *number* of such infringements (and the associated penalties) is explained by the thought that accidents and over-enthusiasm do not strike in the same place an infinite amount of times: more than a few occurrences and it looks deliberate.

More important for us, the proscribed behaviours are now seen as what a player *ought* to do in certain circumstances – further, the idea of 'drawing the foul' means that this is part of the game not only for those who perform this behaviour, but equally for their opponents. This activity is *within* the ethos of basketball – the distinction between the spirit and the letter of the rules (or between principles and rules) seems to break down. This is *not* the suggestion (Chapter 2 p. 36) that cheats are not playing the game at all, because they are not abiding by its constitutive rules. Here, though, rules of the game *regulate* this way of behaving.

While showing nothing in and of themselves, these points sketch good reason to suppose that participation in such a sport (basketball is not alone here) could not possibly be morally educative through the inculcating of moral principles. Here we see some practical possibilities of our investigations. With no place in the moral laboratory, such activities need have none in the Olympics (for instance).

These three cases illustrate one aspect of pursuing the idea of a moral laboratory where it leads, as well as a (potential) normativity to such an idea, one which might be applied elsewhere – say, in schools or in leisure centres – although I have not suggested how! We should now turn to other cases, as well as interrogating the premises of the argument that generates such conclusions.

Outcomes

As noted earlier, this whole argument is a research agenda. If, in offering concrete realizations, sport can function as a moral laboratory for the (particular) engagement with moral concerns, it has the potential for *a* kind of moral educativeness not so far removed from De Coubertin's dream. (Of course, this is at best only one aspect of sport: I am *not* urging that it is the most important.)

Nothing here sustains De Coubertin's optimism about sport: the moral laboratory may teach *immorality*; or some people learn nothing from it – there is no *guarantee* of learning; and also no guarantee, even for those who have picked up the moral dimension of sport, that there will be any transfer to the rest of their behaviour. These are reasons for pessimism about the Olympic Ideal. But they also indicate potentials or possibilities of sport, ways in which sport might help us to transcend our petty concerns with self, and so on; and thus might serve the grand purposes De Coubertin envisaged.

9   The value of sport

This chapter fulfils, in part, two omissions from the previous chapter, in saying more about the value of sport and about the degree to which that value should be thought enduring, in a world where sport changes. For it might seem like an objection to the research agenda sketched in the previous chapter that it dealt, at best, with sport now – at worst, that it assumed some 'essence' for sport.

Of course, the aim here is not to show that sport *has* a value: that is taken for granted, in the light of previous comments. Rather, it is to comment on the nature of that value – on how that 'having a value' might be explained. That will be the topic of much of this chapter. On the second point, one must grasp some nettles: I am personally convinced that the beginnings of sport are fairly recent – that before one has modern sports, there was no sport as such. Whatever one makes of this, the fundamental point is that the concept *sport* has a beginning in time: hence, we can (in principle) imagine a world where sport has disappeared. To this extent, we grant that some activities are examples of sport, some are not, and some are borderline. But there is nothing essentialist in this.

Nor, of course, am I discussing specific *values* that are – or might be – ascribed to sport. Rather, my topic is, roughly, the *point* of sport: its value in that sense (if it has one), where that value is intrinsic.

We have already sketched some accounts of valuing of this sort. Thus, for instance, for Morgan (1994: 277), '[t]o make the good of the game one's own good' is the 'best and most compelling reason one can have to accept' the limitations imposed on one's behaviour by what Morgan (1994: 227) calls 'the internal logic of sport'. And he (rightly?) conceives of that logic as having both formal and normative aspects. Similarly, the idea of *being true to the game* (or sport) might be invoked here, since '[i]f you are engaged in a practice, if you respect a practice, you acquire and assume a new set of interests – those of the practice itself' (Butcher and Schneider 2003: 161). Morgan's focus is on institutions or structures; I focus on the perspective of the athlete or the spectator (and I am less worried by methodological individualism: see McFee [2002: 124–6]). But, in fact, one set of considerations here is that there is really nothing *below*, or more fundamental than, our (intrinsic) valuing of sport – and Wittgenstein offers us appropriate sets of reasons (Chapter 4 pp. 79–81). Yet we will need to consider why there is nothing more fundamental: for example, by looking to other justifications, and to postmodernist rejections of grand narratives (Chapter 10 pp. 168–9).

Once this is done, four substantial worries remain. First, the sorts of valuing discussed earlier (Chapter 8) can seem rather impersonal, rather detached. How it this value for sport *mine*, in the sense both of bearing on me and of being compelling for me? As we will see (p. 154), considerations in practical reason can address this worry. Second, the values do not seem *powerful*: sport does not *seem* to promote regard for others, or fairness, in sports players. In part, this worry relates to the previous one: *I* seem to play sport with no obvious moral imperative – is that a flaw in sport or in me? But it also takes us to the next. For, as a matter of fact, sport does not seem to promote moral thinking or moral behaviour. Thus, third (and relatedly), the values ascribed to sport seem questionably true (especially as worked out in, say, the practice of the IOC). For most observers, the national teams in the Olympic Games do not *all* seem to manifest the kind of commitment to sport (and especially to fair play and the relatively minor importance of victory) that the Olympic oath asserts, nor do all the judges *always* (compare boxing – Jennings 1996: 79–92) strive to reach the standards in their oath. An informed public, in recognizing these facts, also recognizes the many babies in all this bath water. So that he or she does not simply become brainwashed about the possibilities of Olympism. Rather, the virtues asserted are recognized *as* virtues; and the efforts to reach them applauded where these are genuine efforts. (If some spectators are less realistic, and hence less critical, than this, that should be ascribed to the kinds of ignorance Olympic cover-ups generate: see Jennings and Sambrook 2000: 290–306.) So difficulties of this sort indicate human frailty only, with no theoretical importance (Chapter 8 pp. 133–4). Fourth, the values seem to change (or be changed) by/with the passage of time: again, an example might be the values claimed for the Olympic movement (pp. 160–3).

Another general issue comes from acknowledging the variety of sport. Suppose we locate some plausible account of the intrinsic value of sport: what would we make of the counter-cases that the variety of sport suggests? That not all sporting activity fits the bill here may partly reflect on the unity (or otherwise) of sport. It may suggest ways of *selecting* sports for some purposes; for example, educational ones, or for the Olympics, *if*. . . . But it does not undermine the general thesis if some sport does not fit: since the relation is defeasible, we have not required claims to be exceptionless ('[all] cheetahs can run faster than men'); if exceptions defuse claims for '*all* sport . . .', we might still think *sport* was not a very uniform category.

Reasons for participation in sport

Different contexts of sports participation (and watching) reflect the many different reasons one might truly (and justifiably) have for doing (or watching) sport. We should be wary of assuming that all sport, across all times, places and contexts, is always played for one reason, or a small number of reasons. For instance, the football match in the park might have little to do with the fact that it is football (rather than, say, cricket) and a great deal to do with camaraderie and companionship. Indeed, the shared activity might even have been something other than a sport – for instance, a game, or other activity (such as birdwatching).

Still, in thinking about the value of sport, we are considering its value in virtue of its being sport – if it has any such value (which we have assumed). So one quite general issue can be introduced (as above) by recognizing that a concern with, say, health or fitness (and suchlike) is not a reason for doing sport rather than some other activity; hence it cannot offer an *intrinsic* account of sport's value. But only an intrinsic account would give sport the value-role needed – only that would be *sport's* value, as the other values could equally pertain to other activities.

We should notice a misconception about what is needed from a 'moral imperative' account of the value of sport – it might seem that the question is (something like), 'Does sport always do me good?': that is, does it always have a (positive) moral benefit? But it is moral connection, not moral benefit, that is required (Chapter 8 pp. 132–3). And even what is valuable, as (say) friendship is valuable, does not always work out well: if my friend is a spy, I may end up with conflicts resulting from friendship over what to do (betray my friend or betray my country). Further, recognizing such-and-such as a virtue (or as valuable) does not mean I act in accordance with it – even if it gives me reason to.

The thought, then, is that sport is intrinsically valuable; that it should be seen like the virtues of friendship or benevolence – where, if we ask, 'Why do it? What is good about doing it?', we have not understood the *it*. First, only someone who did not understand the virtue of benevolence (and understand it as a virtue) could ask, 'why be benevolent?'; second, if a person gives some self-serving answer to such a question, the action under discussion is not an example of *benevolence* at all – rather, it too is self-serving. So we cannot say what is good about benevolence, once we grant that it is a virtue. For now the discussion will typically use benevolence to exemplify virtue (roughly as the metre rule functioned as an exemplar: Chapter 2 p. 44). In the same way, we may not be able to say what is good about sport, even having explained the nature of the value of sport. But we have seen that the question is best put impartially: the issue is not why *I* play sport, but why sport *should be* played.

Normative and motivating reasons

Some ideas from general philosophy can advance our thinking here. Jonathan Dancy (2000b: 1–5) has introduced in a clear way a common-sense distinction, but one lacking generally agreed nomenclature. So, here, we follow Dancy's usage,[1] presenting the position through extensive quotation. As he explains it:

[t]here are . . . two ways of using the notion of a reason *for* an action, which address different questions. There is the question about what were the considerations in the light of which, or despite which, he acted as he did. This issue about *his reasons for doing it* is a matter of motivation.

(Dancy 2000b: 2)

So Dancy suggests calling these *motivating reasons*. And, of course: '[i]f an agent does a truly bad or silly action, then, he will surely have acted for some reason; he will, that is, have had a motivating reason for doing what he did' (Dancy 2000b: 3).

So when we ask him (or her) why he did such-and-such, the answer we get will typically be a motivating reason. But, in addition:

[t]here is also the question whether there was good reason to act in that way, as we say, *any reason for doing it* at all, perhaps one that made it sensible in the circumstances, morally required, or in some other way recommended, or whether there was more reason than not to do it. . . . This second question raises a normative issue.

(Dancy 2000b: 3)

For that reason, Dancy suggests calling such reasons *normative reasons*: they are the ones 'we try to cite in favour of an action, because they are the ones that should show that the action was sensible or right or whatever' (Dancy 2000b: 2).

Later, though, Dancy (2000b: 2–3) acknowledges that, in our concern with normative reasons, 'we are . . . thinking about whether it is a good reason, one that favours acting in the way proposed'. So we could equally speak of normative reasons as *good reasons*, as 'a mark that we are thinking in normative terms' (Dancy 2000b: 4). But (in line with some of our considerations: Chapter 2 pp. 47–52), he does *not* intend this talk of motivating reasons and normative reasons

to suggest that there are two sorts of reasons, the sort that motivate and the sort that are good. There are not. There are just two [kinds of] questions that we use the single notion of a reason to answer.

(Dancy 2000b: 2)

And this is important because, like Dancy (2000b: 6), an important thesis here will be 'that one and the same reason can be both motivating and normative'.

Of course, the precise account to be given of this possibility might differ, with different intellectual backgrounds. Here, I roughly assume Dancy's account, to which readers can turn for further explication. This is sensible, given this text's previous use of Dancy-style particularism (Chapter 8 p. 141). But all that is absolutely required for the argument here is the possibility of reasons being both motivating and normative:[2] that, as Dancy (2000b: 6) puts it, '[a] reason for acting can be a reason why one acted'.

Of course, that there *are* good reasons (when there are) does not mean that the agent acted from these reasons:

> there may be very good reasons favouring an action although these influence the agent not at all, either because he is simply ignorant of them, or because, though perfectly well aware of them, he is lazy, selfish, pig-headed, or whatever.
>
> (Dancy 2000b: 3)

Further, the talk of normative reasons (good reasons), *in contrast* to motivating ones (which might in some sense 'go through my head'), highlights that the normative reasons need have no place in my psychology. Perhaps there is *a* normative reason to donate to the charity Oxfam; but if I donate simply to stop my wife nagging, that reason was not mine. In a sense, the normative reasons are everyone's: they simply represent a good reason to do such-and-such (say, donate to the charity), even if not the reason I act upon. (Or, better, even if not the reason I truthfully give for my action – for, recall, there is no need for this reason to be 'before my mind': rather, it might be the account I offer after the fact.) So there is no guarantee that one's motivating reasons will be normative reasons too. Still, we will move forward (in the next section) by asking ourselves both (a) when that might occur, and (b) what the outcome of such concurrence would be.

Dancy (2000b: 2) makes a fundamental point in a language strongly reminiscent of Chapter 2 (p. 44): 'Because there are different questions at issue, the answers to them can differ.'

Recognizing this offers the basis of (and the need for) the distinction. Here, we are reusing a device introduced earlier: there, two kinds of *questions* concerning rules allowed us to distinguish two kinds of *uses* of rules, without thinking that there were really two kinds of *rules*. Here, in a similar vein, two kinds of questions about the reasons for action indicate two kinds of *uses* of reasons – in explaining motivation or normativity – without postulating two kinds of reasons.[3]

Of course, this distinction is technical: these words are not generally, and regularly, used in these ways in English. But, since we regularly speak neither of motivating reasons nor of normative reasons, this technical usage should be obvious when we encounter it, a transparent way to mark the common-sense contrast. As Dancy (2000b: 3) points out, it leaves a major verbal awkwardness:

> an agent can act for a reason (a motivating one) that is no reason (no good reason, that is), or that there was no reason to do what he did, even though he did it for a reason. Some motivating reasons, that is, are not good reasons.

But such awkwardness is purely verbal – if we pay attention to what is said at each stage, there should be no difficulty.

Of course, this picture of motivating and normative reasons is already a simplification. For instance, as Dancy (2000b: 4) recognizes, we can have:

> a consideration pulling against the action that I choose to do, but pulling unsuccessfully. I recognize it as a reason, and am influenced by it, but not enough to stop me from acting. As we might say, 'I was moved by her plight, but not enough to do anything about it.'

But, like Dancy, I shall simply put this complication aside.

Thus far, I have urged the distinction between normative reasons (*good* reasons for doing such-and-such) and motivating reasons (*my* reasons for doing such-and-such). But why might this be of importance to us? To understand, we must first recognize that even motivating reasons are not (or need not be) thought of causally. That is to say, when I give you my reasons for doing whatever, those are thought of less as 'what went through my head' prior to doing the thing than as how I would honestly *explain* my doing it. After all, this is the power of Wittgenstein's image of persons as first-and-foremost agents (see Introduction pp. 5–6): 'In the beginning was the deed'. So motivating reasons can be thought of as *after the fact*, at least in typical cases. Even when this *is* what went through my head prior to my acting, that need not be the fundamental feature of that action.

To introduce an imaginary example to which we will return, suppose Martina Navratilova is asked why she has returned to competitive tennis. And suppose too (improbably) that she truthfully replies, 'For the money', and we have no reason to doubt her. Then the *motivating* reason for her return is identified. But, first, there still remains the issue of whether this is a good reason – that is, a normative reason – for her action. (Later we will assume it is.) Second, this case illuminates our comments on the status of motivating reasons as after the fact. In the case imagined, Martina may never have been asked (or asked herself) why she was returning to competitive tennis – she may just have got on and done it! So if one thought (mistakenly) that motivating reasons reflected simply what went through the head – that is, one thought of them causally – one would have to say that there was *no* motivating reason in such a case (since nothing explicitly went through the head). But that would simply be a point about Martina's psychology; and that would be what was *wrong* with it. For what motivates Martina (in the case as imagined) is the financial incentive. And (*ex hypothesi*) this is true *whether or not* she explicitly thinks of it; in this sense, it is after the fact.

Yet if motivating reasons do not operate causally, what I offer (typically after the fact) as my motivating reasons – to explain my behaviour – could be challenged. Some third person might dispute that this was the reason I did such-and-such: we are familiar with this kind of challenge through its use in sociology, where 'what really happened' is explained via, say, power relations.

But these kinds of reasons for action could not play a role in our (intrinsic) justification of sport: as we saw earlier (p. 151), there may be very many reasons of a motivating kind why people might participate in, or watch, sport. That is, there might be a great many reasons offered after the fact for why so-and-so participated in such-and-such a sporting event – and some of these might with justice be challenged by our third party (say, our sociologist of sport). So these cannot relate to an intrinsic aspect of sport.

Instead, we must look to what is internally or intrinsically connected to sport: that amounts to the normative reasons for participation in, or watching of, sporting activities. For what is a *good* reason to do, or to watch, sport – where this is a reason to do or watch sport not shared with (say) all other doing or watching – will be intrinsic to sport.

We should go carefully here. First, there may turn out to be no such good reason, but only the sorts of (extrinsic) reason shared with other activities. Thus, if we think about participation, a concern with health and fitness might provide a good reason here (if, say, we make certain empirical assumptions about the benefits of moderate exercise). But this would not be a good reason to participate *in sport*, in the relevant sense, because it would be equally met by many non-sport activities. (This is a point we must return to.) Second, we cannot simply assume that there will be a single intrinsic reason, even if there is at least one. Third, the explanations of watching and of participating should not be run together: we have no reason to think them the same, and some reasons to consider them as different. Yet recording the difficulties in this way may be enough to keep us alert to them.

With this proviso, we can see that – insofar as our reasons are relevant – the normative reasons for sports participation and watching will be the important ones. Only they could offer (part of) our explanation of the (intrinsic) value of sport. Clearly, finding good reasons to do such-and-such is akin to finding the value of such-and-such. But then the reasons here must be relevant, in so far as they are normative reasons. For those just *are* our good reasons.

Normative reasons, rules and sport

Thus far, I have urged of the normative and motivating reasons for, say, participation in sport (a) that they may coincide – although I have not said when or how; and (b) that when they do not, the issue here concerns *normative* reasons. But when would normative reasons coincide with motivating ones?[4] That is, when would the good reasons for doing such-and-such coincide with the reasons I would truthfully give for my doing it?

The answer, of course, is when I do the activity for a good reason. Of course, as one complication here, I may be self-deceived or some such; so that even what I truthfully offer as my reason is not. But when I am not self-deceived in this way, one consequence of normative and motivating reasons coinciding will be that I am doing the activity for a *good* reason. And when those good reasons are intrinsic to the activity, one will be participating for reasons which connect to the value of that activity. For example, if a good reason to be your friend lies in the value *friendship*, that I am your friend means that this value is a part of my life – that my life is richer in that way.

Of course, there are at least two kinds of good reasons (that is, normative reasons) here. First, those that are good reasons for doing sport, but also for doing a wide range of other activities. Our earlier example concerned health and fitness: these are good reasons for doing sport here but, because they are not intrinsic to sport, they cannot ground a value to sport. (One way to see this: imagine you were justifying the place of sport in a school curriculum – these would not give reasons to include sport in a curriculum already replete with other health/fitness-inducing activities.) So these are good reasons to do sport in contrast to *bad* reasons (rugby gives me the opportunity to hit other people) or *non-reasons* – as if someone said that he or she played sport in order to decorate a bedroom. (Of course, there may turn out to be a connection here; but, on the face of it, this is simply irrelevant to sports-playing.) And, having seen this sort of reason for sports participation, we should also note parallel cases for the watching of sport: good but extrinsic reasons.

Then, second, some good reasons for doing sport might be intrinsic to sport, such that one encountered them only or chiefly through the playing of sport. It would not matter here if the connection was not exclusive, as it might be granted that there were other activities sport-like in this respect; but – to fit the bill – the reasons here should be *necessarily* connected with sport, at least defeasibly (see Chapter 7 p. 124; McFee 1992: 61–3). These would be good reasons for doing *sport*, in the sense of applying to sport and sport only (or nearly only).

An earlier example imagined that – asked about her return to competitive tennis – (improbably) Martina Navratilova has truthfully replied, 'For the money.' So that is her *motivating* reason. Suppose further that this is a *good* reason for her returning to play competitive tennis (a normative reason to do so). Here, the answers to the two kinds of questions coincide: her (motivating) reason is a normative (good) reason. But, of course, the reason is not intrinsic to tennis: if it is a good reason for Martina to return to tennis, it would also be a good reason for her to engage in (at least) other activities where her skill and interest might make her lots of money – such as skiing or volleyball (at which, let it be granted, she is both interested and skillful). So we cannot claim a value for tennis in this way – more exactly, any value is not intrinsic to tennis.

The intrinsic value, then, is the value of the activity for itself, or in its own terms. But if that value is shared with other activities, then the value cannot be intrinsic to this activity, since the content of the activity will not be reflected in it. In speaking of the *content* of the activity, I mean simply the features that it has, whereby it differs from other activities. For sports, we would expect a powerful contribution here from rules in their constitutive use (Chapter 2 p. 44): these are what permit one to serve (in tennis), to hold one's serve, to win the game from deuce, and so on. (Notice, too, that these were the sorts of characteristics Suits was looking for: and we lose nothing if we grant them defeasibly [Chapter 7 p. 124].)

If, in our imaginary cases, we press Martina about what is valuable about tennis *as such* – that is, search for an intrinsic value – we are likely to end up with talk of doing the sport 'for its own sake'; for there to be no *reason*, outside of tennis, for Martina to return to competitive tennis. (And if she phrases this as, 'I just love playing competitive tennis', we should not take the answer as one about enjoyment: that too would be an extrinsic valuing.) Indeed, one might feel (with justice) that any other kind of answer is *likely*, or even *bound*, to be extrinsic to tennis. But my position will amount to exemplifying why, in spite of not perhaps being able to say more at the level of *motivating* reasons, there is more that can be said. For the normative reasons here need not be reasons outside of tennis. Rather, only what is intrinsic or internal would meet the constraints (earlier) on the value of sport. Further, only what is intrinsic will be summed-up as 'for the sake of tennis'. What is needed is some good reason – that is, normative reason – for playing tennis (or returning to tennis) that is intrinsic to *tennis*, that draws on its *content*.

Of course, there *might* be no such reasons. Have we a basis for optimism about such a strategy? Here I have urged at least one such kind of reason, in two versions. Both might be captured by speaking of *the moral imperative of sport*, for no good reason for playing sport could ignore the rules, and so on; basically, no good reason could exclude at least reference to the *fair play* and *level playing field* aspects of sport. On the first, weaker version, sport has the capacity to provide opportunities for moral development because rule-following (of the kind intrinsic to sport) is morally motivated: one must follow intrinsic rules because, roughly, one has contracted into them, for these are the rules in their *constitutive* uses (Chapter 2 p. 44; Chapter 7 p. 123). More importantly, the stronger version emphasizes the role in some sports at least, if not in all, of learning moral principles in concrete settings, through the application of moral metaphors (Chapter 7 p. 114; Chapter 8 p. 136). For any rule-related activities where principles of right conduct apply, our position has been that practice for such activities takes one into the moral sphere, but within an area of minimal risk, offered by sport – our 'moral laboratory' idea. A further intrinsic value to virtues is not needed; and we see how sporting activities may contribute to the acquisition of the virtue(s) of justice or fairness. That is part of the potential of sport here, part of the normative reasons for participation in it. But that potential could be actualized only if I internalize that reason – only if the (motivating) reasons *for me* included this one.

On either version, this *moral imperative* is intrinsic to sport: no-one who engaged in sport could avoid confronting it. So our moral imperative, discussed earlier, gives us a normative reason to participate in sport; and (moreover) one intrinsic to sport. Similar considerations might ground the watching of sport, since (in order to understand the *actions* that make up a particular sporting game or match) I must understand – to some degree, at least – the constitutive rules of that sport. For those rules permit my activity to be, say, the action of scoring a try (in rugby) or serving an ace (in tennis). Those who argue that the rules of a sport are crucial to that sport are right, to this degree: the (potential) value of sport lies in its intrinsic connections to virtues such as justice, and that connection operates through the rules of the sport on their constitutive understanding. Moreover, rules *bear* on my behaviour – the ones I *follow*, as opposed to merely conforming to – at the limit of justification. The rule with which someone conforms provides a reason, or part of a reason, for the agent's act. But that is the level of *good* reasons (*normative* reasons), rather than motivating reasons.

Unfortunately, this account of the nature of the value of sport draws on normative reasons for sports participation. And we have granted that normative reasons might not coincide with motivating ones. Further, that the motivating ones are, as it were, the ones that impinge on who I am: for they are my reasons for engaging in the activity.

That permits us to reformulate our goal, with respect to the moral imperative. Now the target will be to get one's motivating reasons (the reasons I would truthfully offer for doing such-and-such, if asked) to coincide with one's (the) normative reasons (good reasons for doing such-and-such). For this will make the intrinsic value of sport *mine*, internalizing it. But it will also develop my moral understanding, at least to some degree – and, consonant with points made earlier (Chapter 7 p. 116), not necessarily in ways I could describe neutrally; so not necessarily in ways amenable to empirical investigation (compare Jones and McNamee 2003). Practical reasoning (here, about sport) should be recognized as *reasoning*; hence, it escapes causal explanation. For causal explanation – the sort where brainwashing or an injection (as well as socialization) would do just as well – will always be beside the point. At best, it describes the *mechanism* of coming to that conclusion. But our interest is not in *how* a person comes to think such-and-such, but in *why* (that is, in the reason) the person should hold this view. Such a causal account should be contrasted with one where *reason* is operative. The reason-type account imports both the *content* of what is thought (the content of my views here connects with the reasons I hold them), and the possibility of acquiring these thoughts or beliefs *rationally* – say, through education. So we can plausibly see education as means of making normative reasons central: that is, of recognizing more than motivating-type explanation.

Drawing this distinction explains why sport may be beneficial or valuable without its being valuable *for me*: I cannot find in myself those normative reasons for playing sport. It also helps explain why a picture of professional sports players in the philosophical literature can seem so idealized (or unrealistic). Contrast two views of the place of professional players: at stake is 'the conventional wisdom that instrumental athletic types, most notoriously professional players, who place a premium on the external good that can be had by participating in sport are genuine game players' (Morgan 1994: 249 note 41).

The thought here resembles that plausibly ascribed to De Coubertin: that if we play sport for reasons other than sport itself, we will not arrive at those intrinsic benefits. Most writers, though, take professional sports persons as obvious examples of those engaged in sport, whatever their motives. (for instance, this is Suits's view, although not Morgan's). Still, as Morgan (1994: 249 note 41) points out, for Suits (1978: 144), professionals will not count as genuine players unless they take, as the major concern of their career, 'excellence in playing the game, and in playing the game alone'.

These views seem counter-intuitive, in ways my account can explain. For the explanation the players would give would, typically, involve motivating reasons. Since those reasons will typically concern money, fame, and so on, they cannot be intrinsic to sport. Yet 'the good of the game' is intrinsic. Hence, for Morgan, these 'players' are not *genuine* game players for that reason: their commitment to the game is extrinsic. But, of course, if we enquire into their normative reasons, these might be intrinsic: at the least, the mere fact that such a player has extrinsic motivating reasons is beside the point. By contrast, what Suits recognized is that, for his archetypal players at least, the reason for participation must be both a normative reason and an intrinsic one. But then the players' concern will indeed be for the game alone: they will be playing for what are good, intrinsic reasons. So Suits's strategy is, in effect, to *stipulate* that only those meeting his criteria count, for *his* purposes.

This is a practical example of my strategy: I can explain the plausibility of both insights (or positions) but without there being a middle way – instead, this is Ramsey's Maxim,[5] such that: 'wherever there is a violent and persistent philosophical dispute there is likely to be a false assumption shared by both parties'.

I am identifying an assumption shared by both Suits and Morgan: namely, that the reasons most professional sportsplayers are . . . well, *professional* relate to extrinsic goods, such as fame or the financial. Then Morgan denies that they are genuine games players; while Suits stipulates that these are not the ones he is discussing. My view concedes these as motivating reasons, but argues, first, that such sportsplayers might also have normative reasons, where these normative reasons might be intrinsic; and, second, that one's normative reasons are the important ones for reaping (or otherwise) the *moral* benefits of sport.

Here, then, we have addressed two of the areas of puzzlement introduced initially in this chapter: we have seen how the value of sport might be explicated – sport is (intrinsically) valuable through its moral imperative – and how that fact might escape many sports players, in two ways. First, our sports players may not find this in their motivating reasons for participation, in which case the (moral) potential of sport will not be actualized; what is valuable will not be valuable *to*, or *for*, them. Second, we cannot readily say where the value of sport lies, except that it lies in sport: for that value is intrinsic.

This leads us to the other two questions posed initially: that concerning the enduring value of sport, and that relating that value to the formulation of ideals for sport, such as the Olympic Ideal – what I earlier called *value formulations*.

The persistence of value

It sometimes seems a simple matter to see whether or not the values of, say, the Olympic movement have been adhered to on a particular occasion, or whether they have changed over time. We have seen (above) that adherence can be conceded even when human frailty is acknowledged; much turns on the account given of the persistence of such values. Simple accounts assume that what is and what is not the persistence of a value is, in and of itself, uncontentious. But, instead, I urge that the values *claimed* for successive Olympic Games are subject to what Alan Tomlinson (1999: 218) has called 'a necessary arrogation': the values were seized, and made anew (or remade), by each Games. A clear example here, of course, are the Olympic 'traditions' claimed – in the case of David Coleman's claim (in 1984) regarding the 'tradition' of an opening ceremony at which the host nation displayed its history and culture, a tradition eight years old! How should such changes in sets of 'defining' values be understood?

If it is granted that the history of the Olympic movement is a history of the 'necessary arrogation' – that is, necessary remakings – of the central values (of the Olympic Ideal, as it were), we ask: *is such remaking a species of persistence?* Speaking of the remaking of certain values implies *some* sense of their persisting through that 'remaking'. Indeed, both the term 'remaking' and the term 'persistence' imply a *kind* of continuity, although remaking also implies some non-continuous aspects. Clearly the sort of persistence of values implied by the remaking of those values cannot mean that all implications from a previous account of those values would carry-over into the new account: that is tautological, from the very idea of *remaking*.

So does 'remaking' describe *change*? Certainly, we should expect a complex relationship here between what *persists* (enough to give some substance to the claim that it is *the same* value) and what *changes* for this to count as modification rather than replacement.

But from whose perspective? That of the philosopher or that of the practitioner? As Feyerabend (1987: 272; McFee 1992: 307) notes, a difficulty for philosophers may not be one for practitioners (in his case, scientists). For instance, any contemporary scientist, looking back at the claims of his scientific forebears, may think them wrong (and correctly) while his detachment allows philosophers to recognize these forebears' claims as incommensurable with those of the contemporary scientist: *incommensurable*, that is, in the strict sense of being unable to be put into one-to-one correspondence with one another.[6] So part of the solution here is to recognize that practitioners may see *persistence* where philosophers (for analytical purposes?) see *change*, or vice versa. Then sports players and officials might think of the *persistence* of the value (that is, the same value was under consideration, now better understood) in a case where philosophers might recognize a *change*. For instance, the practitioners might claim that sponsorship had always been an issue at the Olympic Games, right back to the sponsorship of members of the British team for 1908 by Oxo beef stock cubes![7] But philosophers might urge the transforming effect of introducing television sponsorship on a massive scale – that this was really a different thing. Or the opposite might occur: the value might be re-presented, in a modern context, or with a modern explanation – as when the Olympic concern with equality of opportunity led first to a commitment to amateurism and later away from it. Then sports players and officials might think there had been a *change* in a case where philosophers urge the *persistence* of the value.

Does what is truly an Olympic value depend on the time (and perhaps place) of asking? It is tempting to treat these Olympic values relativistically. As is well known (but the argument is rehearsed in Chapter 10 anyway!), naive relativism is self-refuting. Might a more sophisticated version succeed? In part, the argument here and in Chapter 10 attempts to put aside the lure of such relativism, by finding another account both of value change and of our tolerance for the views of others.

One element of that answer lies in identifying the inevitability of such change. For what sense is the remaking of Olympic values 'necessary' (Tomlinson's expression)? In part, it is necessary *just* as a response to changing social and emotional conditions, to a changing social and emotional world. Schematically, the passage of time is operative in at least two different ways, for judgements are located historically, so that some can only be made with hindsight. Time's passage generates a number of new truths, but there is also the development of new conceptual structures. Either might be treated as examples of necessary remaking. Thus, historical percipience is needed to assert that in such-and-such a house is presently being born the greatest physicist of the twentieth century – suppose both that one is pointing to Einstein's birthplace, at his birth-time, and that Einstein is the greatest physicist of the twentieth century: this judgement requires hindsight, because only the passage of time proves it true (or false). In contrast, the judgement that the creator of the theory of relativity is presently being born in the house makes no sense. More than *mere* hindsight is required to assert it, as the expression 'theory of relativity' requires later conceptual events even to be meaningful. The concepts to make sense of that assertion are only available to us at a certain time and place. Yet with those concepts in place, the assertion is (or can be) true; and earlier persons could not deny the assertion, since to them it would make no sense. In this way, the judgements pass one another by: they are *incommensurable* in the strict sense of being unable to be put into one-to-one correspondence with one another. What counts as possible now (and hence as true or false) depends in part on the concepts available now – and we should not under-estimate the epistemological significance of this fact for talk of *all* possibilities (or of a finite totality of possibilities: compare Chapter 2 p. 47).

As an example, let us return explicitly to the idea of an Olympic Ideal, comprised of (say) the goals De Coubertin originally set out (Chapter 8 p. 131). Here the idea of amateurism (mentioned above) seems a good example of change within the Olympic Ideal. As Loland (2002: 62) notes:

> The word 'amateur' itself disappeared from the Olympic Charter in 1974. In 1968, the IOC left it to the international sports federations to decide whether to allow professional athletes into Olympic competitions. In the 1988 winter Games in Calgary, Canada, professional ice hockey players took part. In the 1992 Barcelona Games, all rules against professionalism of athletes were in practice abandoned. The International Basketball Federation (FIBA) allowed the multi-millionaires of the American NBA to compete against teams from poor countries.

And we should add a note on tennis in Seoul in 1988 – Steffi Graff as champion: the principle seemed to be, 'not *yet* multi-millionaires'.

But, on closer investigation, De Coubertin was never committed to amateurism *as such*. Instead amateurism had, for De Coubertin, two purposes. First, it supported the educational aim of the Olympics ('athletics for its own sake'), since he feared – perhaps rightly – that competing for one's livelihood was difficult to combine with competing for the sake of the sporting activity. Second, amateurism was seen as a way of ensuring equality, so that no-one would be advantaged by being full-time. Of course, that did not happen: in practice, that meant that some get sponsorship, while others lack the training shoes that come with sponsorship (even ignoring the differences in basic facilities in different nation-states!). The *values* might seem enduring, even if the ways of actualizing them were flawed. But, also, recent changes have required some rethinking of the Olympic agenda. Realistically, current[8] successful host cities must be (a) first-world, (b) rich, (c) democratic (Hill 1992: 241, 247). So what price the principle to rotate host cities? Clearly, such values have their origin in (roughly) Western European thought – for example, through the Baron's *influences*, as well as his influence! But the *origin* of values is not, strictly speaking, relevant: the question is better formulated by asking if there are contexts where these values have a place – and, for *some* at least, the answer must be 'yes'. Of course, certain values may have arrived in certain locations (say) under colonialism. But if they are appropriate values for the activities, that is just an irrelevance. Ultimately, such issues concern the causal history of the values only.

In contrast, a *big* question for us asks: what is it for certain values to persist? (What needs to be 'the same' for it to count as *the same value*?) Clearly, using the same words to describe or characterize them will not do – that is a recipe for the remaking (the arrogation) of value-formulations! It is also a big problem for (supposedly) timeless statements of values: for example, a statement of the Olympic Ideal.

The remaking of value-formulations

Later changes – our example above has been the dropping of amateurism – might seem to require a change in the values from the Olympic Ideal. But do they? Here it is important not to confuse *values* as such with *value-formulations* – the problem *from* rules, where rules and rule-formulations are confused. As we saw (Chapter 3 p. 68), either too closely identifying these or too forcefully separating them is a mistake. Here, what had *seemed* central to Olympism (say, amateurism) now no longer does. But the same underlying value is in place. This is sometimes better regarded as the arrogation of *value-formulations*, rather than of the values themselves. If I could wave my magic wand, I would ban such value-formulations: like rule-formulations (Chapter 3 p. 70), they give the illusion of a clarity not possible – seeming to imply that one can always determine, from the formulation, whether or nor a value is being implemented. And this is manifestly not true.

Of course, there is no magic wand: but the point is clear enough – that value-formulations are always open to remaking, in changing circumstances. We might well expect it: certainly, we should be unsurprised to find it. Equally, this is a site for contestation, where you say that this is a legitimate way to read the value-formulation and I deny that it is. The debate between us might turn on the way each understands the changing economic or historical situation. But that debate takes place in an arena circumscribed by our previous value commitments: by the traditions of value-making and value-explaining we share (to the extent that we do). These are ways of referring to what, above, we spoke of as *traditions*.

So the remaking of value is a species of persistence (for the practitioner) – though what persists is sometimes little more than the value-formulation – but also a species of change, from the philosopher's perspective. And re-makings of value are often no more than arrogations of value-formulation. So value-remaking does consist both:

- Of treating change as continuity because there is *formulation* continuity, and
- Of treating *as change* what is, from the practitioner's perspective, continuity (or vice versa).

In a sense, I am responding both to those who deny that there are *abiding* Olympic values and to those who think that the invention of so-called 'traditions' *automatically* gives them a place in the Olympic Ideal, although not by denying what either group assert. Rather, in line with Ramsey's Maxim (p. 159), my strategy involves denying some theses about the persistence of value shared by both my opponents, although these theses are merely assumed, rather than stated or argued for: in particular, the thesis that persistence requires constant application of trans-historical value-formulations. My opponents differ as to whether there *is* such constant application, but agree that *if* there were, there would be persistence of value: and if not, not. And hence one side, failing to find such a formulation, infers that there are not abiding or persisting values. Equally, those that take appeal to (newly created) Olympic traditions to *assure* the persistence of values do so *because* they take such traditions to constitute just these trans-historical value-formulations.

But what this thesis assumes (namely, that for values to persist there must be some trans-historical value-formulation that persists) is neither necessary nor sufficient for such persistence. Formulations may be subject to remaking; and hence *amount* to something different. Equally, values might be thought to persist (from the *practitioners'* perspective) even though (from the *philosophers'* perspective) there was no trans-historical formulation. My point here is that, given these contexts, value-persistence is contestable, debatable. . . .

Moreover, explicit philosophical conclusions are implicit in thinking that only one perspective represented truth, and about the epistemology of finite totalities (see Chapter 10): these are matters fraught with potential to mislead, which have misled some writers! In addition, it is a philosophical thesis, contested here, that (crude) relativism and absolutism about values exhaust the alternatives. And this idea too is widely and uncritically assumed by writers on philosophy.

10 Relativism, objectivity and truth

Thus far, Part III has urged the value of sport from a philosophical position granting both the reality of value (in general) – and hence only disputing whether or not it is instantiated here – and the possibility of speaking truly in explanation of sporting phenomena and sporting institutions: and, on these assumptions, of justifying and explaining their value! But both of these assumptions have been contested. As we saw earlier (Chapter 3 p. 62), the threat of a general relativism is visible in the literature. Exploring this topic requires some brief comment on the project itself (in particular, further discussion of the need both to invoke an intrinsic value for sport and towards a rigorous understanding of the term 'meaning') as well as a more sustained consideration of key themes founding scepticism concerning my fundamental ideas.

It is important to be clear about, for example, claims for *the meaning of sport* – what this expression does and does not amount to! For conflating meaning and value will lead, at best, to a confusing presentation, by suggesting an unwarranted parallel with *genuine* meaning (that is, meaning in, say, language). Roughly, the term *meaning* in such a context usually amounts to something like 'social significance', because sport cannot have a *meaning* in the literal sense in which, say, utterances are meaning-bearing. With *meaning* as it applies in language, we can typically ask what is meant, and relate this to the intention to *mean* such-and-such (Best 1978: 139–41). But the issue here more closely resembles what observers make of (or take from) events: thus, cracks in a wall cannot literally *mean* anything, although they might (a) indicate something, of which they were symptomatic (say, subsidence), or (b) have some social significance for some person – say, if the cracks resembled the name of a loved one. But avoiding misconstrual is not straightforward.

For example, a standard view urges that games typically 'do not signify anything *outside* the game [since] . . . [t]he game can obviously be played without assigning any "interpretation" to the pieces or to their various positions on the board' (Nagel and Newman 1958: 34; my order). Much turns on the term 'signify': chess does not – as it were – *apply* to features of the world. We do not, for instance, see the pieces in terms of the disbursement of an army. And this conclusion would not preclude playing chess with Death, in Ingmar Bergman's *The Seventh Seal* (1957), nor playing Battleships, Cluedo and Twister against Death, as in *Bill and Ted's Bogus Journey* (1991: director Peter Hewitt). For such cases just *assign* to chess – or whatever – a value not implicit in the game. But doing so does not undermine the thesis here: that mastery of (say) chess involves morally relevant mastery, because it involves recognition of the constraints on rule-following as moral constraints (Chapter 7 p. 126); and that case is even stronger when – for sport – more is at stake than there could be within the chess game.

Sport is trivialized if seen exclusively in these terms. But saying more in an abstract way is difficult. We should stress both that the world of sport is one world (see pp. 175–6), and that the notions of significance *within* sport have a life in civilian dress ('in mufti', as Wittgenstein put it, for mathematical notions: RFM V §2).[1] So even when moral metaphors (Chapter 8 p. 136) come from sport, their application outside it is crucial to their overall role. And then stressing the value of sport recognizes its connections to the intrinsically valuable: and hence (as urged earlier) to moral insight – where the contrast is with the widespread human valuing of what is intrinsically worthless (or of little worth), my candidate examples being television soap operas.

Nevertheless, some wholly general problems concerning the truth of claims about sport might be considered. In doing so, we discuss not how sport is understood but how it is theorized. For the primary topic concerns the (logical) underpinning of any claims; and even those claims are likely to be heavily theorized. Postmodern thinking amounts to the most *radical* way of undermining the claims thus far: it disputes that there are some 'facts of the matter' here, which might, then, be understood or misunderstood. But that is exactly how I have presented the world of sport; as objective in this sense.

Now, postmodernism viewed as, on the one hand, a mode of conceptualizing the state of the world, or society, or knowledge (the *postmodern condition*) should be contrasted, on the other hand, with a particular view of (or, worse, recognition of the nature of) *certain* sports, but not others.

Often, writers on sport wishing to avoid relativist tendencies end up adopting some kind of absolutist conception of truth, which casts postmodern thinking as unadulterated nonsense. That is not the position here. Instead, while central theses concerning a postmodern condition must be rejected, (properly understood) there are insights into the nature and limits of knowledge: hence insights any account of *sporting* knowledge must accommodate. An argument here concerns the possibility of truth in social contexts – but, if successful, this line of argument will undercut many of the positions advanced throughout this work.

Getting the first of these topics right circumscribes what can usefully be said – for philosophical purposes – about sport. On this conception, postmodern sports are simply sports with another way to conceptualize their past, or their history, or some such. For we put aside any fundamental objections to accurate and reliable description and explanation. Of course, for some theorists, the postmodern condition explains why certain new (or newish) sports have developed as they have. But we need not comment on this, since (at best) it simply represents another way to consider *sport*.

Three (new?) related issues might seem foregrounded. First, the idea of *objectivity* as it applies in, for instance, the context of *proof*: if I claim that arguments of the chapters of this work *prove* such-and-such, might that be dismissed as, say, simply my opinion? In this way, we question to what degree the nature and scope of philosophy demands 'one right answer' or the search for 'universal commensuration in a final vocabulary' (Rorty 1979: 368). The second issue concerns the *public* nature of those judgements or proofs: they are available to the scrutiny of others. Hence, what is or is not a sporting activity cannot be simply a personal matter: we cannot with good grace pay much attention to what is (or is not) *sport-for-me*. A third issue relates to my judgements of sporting events: in what sense are they *true*?

Having considered the issue of objectivity quite generally (Chapter 5 pp. 92–7), this chapter discusses the issues of publicity and objectivity as they apply to judgements of sport, with some discussion of the larger topic of *truth* (in contrast to relativism); fuller discussion of judgement within the context of philosophy will appear in the Conclusion.

With respect to decisions about the application of rules (discussed in Part II) or about what is or is not sport (addressed in Part I), can one *really* hold what 'opinions' one likes? Is there no fact of the matter in such cases? Here, the argument cannot be that something *in this case* precludes its being resolved – that is, something which applies here but could not apply to at least some other human activities. That the argument would simply raise a problem in this case, not generate reasons for a more general doubt or scepticism. (So this is the converse of the 'sport-shaped hole' case: Chapter 8 pp. 131–2.)

No simple account can capture the relationship between (say) sport and society. As Clement Greenberg (1993: 94) put the corresponding point for art: 'Society contains and throws light on art, receiving light in return, but this reciprocity does not completely explain either art or society.' So some simply-put relationship cannot be here: not as some unidimensional process of mirroring or representing, nor as just the development of a cultural practice. Rather, complex sets of interconnections are to be expected, some normative, some descriptive.

We need to consider the conception of the world of sport – indeed, of the world of fact and knowledge – that such a position supports, as well as that it aims to undermine.

The denial of the coherence of relativism

Since the opponent is relativism, what must one believe (or assert) in order to count as a relativist? On my account (McFee 1992: 301–9), relativists must accept the following possibility: that two people be in genuine (and not merely apparent) *disagreement*, and that both be *right* (relative to some culture, time, place or whatever). As this formulation shows, the charge of relativism might be defused in two ways: namely, by finding that there was no *real* dispute/disagreement, but only an apparent one (that the claim that it was or was not raining *here* was made true by two different 'heres' being invoked, say) or by recognizing that only one of the assertions can be true (even if we do not [yet?] know which). The first of these possibilities, in which two claims pass one another by, is the important one, for it offers diversity without relativism.

With these points in mind, relativism is less attractive than it at first appears, despite its obvious tolerance for others. But this is progress. When we recognize such relativism as self-refuting, we must look to some other ground for tolerance. To see that it *is* self-refuting, notice that the relativist really claims that there are no universal truths since, for him, any truth might be asserted by one person while being denied by another and both be right, both be speaking 'the truth' (relative to . . . something). So no truth can be *un-relative*: but what about the truth of relativism? If, consistently, he urges that relativism itself is not universally true, why should we believe him when he claims that it applies *here*? Indeed, what *precisely* would he then be asserting? Presumably, that there are some universal truths (since not all truth-claims behave as relativists assume): but then he is not a relativist – he accepts universal truths. If instead he asserts that relativism *is* universally true, he is no relativist either. For *that* is then urged as a universal truth. (Or, at least, a lot of further argument is required to make sense of his position.)

Our argumentative strategy against the relativist simply involves claiming, 'relativism is not true-for-me'. Since he accepts no truth *other than* truth-for-me (or someone else), he has nothing to say. Anyone who, faced with this remark, wants to debate with you – that is, to contest the remark – is not a relativist: but, were a thinker so easily discomforted, we might worry about the value of his theses. And denying that there is any such thing as truth must count against the *truth* of relativism as a philosophical thesis.

So the insights of postmodernism can be overplayed. To bring this point to the fore, we can begin from Lyotard's account of the postmodern condition.[2] Exploring these topics takes us fairly far from the world of sport, but some discussion here is essential to avoid misunderstanding and to locate our position amongst competitors.

The postmodern challenge: incredulity towards metanarratives

In his most general (and widely familiar) formulation, Lyotard (1984: xxiii) characterizes the postmodern in terms of 'incredulity towards metanarratives', citing Freudianism and Marxism as examples of such metanarratives, explained as those 'which describe or predict the activities of such entities as the noumenal self, the Absolute Spirit or the Proletariat' (Rorty 1991: 199). Such metanarratives (or 'Grand Narratives') seek all-embracing explanation: as Rorty (1979: 368) puts it (recall), they 'search for universal commensuration in a final vocabulary'.

Lyotard (1984: 60) seems to believe that the postmodern condition requires new conceptualizations of (for example) knowledge or science, in a way inevitable (and perhaps therefore correct) in the postmodern condition. So this suggests, not the identification of a *mistaken* view previously held, but a new situation, a 'condition' where the whole idea of knowledge or of science *can*, and perhaps *must*, be understood differently.[3] So (on this view) the old account *was* accurate, but *no longer* is.

Whatever its merits as a sociological thesis, this is decidedly odd as a philosophical thesis: if, at one time, there were arguments for (or against) some view of the nature of (say) science, surely they are arguments *now*. And if there are *now* counter-arguments, there were such arguments then! For instance, if later changes in social understanding or scientific theory make us doubt the explanatory adequacy of some metanarrative, surely that shows that it was *always* false (in its full generality) but that its falsity was not *clear* previously.

So characterizing the postmodern condition in terms of 'incredulity towards metanarratives' (Lyotard 1984: xxiii) raises two difficulties. Suppose, with Lyotard, we doubt the possibility of such perfectly general explanation of every event. Then postmodernist theory seeks to contest some traditional claims about the nature of understanding. But many philosophers have been incredulous about metanarratives (if not in those words). For example, J. L. Austin (who died in 1960) was incredulous about metanarratives – in a principled way – before any more general postmodern condition was claimed. Thus Austin (1970: 203[4]) noted that 'there is no necessity whatsoever that the various models . . . should all fit together neatly as parts into one single, total model or scheme'. So there is no reason to assume such a general theory: hence reason to be incredulous about one offered us by some theorist.

Of course, some elements of our world lend themselves to this historical treatment. For example, a change in artistic fashion is one thing (McFee 1998b: 81–2). But the issue for philosophy seems (prima facie) to concern truth: Austin's *incredulity* does not attack or dispense with the concept 'truth'. So the first difficulty is the basis for the incredulity: might we not (like Austin) be genuinely incredulous, without invoking a postmodern condition?

The second difficulty concerns what *action* follows from incredulity. Justified suspicion of 'one right answer' does not *automatically* lead to the 'anything goes' of subjectivism or relativism – as multiple figures from psychology (for example the old crone/young woman: see Chapter 5 p. 95) illustrate. One might give up the *grand* project *without* concluding that nothing can *ever* be explained. So where exactly does being *incredulous* about

metanarratives get you? Denying the possibility of such overarching explanatory schemes can mean that *no* explanatory scheme is possible, or
merely that explanatory schemes must not be overarching. (The second should
not worry us.) For example, nothing seems rendered problematic for *these*
reasons about what Luntley (1995: 110) calls 'simple truth', explained as:

> the concept of things continuing to exist independently of our thought
> about them. . . . I judge that there is £2,000 in my bank account, but
> I acknowledge that there is a fact of the matter independent of my
> judgement.

In this way, mere incredulity, and especially incredulity explained simply
historically, does not *yet* strike us as challenging. So the precise *challenge* of
postmodernism is difficult to grasp. For postmodernism owes us – but does
not typically provide – a reply to both worries.

These considerations from Lyotard and his acolytes are often taken to
show far more than they actually do. The fact that language has no foundation in the facts of the world might *seem* to imply that all truth-claims are
ultimately arbitrary: this would undermine the notion of truth. Thus, it is
sometimes suggested that this 'arbitrariness of the sign' means we are *really*
dealing with words only. As Williams (2002: 6) notes, this view typically
begins from a misunderstanding (he says 'mangling') of Saussure:

> to the general effect that language consists of 'arbitrary signs' which 'get
> their meaning' from their relations to other signs, and since this is so, it
> [language] cannot refer to a non-linguistic world.

But he recognizes that this is a weak argument:

> if *dog* is an 'arbitrary' sign for a dog, it is at any rate a sign for a dog,
> and that must mean it can refer to a dog: and a dog is a dog, not
> a word.
>
> (Williams 2002: 6)

So the supposed arbitrariness cannot pry words from the world. Further, no
account could offer more by way of rejecting universalism about the meaning of expressions than has been granted by our contextualist account of
occasion-sensitivity (Chapter 2 pp. 49–52). Yet that view recognizes truths.
Moreover, at best, an *image* of truth (and so on) is undermined by these
points, not *truth* itself. Scientific description of the world around us has a
reductive tendency, treating colours as optical effects, sensations and emotions
as brain states and so on. Certainly the world of theoretical physics is not
coloured: but need that affect us? Are there *really* red post boxes, blue cars,
toothaches, depressions and loves? Once we recognize these as contingent
features of our contemporary account of the world, natural science may

have seemed to offer a preferable alternative – a view of how the world *is*, abstracted from any particular historical or cultural position: *the View from Nowhere* (Nagel 1986). Then postmodernism has been presented in terms of the failure of such a project 'to attain absolute truth, the truth that transcends local points of view . . . the truth that makes up the grand narrative about the whole of creation' (Luntley 1995: 11–12). But the project thereby undermined was committed to *one right answer*, not just to *an* answer. Giving up *that* aspect of the project need not amount to giving up the notion of truth.

Luntley's strategy, therefore, returns to such commitments to the colour of post boxes and cars, as well as the reality of pain, depression and love; to what (as above) he calls 'simple truths': 'to the idea that things go on independently of our thinking of them' (Luntley 1995: 107). Such truths are accepted by postmodernists, at least through their actions. For why else 'do they wear seat-belts in their cars, go to the dentist when they have a toothache, or go to the bank manager for a loan?' (Luntley 1995: 107).

This account makes plain some of the attractions of postmodernism, although putting them more soberly: postmodernism's 'insight' is only that the *God's-eye view* conception of truth is misconceived. But we do not need postmodernism to explain or understand that.

Understanding and the concrete

Recognition that we are ineliminably in the fishbowl (that there is no external perspective) is only worrying if our account of reason or of truth would thereby be undermined: and why should that be? The relativist and his absolutist opponent both accept a demand for determinacy. To reject it, we need a more plausible model of the rational. As John Wisdom (1965: 102) comments, 'at the bar of reason, always the final appeal is to cases'. Here there is the promise of an account of rationality with a particularist tendency, stressing the connection of objectivity to the public nature of rationality. Wisdom elaborates the idea by contrasting what he calls 'the mother's method' of explanation with 'the father's method'. Asked what a greyhound is, the father replies with a kind of 'definition', that a greyhound is 'a dog of such-and-such a type'. Wisdom comments: 'Short, conclusive, the father's procedure. That's more what one might call a proof' (Wisdom 1991: 48). In contrast, the mother says (pointing):

> that's a greyhound, and you remember your uncle's dog, Entry Badge, well that was a greyhound. But now that [she says, pointing to a Borzoi] is not a greyhound, and even that [she says, pointing to a whippet] is not.
>
> (Wisdom 1965: 69)

Wisdom (1965: 69) also imagines that she might offer the rhyme:

A foot like a cat, a tail like a rat,
A back like a rake, a head like a snake.

He concludes that the mother 'replies with instances of what is and what is not a greyhound or by comparing greyhounds with what they are not, and these two procedures merge into one' (Wisdom 1965: 70).

Attempts to force knowledge and understanding into the straitjacket of a set of criteria – the sort of thing 'the father's method' offered – seem doomed to failure. But this is no cause for complaint, since the mother's method is the typical route to genuine, public, discussible claims – that is, to objectivity (Chapter 5 pp. 96–7). And the route is clearly that of particularism (Chapter 8 pp. 141–4), in line with the commitment to occasion-sensitivity (Chapter 2 pp. 49–52).[5]

Consider, for instance, the place of traditions of value-making and value-explaining (with Olympism as one such). The 'mother's method' appeals to what we know and understand, to familiar cases: and these derive from the history of the concepts in question. In this vein, we recognize traditions as ways of articulating a relevant reason here – that is, of clarifying relevance – as what allows us to identify a certain claim as being a reason in the context of Olympism: as being *Olympic reasons*, as we might say. Equally, appeals to tradition are ways of not explaining: saying that this action or event was traditional, or seeing it as part of some tradition, justified it. For instance: 'The point about traditions is that you don't really have to justify them: they contain their own truth' (Giddens 1994: 6). That is, the appeal to traditions was part of both value-making and value-explaining. In plotting an Olympic tradition, then, we sketch a narrative within which certain values obtain, values which *define* our thinking as appropriate by linking it to the Olympic Ideal. To count as an *Olympic reason* is to be appropriately related to the history of Olympism. For we understand *Olympism* only by reference to what has happened *previously* as Olympism – although some such reference (as with revolutionaries) proceeds through denial.

In this way, the appeal to traditions and histories – when not gratuitous – is an appeal to practices worth preserving, 'having the weight of . . . something that has flourished' (Scruton 1980: 42),[6] where such flourishing gives us reason to esteem them. But the justificatory force of such appeals to tradition is fragile: Giddens (1994: 6), among others, notes this fragility in recording the forces that undermine such appeals to the justificatory weight of *tradition*.

What have we recognized about value? We have seen the objectivity of value as consistent both with divergence in specific contexts, and with a characterization of values through concrete cases rather than formulae: also, the potential of tradition to hold such values in place, and to explain them. These are the insights behind relativism, without thereby making us relativists.

The postmodern challenge II: reason and science

Another, related, thread in Lyotard takes a metanarrative as concerned with 'legitimation with respect to its own status' (Lyotard 1984: 8). Then, having recognized that we speak and judge as 'the contingent historical selves we find ourselves to be' (Rorty 1991: 214), why should such (historically-rooted and contingent) judgements carry any weight for others (much less be compelling on them)? Rather (Lyotard thinks) we should deny any single discourse the right to judge others on its terms: all discourses are equal! Faced with a search for some tribunal of Pure Reason, Lyotard asks rhetorically, 'What language do the judges speak?'. Any answer *seems* to import arbitrariness into the heart of human judgement.

Theses such as Lyotard's *appear* to commit postmodernists to attacks on the concept of truth. With no metanarratives, no overarching explanatory frameworks, the model of knowledge based on the (supposed) qualities of scientific knowledge is undermined if – as is the postmodernist tendency – science is claimed as just another narrative: that is, as just one among many, with no further claim to authority. In part, this recognizes a general (and agreed) characteristic of science: namely, the *inherently* changeable nature of the truths of science and technology, in a world where theories can change.

If successful, this argument only proves that scientific knowledge cannot be our model: but the argument might *seem* to show more. It might be thought that '[o]nly descriptions of the world can be true or false' (Rorty 1989: 5). Then 'it is difficult to think of the world as deciding between' (Rorty 1989: 5) alternative descriptions of events, once these are seen as *whole* ways of describing – 'the jargon of Newton versus that of Aristotle' (Rorty 1989: 5), for example. Then we recognize 'that socialization, and thus historical circumstance, goes all the way down – that there is nothing "beneath" socialization or prior to history which is definitory of the human' (Rorty 1989: xiii).

So, it might be thought that 'Truth cannot be out there ... because sentences cannot so exist, or be out there' (Rorty 1989: 5). Thus truth is 'free-floating': that is tantamount to claiming that there is no truth. (Rorty acknowledges this conclusion by taking as his hero the ' "strong poet" rather than ... the truth-seeking "logical", "objective" scientist' [Rorty 1989: 53] – where the scare quotes indicate his hesitation about the possibilities of *objectivity*, and the like.)

As traditionally viewed, scientific description of the world around us has a reductive tendency, offering a *View from Nowhere*, abstracted from any particular historical or cultural position. Rejecting such a position, postmodernism reiterates its assumption that the alternatives here are *one right answer* or *anything goes*: each of these positions then chooses one alternative by rejecting (with justice) the other. So, having rejected one right answer, the postmodernist concludes that anything goes – just as the absolutist might arrive at one right answer by rejecting (with justice: Chapter 5 pp. 94–6) the idea that anything goes. But the mistake here lies in that reasoning: from the fact that there was *not* 'one right answer', the conclusion 'anything goes' simply does not follow (nor vice versa). Such theorizing assumes (mistakenly) that what is not *independently* legitimated is thereby guaranteed to be arbitrary. So Lyotard's key argumentative strategy is unsound: from a rejection of the search for 'universal commensuration in a final vocabulary' (Rorty 1979: 368), nothing follows about issues of objectivity.

Furthermore, the postmodernist rejection of *truth* is supposed to carry over to *rationality* also. But this too is a problematic move: it can fall into 'the trap of concluding that all rational argument is mere rationalization and then proceeding to *argue rationally* for this position' (Putnam 1981: 161). Even the first element of this trap is problematic: suppose I claim to attend philosophy conferences to disseminate my wisdom, but this is a rationalization – I really come to conferences hoping to banter and drink with friends. Now my rationalization does not give the real reason for my behaviour, but there *is* a real reason. Putnam identifies, of course, that one cannot justify rationally one's accusation that all rational argument is mere rationalization: for, by its own lights, any putative justification could be dismissed as mere rationalization. That the position is so easily put aside must make its attractions (if any) doubtful.

A more realistic reading of the objection here would argue, not that there is no rational argument (which, as we saw, precludes one saying *why*), but that rational argument is different than is sometimes supposed – the objector urges that it is different from how I suppose it is. But now his position depends on accurately capturing how *I* regard logical or rational argument: if he is wrong about this, his objection will bypass my position.

Perhaps our account of rationality *is* flawed. No doubt there are problems about 'our' understanding of the world; yet these 'require not only rational reconstruction but criticism. But criticism requires argument, not the abandonment of argument' (Putnam 1992: 130). To attacks on logocentrism (Norris 1987: 28, 57), we reply that, while our account of rationality may need modifying, we cannot do without *some* such account – criticism is needed to motivate and to direct any modification, and pointing to the features of some phase of human development, some postmodern condition, cannot provide this. Indeed, as Putnam (1992: 124) urges:

> the collapse of a certain picture of the world, and of conceptions of representation and truth that went with that picture of the world, is very far from being a collapse of the notions of representation and truth.

Finding that a certain metaphysical picture is *now* bankrupt is (probably or typically) a way of noting that – for all its apparent successes – it was *always* bankrupt: its successes are indeed only apparent (and probably best explained in some other way).

One sporting world?

Earlier, the question of whether or not it was right to think of theoretical claims about sport as ever (in principle) *true* was raised. Two central thoughts here, to arrive at a 'yes' answer, are that we should dispense with some grandiose view of truth (truth with a capital 'T', conceived of as timeless and omnipresent) and that recognition of truths is compatible with diversity (especially the diversity of interests, concerns and perspectives).

First, in order to recognize that claims in social theory (for example, concerning sport) might be *true*, we must acknowledge this as a thesis about what is *possible*. We are not urging that any such claims are (or are not) true: merely that they are candidates for truth – the possibility of truth cannot be ruled out prior to actual investigation. Further, the sorts of truths here are equivalent to, say, the claim that so-and-so has an overdraft: no overarching grand theory is being imported. We are only urging that, say, it is *true* (or part of the truth) that '[a] species of internationalism constitutes a chief rationale of the Olympic movement' (Hargreaves 2000: 113). Or, if it is not true (something we might discover by detailed analysis), that is because it is false! Moreover, central to such an everyday conception of truth (and falsity) are ideas of showing, or of finding out, that such-and-such was true (or part of the truth), where these are not simply made so by our wanting (or wishing for) it.

Our discussion might be augmented by recognizing the diversity it tolerates: what is rejected here is the position that anything goes (that any view is as good as any other). Multiple-figures from psychology (such as the 'old woman/young woman'; Chapter 5 p. 95) have offered a model for diversity, answerability to features of the case, and a rejection of *anything goes*. On this view, the notion of truth here would be unthreatening. Moreover, the true will generally be preferable to the false, and for that reason – and 'the truth' here seems unitary. This is how the operation of explanations of, say, sporting events is conceptualized.

Equally, it seems unlikely that a single framework would unify all the issues: in a language recently fashionable, there seems little hope for a 'grand narrative' (Lyotard 1984: xxiv). To offer a simple model, we would not expect the concerns about my sports-activity expressed by my doctor and my friend to have the same basic structure: the friend is interested in what I can do – say, can I play soccer on Saturday? But, while the question here *might* be better put as asking whether or not I *can* play soccer (full stop), it is more likely that the range of answers will draw on something like: do I have the time? (Am I going to another friend's party?) Do I have the money to get to the venue, or the requisite clothing? And so on. Of course, on that list will be a question the doctor might have asked: have I recovered from the hamstring injury? Yet the other range does not address anything the doctor's methodologies give him access to. In this way, what seemed like *one* request (whether I could play soccer on Saturday) becomes visible as

– potentially – *numerous* requests. So we cannot expect one unified set of (candidate) answers to questions about whether so-and-so can play *soccer* (let alone *sport*) on Saturday: that form of words can embrace numerous different questions. In this vein, then, we cannot expect a single 'overarching' theory to incorporate *all* the soccer-playing-on-Saturday issues, for there is no *all* here, no finite totality of issues (McFee 2000a: 121–3). Once we recognize this point for one such topic, we can hardly hope for more from a general consideration of sport.

Thus, for example, suppose we conclude that such-and-such (say, power conceived in class-based terms) was crucial for understanding sport in so-and-so context (say, Britain during the last century and a half: see Hargreaves [1986: 209]): have we thereby precluded other explanations? No, because, in locating *this* as an explanation in this case, we are not insisting that it be explanatory in all cases – it might, but it might not. So other contexts might require reference to power-relations conceptualized in terms of gender, ethnicity, etc., in ways not simply reducible to social class. We have not even concluded that the explanatory tool will *always* be power. Further, in taking this to answer *our* question, we have not precluded other questions being asked (even in the same, or similar forms of words): so different preoccupations might lead to a (slightly) different question, and hence a different form of answer, even when discussing (say) Britain in the last century and a half.

This discussion might be summarized as saying that there is one world; more specifically, one sporting world – that the diversities within our ana-lysis of that world, within the concerns we might have for it, the values we might locate in it, speak directly to the idea of a single locus of attention: as Virginia Woolf is supposed to have remarked, 'one of the bloody things is enough'! But we also see why the metaphor of 'many worlds' might seem attractive, as a way to recognize diversity.

Conclusion
Sport, rules and philosophy

The text as a whole urges that mistaken conceptions both of the nature of rules and of philosophical investigation – with its associated determinacy – preclude a realistic understanding of sport: indeed, that such misconceptions dog the literature on sport. These ideas were explored in Part I. Further, both the decision-process of judges, umpires and referees and the overall value (to human kind, but intrinsically) of sport make sense once the *moral imperative* implicit in how sporting activities relate to the rules of those activities is recognized. This was considered in Part II. Moreover, there is an explanation – also drawing on that moral imperative – of how an intrinsic value for sport might be characterized. Part III deployed a variety of considerations in this area. Enough has been done if this account of the value of sport is *arguable* – most alternative accounts are already refuted by arguments rehearsed earlier.

One danger of almost all theoretical writing – especially in a text like this – is of critics taking forward (at best) simplified versions of the key ideas. For example, Freud[1] foresaw this outcome for his own work, where:

> qualifications and exact particularisation are of little use with the general public; there is very little room in the memory of the multitude; it retains only the bare gist of any thesis and fabricates an extreme version which is easy to remember.

Freud's point is that something inexact is *taken* from his theoretically-precise accounts of human beings, with that inexactness following from how his works are presented to a general audience.

Applied here, I imagine that misunderstandings will focus on the strategies of this text, and therefore on its achievements. It will be presented as having a number of precise (or fairly precise) *theses*, then shown to be not exceptionless. This is already a misreading, in two ways. To find exceptions cannot (alone) be to criticize, since such exceptions are granted: the 'claims' here were never intended as exceptionless – as the text makes plain! But, equally, they were never *claims* or theses either. At best, some slogans[2] were offered to break the grip of thinking that sport *must* be seen a certain way, by offering '*objects of comparison*' (PI §130).

In this vein, cases have, for instance, illustrated someone mistaking how closely the rules of a sport constrained the behaviours permitted within that sport, or how much (or little) could be achieved by modification of the sport's rules. Further, considering someone who thought referees and umpires were becoming *lawmakers* (rather than just law-enforcers) has shown how a comparison with other cases might dissolve that suspicion, without denying the resources on which the umpire can draw. This kind of case draws attention to the role of *principles*.

Of course, in part, this offers an account of the nature of sport. And doing so may seem to transgress some of my own strictures (from Chapter 1) about definiteness. Do I think the world of sport is *like* this? Is this *the* mystery of sport unravelled, *the* value of sport exposed?

Consonant with my philosophical commitments, the answer here is 'no'; but in a guarded way. First, on many occasions, merely reminding oneself that sport can be thought of as embodying a *moral imperative* will be revealing: it prevents us mistaking sport in various ways. In particular, it focuses our minds on the issue of *intrinsic* value. That will sometimes be clarifying, especially if the emphasis were on some extrinsic properties of a particular sporting situation: for instance, the amount of money to be made! Then, second, this is a plausible view of what is typically valuable in *some* sport. Compared to other views of the value of sport, I prefer that others hold this view; and offer reasons why they might profitably do so. (Most of which will be collected under my first point here.)

Third, the intrinsic character of my picture of the value of sport remains important. I recognize the variety of sporting situations and contexts: much of the value of playing or watching sports on particular occasions may have little or nothing to do with the value of sport. Rather, it may reflect one's enjoyment of others and others' company, of one's (pleasurable) obligations as friend, parent, colleague. It may spill over, through fandom, into connections with one's home town or country. And one cannot deny the benefits of exercise both for health (if taken in moderation) and for one's sense of well-being. So it is always important to value sport as part of a life, as part of what it *can* be to live well (in this sense, as *eudaimonic*: see Nussbaum [2001: 32]).

None of this is denied by the account of sport offered here. For many of the activities just cited have little or no connection to *sport* as such; sporting activity, at best, is the *occasion* for them – one occasion among many, with luck – and not a unique provider of that occasion. So, as far as these are explanations for participation in sport, one's life could lack *sport* and still be equally full, rich and complete. To see this, we need only replace the sporting occasion in each of the examples above with some *other* occasion. I can play chess with my grandson as well as cricket – or instead; I can swim and jog for exercise – even for health – without taking these activities as sport; I can enjoy conversation with colleagues at the book club (or in the bar) as fruitfully – and perhaps more easily – than on the tennis court; I can even come to value my town or country for its other activities; and so on. Thus, on all these bases, participation in sport may turn out to be part of a good life, but only contingently. The virtues (of friendship, and so on) are only *accidentally* connected with sporting activities.

In contrast, my account stresses a value sport may have; and, when it does, this will necessarily conduce to a good life. Of course, it will only be one part of that life, at best. But it *will* be that part. So that, for the person who can see sport in this way (and internalize that insight), sport will necessarily be a part of what it is to live well; and that person's life would be poorer were sport removed from it.

To summarize, then: my account does not take the form *this is how sport should be thought of*. Rather, it stresses the benefits or insights from seeing or thinking about sport this way. But an *even* better (because more Wittgensteinian) formulation would be: *resolve or dissolve some of your perplexities about sport by seeing it this way*. Of course, a particular person might either have *no* perplexity about sport or have *others* than the ones explored here. Then this would not be the text for such a person. (And perhaps, in years to come, other texts might be written for that person's perplexity – I might even write some of them myself!)

But the perplexities resolved or dissolved here are those fuelled by other writing and by other theorists in particular – even when those theorists are not named explicitly (often to avoid giving this work too scholarly a cast). Perhaps, for that reason, I should not insist on its pedigree in *others'* writing. Let us say, then, that it responds to challenges I have encountered, first, in saloon bars around the world and, second, in my own tendencies to explain: that it comes 'from philosophers and from the philosopher in us' (Ms 219 p. 11).

One feature of my position – visible both in the form and the content of this work – is that discussion of sport depends on more general philosophical issues: issues in respect of sport are either *ethical* issues concerning sport or issues from general philosophy with sporting examples.[3] So most chapters contain at least one section which could equally be located in a work of general philosophy, merely offering sporting examples. As elsewhere (McFee 1998a: 12), part of my point is that one cannot genuinely be a philosopher *of sport* but only a philosopher with interests in sport.

But, in part, this text illustrates how even the two options above might come to the same thing: ethical issues too depend to some degree on conceptions of ethics discussed fully only in (general) philosophy. And even when that theory (from philosophy more generally) turns on ethical concerns within sport, the point is not typically for sport *only*. Again, and at the least, the *structure* of this text should be seen as (partially) constitutive of an argument for that conclusion. Adherents of my position would expect philosophical conclusions concerning sport to be underpinned by more general considerations: that is what they would find exemplified here.

Most chapters, then, show the application of some philosophical insights to issues from sport. Which? These insights might be roughly sketched as follows:

- *Chapter One* contains standard arguments against definability but, more important, arguments against the philosophical *importance* of definiteness: and also of hiddenness; it rejects the philosophical project of analysis.
- *Chapter Two* includes a picture of rule-following, the introduction of context-sensitivity – crucial to the account of understanding throughout – plus the focus on the *use* (rather than the *nature*) of rules.
- *Chapter Three* explores the identification of normativity as a (possible) issue, once we recognize how views which dispute the *thesis* of formalism (in Suits's version) may still adopt its *project*.
- *Chapter Four* contains reflection (largely negative) on MacIntyre's influential account of *practices*, if used as an explanation for normativity: that was not MacIntyre's purpose, nor could his thinking do that job.
- *Chapter Five* turns on the rejection of subjectivism – permitting diversity does not require that anything goes. And recognizing this point is granting both that we may *differ* without losing answerability to the features of events, and that recognition of such features may be beyond some people.
- *Chapter Six* begins from recognition of the role of sport's rules in the (true) description of sporting events, leading to a consideration of the *principles* underlying such rules.
- *Chapter Seven* introduces the central moral imperative, developed from the nature of rule-obedience.
- *Chapter Eight* supports a stronger reading of the moral imperative of sport, in at least *some* cases, through the particularization of moral judgement.
- *Chapter Nine* includes Dancy's distinction between *normative reasons* ('good reasons') and *motivating reasons* ('my reasons'): the first are crucial to our investigation, and do not merely turn on features of my psychology.
- *Chapter Ten* contains a rejection of postmodernism, stressing the idea of 'simple truths'.

Of course, this is not *strictly* an argument for that conclusion about the relationship of sporting issues to (general) philosophy, even if it suggests a reason to accept it: the conclusion might (in theory) have been reached by other routes. But it is much harder to conceptualize that point concretely in other terms. Granting that this structure *might have* some other explanation (in principle), it is not obvious what it might be (in practice).

Part of the thought here relates to the thoroughness of my consideration of relevant issues (as manifest here) – my taking their diversity seriously, and (yet) arriving where I have. Of course, the conclusion might be explained away as an idiosyncrasy of mine: the reference to (general) theory is not *required* by the logic of the arguments; it is gratuitous, in that sense. But close investigation of the arguments does not support that conclusion. For example, the *reason* for the openness of rule-structures is only understood once we turn to, say, occasion-sensitivity (Chapter 2 pp. 47–52). And similar points might be made for the theoretical interventions in *any* chapter.

However, there are three points to draw from the classification given above. First, the philosophical points (or the philosophical conclusions) might be reached with no reference to sport – roughly, as I have stated them here. Second, in the opposite direction, these points have a direct bearing on how the *nature of sport* is understood: they amount to a view of sport. Third, these views constitute a unified package: although one might reject (or modify) *parts* without rejecting the whole, it *is* a whole – a *philosophical* position on understanding, rule-following and aspects of moral philosophy, and (perhaps) more. So that grasping the *arguments* here requires philosophical sophistication at least to that level. As noted initially (Introduction pp. 11–12), a high level of sophistication is not needed. But one may misunderstand the detail by failing to see its underpinning in the philosophical project.

Thus, for instance, the view here respects individualism (as a methodological doctrine) in not requiring – for the explanation of social phenomena, such as sport – supra-individual concepts. The explanation here might lie in the (justified) commitment to parsimoniousness in theory-construction. But it implicitly takes a *rich*, rather than an attenuated, view of the nature of these individuals (see McFee 2002: 125–6). In particular, it does not invoke community agreement. Instead, it sees people as fundamentally *agents*; moreover, as *morally* implicated. Further, its account of the normative deploys the central authorless-ness of rule-following obligations (McFee 2002: 128–32), even in a world of authoritative bodies of sporting institutions. And each of these points may be tracked to a commitment explicitly voiced here.

To conclude autobiographically, when the idea for this text was first under discussion, both the general editors and the publisher encouraged me to use it to develop my *distinctive* account of sport from my *distinctive* picture of philosophy and *its* project. That picture of sport draws on the work of others. As such (and unsurprisingly), it ends up agreeing with the conclusions of some of those others. But four points are of the greatest importance here. First, agreement in conclusions can accompany profound disagreement in reasons – and hence difference in position. Second, any commonality of conclusion here should not conceal that this is a *distinctive* view, one which takes issue with the standard views by taking issue with their assumptions. Putting aside such assumptions will mean putting aside the positions they imply. And central here will be the rejection of the project of determinacy, and recognizing both the occasion-sensitivity of rule-following and (moral) particularism. So, third, if this picture is ever mistaken for one seeking middle ground among competing views, the methodological device to stress here is Ramsey's Maxim (quoted in Chapter 9 p. 159): 'wherever there is a violent and persistent philosophical dispute there is likely to be a false assumption shared by both parties' (Bambrough 1969: 10).

The strategy, therefore, is to undermine *both* of a pair of standard oppositions by rejecting an assumption they both share. At its simplest, we see this at work in the disputes between Suits, Meier and D'Agostino (Chapter 3): all share an assumption about determinacy which should be rejected. Nevertheless, and fourth, the general attitude to those discussed here is not antagonistic – I would not be giving houseroom to views unless the views mentioned were both clearly expressed and had their attractions: they should be tempting, in this sense. For my account of philosophy sees them as (centrally) my temptations or puzzlements. Or, at the least, temptations or puzzlements that I can understand in that way – hence cannot simply *dismiss*. Thus a longer treatment would address the manner of treating 'opponents', plus selection of 'opponents' (that is, of those I choose to comment on). My view takes those discussed more as collaborators in some joint project towards understanding than as objects for target practice. Certainly, they are not fools to be refuted. But this is not the way one's opponents are sometimes treated.

It must be granted that this text only contains an argument for a certain conclusion (or set of them), which depends both on a certain conception of philosophy (expanded above) and a satisfactory outcome of a research agenda (sketched in Chapter 8). It does not explore some other construals of the sporting events considered. And it does not give due weight either to alternative conceptions of philosophy or to variant readings of both sporting events and the philosophical insights to be applied to them. In an ideal world, where books were allowed to be *far* longer, it might. But its central purpose is achieved if it generates in readers the desire to travel down even some of these avenues.

Notes

Introduction: Sports, rules and values

1 In addition to the ones specifically discussed in this text, classic presentations include Pearson 1973; Delattre 1976; Reddiford 1985.
2 The following abbreviations are used to refer to works of Wittgenstein:

Wittgenstein 1953 – PI
Wittgenstein 1967 – Z
Wittgenstein 1969 – OC
Wittgenstein 1978 – RFM
Wittgenstein 1980 – CV
Wittgenstein 1993 – PO

References to Wittgenstein's unpublished writings use the manuscript numbers (Ms) in the usual catalogue, found in PO.
3 I differ from Danto over what it means to *apply* to all cases: I do not assume that this will always be in the *same* way. For related discussion, see McFee (forthcoming).
4 For a clear statement, see Critcher 1995: 5.
5 It has become fashionable to designate as *practices* at least some of what I am calling 'institutions' – the impetus for the move to the 'practice' language standardly comes from MacIntyre 1985 (see Chapter 4 pp. 73–4).
6 A revealing parallel: for medicine, philosophical investigations are almost exclusively in the field of medical *ethics*.
7 See the discussion of the culturally-valued status of sport in Alderson and Crutchley 1990.
8 As Wittgenstein recognizes explicitly: PI §402 – contrary to what is asserted of him by those critics who did not bother with his writings! Followers of Popper have perhaps been the worst offenders here.
9 Note also the diversity of issues, not mentioned here, that 'philosophy of sport' might address eventually. It is partly the diversity of examples where insights into, for instance, agency might have application: see McFee 2002 for some, Morgan 1994 (a text with which I am in considerable agreement) for others.

1 Definiteness and defining sport

1 If one were, for instance, to take turns choosing, one would be making each choice in (potentially) very different situations of climate, ground conditions, and so on.
2 This is, of course, something I deny, at least as a thesis applied to philosophy – deploying the idea of defeasibility: McFee 1992: 61–3.

3 For example, Suits (1995b) has amended the relationship between play (on the one hand) and games and sports (on the other). He maintains that this does not seriously affect the two definitions given here, although he wants to grant that not all sports are games – hence that there are at least two kinds of sports.

4 The capitalization here indicates that a particular model of analysis, based on the finding of conditions individually necessary and jointly sufficient, has typically been assumed: see McFee (forthcoming).

5 Suits (1978: 41) summarizes his own definition as 'playing a game is the voluntary attempt to overcome unnecessary obstacles' – this is an unobvious 'feature': I certainly do not appeal to it in deciding whether or not such-and-such is a game. Indeed, I never thought along these lines until reading Suits.

6 See Margolis (1999: 67) and footnote for a discussion of some of them.

2   Rule-following and formalism in sport

1 As far as I can tell, D'Agostino (1995) invented this term.

2 Even this may not be quite right: consider 'advantage rules', p. 120.

3 Here, I pay closer attention to the *detail* of other writings than elsewhere, consonant with my commitment to fundamentals. For such complex issues can only be faced in concrete instantiations – which means in arguments from the writings of others. Again, I concentrate on two classic texts in the literature of philosophy of sport. This policy, which continues into the next chapter too, is partly warranted by the fact that the *puzzlement* arises from philosophy.

4 D'Agostino (1995: 45) calls this 'The Dichotomization Thesis'.

5 In clarification, we contrast (as above) two activities which cannot be distinguished on *this* occasion – say, because the differentiating rule does not have to be invoked – from the idea of *identity* here: *identity* means that there is, in reality, only one activity. And Morgan's argument cannot demonstrate that.

6 But this discussion of rule-following was never meant to describe the agents' psychology: 'In the beginning . . .' (OC §402).

7 I have modified the example here; but the point is the same.

8 As Travis (1996: 457 note) says, of the same point but a different example (roundness): 'I will not pause to argue against the heroic view that that just means that no one can ever speak truth in calling something round.'

9 Compare Baker and Hacker (1980: 79–80) on completeness of explanations – because (a) there is no absolute standard of completeness, but rather completeness is always explained by the contrasting sense of what is incomplete, and (b) incompleteness must be understood as relative to some purpose, so *incomplete* 'wears the trousers' (Austin 1962: 70–1).

3   Rule-following and rule-formulations

1 One might even include here the NFL decision to veto the Jacksonville Jaguars' plan for 'painting a Santa Claus hat in the Jaguar head on the 50–yard line at Alltel Stadium' (*Los Angeles Times, Sports* 2002a: D2).

2 Contrast boycotts based on other activities of states: for instance, the USA-led boycott of the Moscow Olympics seems simply political, although 'excused' by the USSR's support for the elected government in Afghanistan, then portrayed as an invasion!

3 *Essentialism* here is the view that concepts are sharply bounded, necessarily having some *essence* (identifiable via conditions individually necessary and jointly sufficient): that is, some set of properties shared by all instances of that concept, in virtue of which they are instances.

4 A style of 'Wittgensteinian' writing – that is, writing with lots of quotations from, and citations to, Wittgenstein – places emphasis on just *these* elements. A 'typical theorist' here is D. Z. Phillips (1970), Phillips and Mounce (1969); typical topics (again, represented in works by Phillips) include philosophy of religion and moral philosophy.

5 As Wittgenstein (PI §692) of a similar context: ' "to mean it" did not mean: to think of it'.

6 Of course, this reflects a view of Wittgenstein's so-called 'Private Language Argument' (Baker 1998), but not the most widely endorsed version.

7 Of course, Morgan might be happy to grant all this. Then his position would not differ appreciably from mine. In fact, I regularly think that we do agree in just this way – and I would be happy were this so, given my high regard for Morgan's work and my specific admiration for his account of how some of these ideas impinge on sociology (Morgan 1994: but see McFee 2002 for some criticisms, too). But there is little or no evidence that this is the right way to read Morgan: in particular, the adherence to Wittgenstein which is, for me, fundamental to my thinking on these topics is conspicuous by its absence.

8 From Gordon Baker's unpublished D.Phil. thesis, 'The Logic of Vagueness', University of Oxford, 1970: 413–14. Thanks – too late – to Gordon for making a copy available (many years ago!), and subsequently discussing this material.

9 See also Austin's remark (1970: 84): 'Enough is enough: it doesn't mean everything.'

4 Practices and normativity in sport

1 Such a community view has also been elaborated to characterize Wittgenstein's view of language-mastery. Against it, see Baker and Hacker (1985b).

2 Translation from Baker (2002: 63). A major issue (Baker 2002: 63–4) involves doing justice to the difference in the German between this and PI §202. (I follow Baker's comments.)

3 The discussion here draws heavily on Baker (1999), and on a (presently) unpublished paper, 'To follow a rule . . . is a *custom*', with thanks.

4 Indeed, such a social reading (compare Malcolm 1995: 158) makes this point equivalent to the later remark (PI §202) that: ' "obeying a rule" is a practice' (again, the scare-quotes are ignored! See Baker [2002: 63–4]).

5 PI §201: 'we ought to restrict the term "interpretation" to the substitution of one expression of the rule for another'.

6 See Ms 180 (a) p. 35r: 'The general cannot take the place of the particular.'

5 Aesthetic sports, publicity and judgement calls

1 This may not be quite correct: one of the officials involved was removed from the team scheduled to officiate at this year's Superbowl (*Los Angeles Times, Sports* 2003c: D8).

2 These arguments are put slightly differently in McFee 1992: 25–33.

6 Principles and the application of rules

1 See Dworkin (1978: 72) for his own comments on the distinction, and its importance.

2 See also Dworkin (1986: 15–20) for a discussion of Elmer.

3 For this reason, 'we should not look for this kind of universal truth in ethics' (McDowell 1998: 27) – although, as McDowell concedes in a note, Aristotle makes an exception for those actions – such as murder – where 'badness is part of the very idea of such actions' (McDowell 1998: 27 note).

4 Is Dworkin's distinction between rules and principles 'untenable' (Dworkin 1978: 47)? For answer, see his p. 71 ff.
5 Dworkin is, of course, alive to the number of exceptions which must be recorded for a 'full' statement of this rule.
6 Both in Dworkin (1978: 81–130) and in Dworkin (1986): see McDowell (1998: 62 esp. note).
7 See Dworkin (1996: 295ff.) where there are what seem like four versions of what framers might have *thought*.
8 See, for instance, 'Postscript' to Hart (1994: 238–76).

7 Spoiling, cheating and playing the game

1 Two points, which may be related: first, cricket is regarded as an *especially* suitable model of the moral since, while other sports may implicate morality, cricket illustrates this in some distinctive way. So that Neville Cardus (in Birley 1979: 11) claims:

> If everything else in this nation of ours were lost but cricket – her constitution and the laws of England of Lord Halsbury – it would be possible to reconstruct from the theory and practice of cricket all the eternal Englishness which has gone to the establishment of that Constitution and the laws aforesaid.

Second, while most sports are representable as zero-sum games, this is not true of cricket at the highest level, since there can be *draws* that are not *ties* – that is, where the scores between the sides are not equal (see Skillen 1998: 169–81, especially p. 171). This may be one reason why spoiling is visible in cricket when it is less visible elsewhere.
2 The term 'sledging' really covers any behaviour designed to unsettle the opposing player: say, by loudly commenting on his skill as a batsman or his mother's virtue.
3 If one thought that the Summer Olympics were too large, one might use this to select Olympic sports: those with a role in the moral laboratory are in, the others are out. In this way, some of de Coubertin's commitments might be maintained.
4 A revealing confusion: *sportsmanship* here is a positive term, *gamesmanship* is not – a 'politically correct' version, calling the players 'sportspersons', can obscure this contrast.
5 If a slogan identifying a central purpose for language were needed, we might do worse than go with Dummett (1993: 176): that language was an instrument of thought and a vehicle of communication. But even this would be hopelessly crude, in assigning a single(-ish) purpose for *all* language.
6 As Blackburn (2001: 38–40) illustrates, the history of drives, etc., does not show that moral prohibitions are not real.
7 Of course 'moral' here really means morally-involved: for clearly we can break our promises – but we *ought* not to!
8 Loland (1998: 93):

> When we voluntarily engage in a rule-governed practice, we enter a more or less tacit social contract in which a moral obligation arises: keep the formal playing rules of the game! Here we have the core justification of the fairness ideal.

This seems right, but does not take us into a complex theorization of the nature of such obligation: contrast Loland (2002: 37).

8 The project of a moral laboratory; and particularism

1 The explanation does not have to be good in either case (although often it is very good): my point is that each would be equally good; and for the same reasons.
2 Obeying rules for, say, fear of punishment (hence, prudentially) is not recognizing that one ought (morally) to act in that way: compare Nagel (1986: 132–3).
3 Jennings (1996: 237) quotes from the *Olympic Review* (1981: 158): 'the Olympic Games in Moscow had been the most "pure". Proof of this is the fact that not one case of doping was registered'. Although later withdrawn, this comment (attributed to Prince de Merode) indicates a certain attitude to evidence: there was no drug taking because none was found! This is just what sponsors want to hear!
4 It might seem that one cannot, say, bring a machine gun onto the rugby field: that this is *absolutely* precluded. But we can imagine cases where the object is not classified as a machine gun (but as, say, a peculiar kind of watch), where the prohibition focuses most strongly on what players (rather than referees) bring onto the pitch. And now the prohibition can begin to look like a border-line case – certainly no longer *absolute*!
5 Conversations with Sigmund Loland over the years certainly influenced my thinking, as did his arguments (Loland 1998). However, I cannot subscribe to the project of Loland (2002): this attempt to produce norms is also based on unsustainable assumptions about determinacy (witness, for instance, its taxonomic intentions). The intention to deal with *all* cases through norms is problematic, if there is no *all*: when not exceptionless, these norms still function generally, with application to all cases, even if they 'have the character of guidelines' (Loland 2002: 33) – that will be fine if thought of as a codified (non-contextual) guidance for coaches; a bit like, 'Honesty is the best policy' in a corrupt world.
6 Perhaps, as Jones and McNamee (2003: 42) suggest, this idea was first formulated in Parry (1988): I certainly *thought* I had come to it independently; and our uses of it differ.
7 After I had been working with this idea for some time, I read Nussbaum (2001: 238), in which she writes that '[n]arrative play . . . provides the child with a "potential space" in which to explore life's possibilities'. My thought was to see sport offering something similar, but (a) for adults, and (b) in the limited sphere of (some) moral possibilities – at least on the stronger reading of what is available for my moral laboratory.
8 See Sugden (1996), where this is the title of Chapter Three. My point here could be exemplified by seeing how – having described boxing's political economy in general terms, and engaged in careful ethnographies – its last chapter is a discussion of boxing and society, concluding with an analysis of boxing in relation to inequality and poverty: as we are told, 'The boxing subculture grows when poverty stands in the shadow of affluence' (Sugden 1996: 195). This comment – arguably, *profound* – concerns what boxing can 'tell us' about the global social order: boxing is here our 'sensitive cultural lens' (Beckles 1995: 1 [quoted earlier]).
9 As recorded in Ebert and Cheatum (1977: 4), to instantiate the principle 'no tackling or other rough conduct'. A more modern commentator expressly discusses this idea in terms of personal fouls, rather than the prohibition against contact: see Wilkes (1994: 96):

> A *personal foul* results when contact is made with an opponent while the ball is alive.
>   In general, the personal foul is charged to any player who causes bodily contact . . . [with an opponent].
>
> (Wilkes 1994: 97)

9 The value of sport

1 Distinctions of this sort are found in other writers, of course. Some are discussed in Dancy (2000b: 6–7).
2 As Dancy (2000b: 6) notes, 'This should not look very surprising . . . until one notices that most contemporary philosophers take it to be impossible.' Readers can turn to Dancy for replies to such philosophers.
3 And this was what the 'contemporary philosophers' (see note 2 above) who opposed this position denied was possible.
4 For the reasons the answer might be 'never', see Dancy (2000b: 2–4).
5 The term is Renford Bambrough's: see Bambrough (1969: 10): see also Ramsey (1931: 115–16, 1978: 20–1).
6 Thus Kuhn (2000: 189):

> In applying the term 'incommensurability' to theories, I'd intended only to insist that there was no common language within which both could be fully expressed and which could therefore be used in a point-by-point comparison between them.

Also, with Feyerabend (1987: 272), I take incommensurability to be a rare occurrence (McFee 1992: 306).
7 See 'Chariots for Higher', *Diverse Reports*, BBC television, 1984.
8 For the 1984 Games, the only bidding-city (apart from Los Angeles) was Tehran – and it dropped out! (Hill 1992: 158). But since then the Games have been attractive.

10 Relativism, objectivity and truth

1 RFM V §2:

> I want to say; it is essential to mathematics that its signs are also employed *in mufti*. It is the use outside of mathematics, and so the *meaning* of the signs, that makes the sign-game into mathematics.

2 Why choose Lyotard as a theorist here: perhaps, say, Baudrillard's ideas would be more fruitful? Lyotard was selected because, first, his is a strong position here, one worthy of contesting; second, his position is widely used (and thus representative?); third, it is a position supported by (candidate) arguments and examples.
3 Lyotard seems entranced by the very variety of language-games. But Wittgenstein's idea of a language-game (which he identifies as methodologically central: Lyotard [1984: 9]) cannot support Lyotard's use of it: language-games are not game-like in the sense of being *non-serious* (of being part of 'agonistics': Lyotard [1984: 10]). Contrast Baker and Hacker (1980: 86–98).
4 NB this is the Austin of *Philosophical Papers* (1970) and not necessarily of his later work (Austin 1975).
5 Adopting this model allows us to contrast disputes about *thin* moral concepts ('Is chastity really a virtue?') with disputes about *thick* moral concepts ('Is this behaviour chaste?'): compare Putnam 1992: 164–5.
6 As Scruton (1980: 42) continues, such practices must 'engage the loyalty of their participants' (as Olympism clearly has), and 'must point to something durable, something which survives and gives meaning to the acts that emerge from it'.

Conclusion

1 Freud 'On Psychotherapy' [1905] (Freud 1966, 7: 267).
2 On the slogans/theses contrast, see McFee 2001: 110–13.
3 The major exception concerns the aesthetic in sport (basically, not confusing sport with art), one issue 'solved' (or resolved) by Best (1978: 99–122); see McFee (1998a: 8).

Bibliography

Adande, J. A. (2002) 'Tweet and sour', *Los Angeles Times, Sports*, Tuesday 17 December: D1, D7.

—— (2003) 'Any misgiven Sunday', *Los Angeles Times, Sports*, Tuesday 7 January: D1, D8.

Alderson, J. and Crutchley, D. (1990) 'Physical education and the National Curriculum', in Neil Armstrong (ed.) *New Directions in Physical Education Vol. 1*, Rawdon: Human Kinetics Publishers.

Anscombe, G. E. M. (1981) 'On brute facts', in G. E. M. Anscombe *Ethics, Religion and Politics: Collected Philosophical Papers Volume III*, Oxford: Blackwell.

Austin, J. L. (1962) *Sense and Sensibilia*, Oxford: Oxford University Press.

—— (1970) *Philosophical Papers*, second edn, Oxford: Oxford University Press.

—— (1975) *How to Do Things with Words*, third edn, Oxford: Clarendon Press.

Baker, G. (1981) 'Following Wittgenstein: Some signposts for *Philosophical Investigations* §§ 143–242', in S. Holtzman and C. Leich (eds) *Wittgenstein: To Follow A Rule*, London: Routledge.

—— (1998) 'The private language argument', *Language and Communication*, 18: 325–56.

—— (1999) 'Italics in Wittgenstein', *Language and Communication*, 19: 181–211.

—— (2002) 'Quotation-marks in *Philosophical Investigations* Part I', *Language and Communication*, 22: 37–68.

Baker, G. P. and Hacker, P. M. S. (1980) *Wittgenstein: Understanding and Meaning – An Analytical Commentary on the Philosophical Investigations*, Oxford: Blackwell.

—— (1984) *Language, Sense and Nonsense*, Oxford: Blackwell.

—— (1985a) *Wittgenstein: Rules Grammar and Necessity – Volume 2 of an Analytical Commentary on the Philosophical Investigations*, Oxford: Blackwell.

—— (1985b) *Scepticism, Rules and Language*, Oxford: Blackwell.

Baker, G. and Morris, K. (1996) *Descartes' Dualism*, London: Routledge.

Bambrough, R. (1969) *Reason, Truth and God*, London: Methuen.

—— (1979) *Moral Scepticism and Moral Knowledge*, London: Routledge, Kegan Paul.

Beckles, H. McD. (1995) 'Introduction', in Beckles, H. McD. and Stoddart, B. (eds) *Liberation Cricket: West Indies Cricket Culture*. Manchester: Manchester University Press.

Best, D. (1978) *Philosophy and Human Movement*, London: George Allen & Unwin.

—— (1999) 'Dance before you think', in G. McFee (ed.) *Dance, Philosophy and Education*, Aachen: Meyer and Meyer.

Birley, D. (1979) *The Willow Wand*, New York: Simon and Schuster.

Blackburn, S. (2001) *Being Good*, Oxford: Oxford University Press.

Brearley, M. (2002) 'How to stand firm under appeal', *The Observer, Sport*, Sunday 28 July: 8–9.

Butcher, R. and Schneider, A. (2003) 'Fair play as respect for the game', in J. Boxill (ed.) *Sports Ethics: An Anthology*, Oxford: Blackwell.

Cavell, S. (1969) *Must We Mean What We Say?*, New York: Scribners.

—— (1981) *The Senses of Walden*, expanded edn, San Francisco: North Point.

Critcher, C. (1995) 'Running the rule over sport: A sociologist's view of ethics', in A. Tomlinson and S. Fleming (eds) *Ethics, Sport and Leisure: Crises and Critiques*, (reissued 1997) Aachen: Meyer & Meyer.

D'Agostino, F. (1995) 'The ethos of games', in W. J. Morgan and K. V. Meier (eds) *Philosophic Inquiry in Sport*, second edn, Champaign, IL: Human Kinetics.

Dancy, J. (1993) *Moral Reasons*, Oxford: Blackwell.

—— (2000a) 'The particularist's progress', in Brad Hooker and Margaret Little (eds) *Moral Particularism*, Oxford: Clarendon Press.

—— (2000b) *Practical Reality*, Oxford: Oxford University Press.

Danto, A. C. (1993) 'Responses and replies', in Mark Rollins (ed.) *Danto and His Critics*, Oxford: Blackwell.

Davis, Lindsey (1998) *Two for the Lions*, New York: Warner Books.

De Coubertin, P. (2000) *Olympism: Selected Writings*, Lausanne: International Olympic Committee.

Delattre, E. J. (1976) 'Some reflections on success and failure in competitive athletics', *Journal of the Philosophy of Sport*, 2: 133–9: reprinted (1995) in W. J. Morgan and K. V. Meier (eds) *Philosophic Inquiry in Sport*, second edn, Champaign, IL: Human Kinetics.

Dummett, M. (1993) *The Seas of Language*, Oxford: Clarendon Press.

Dunning, E. and Sheard, K. (1979) *Barbarians, Gentlemen and Players: A Sociological Study of the Development of Rugby Football*, New York: New York University Press.

Dworkin, R. (1978) *Taking Rights Seriously*, Cambridge, MA: Harvard University Press.

—— (1985) *A Matter of Principle*, Cambridge, MA: Harvard University Press.

—— (1986) *Law's Empire*, Cambridge, MA: Harvard University Press.

—— (1996) *Freedom's Law: The Moral Reading of the American Constitution*, Cambridge, MA: Harvard University Press.

Ebert, F. H. and Cheatum, B. A. (1977) *Basketball*, second edn, Philadelphia, PA: W. B. Saunders Co.

Feyerabend, P. K. (1987) *Farewell to Reason*, London: Verso.

Flint, J. and North, F. (1970) *Tiger Bridge*, London: Hodder & Stoughton.

Frege, G. (1960) *Philosophical Writings of Gottlob Frege*, trans. P. Geach and M. Black, second edn, Oxford: Blackwell.

Freud, S. (1966) *The Standard Edition of the Complete Psychological Works* (twenty four volumes), London: Hogarth Press.

Gibbard, A. (2002) 'The reasons of a living being', *Proceedings and Addresses of the American Philosophical Association*, 76: 2: 49–60.

Giddens, A. (1994) *Beyond Left and Right: The Future of Radical Politics*, Cambridge: Polity.

Goodman, N. (1968) *Languages of Art*, Indianapolis, NY: Bobbs-Merrill.

Greenberg, C. (1993) 'Review of *The Social History of Art*, by Arnold Hauser', in his *Collected Essays and Criticism*, Volume 3, Chicago: University of Chicago Press.

Hargreaves, J. (1986) *Sport, Power and Culture*, Cambridge: Polity.

—— (2000) *Freedom for Catalonia?: Catalan Nationalism, Spanish Identity and the Barcelona Olympic Games*, Cambridge: Cambridge University Press.

Hart, H. L. A. (1994) *The Concept of Law*, second edn, Oxford: Clarendon Press.

Haugeland, J. (1998) *Having Thought*, Cambridge, MA: Harvard University Press.

Henderson, J. (2002) 'You cannot be serious', *The Observer, Sport*, Sunday 3 March: 16.

Hill, C. (1992) *Olympic Politics*, Manchester: Manchester University Press.

Jennings, A. (1996) *The New Lords of the Rings*, London: Simon and Schuster.

Jennings, A. and Sambrook, C. (2000) *The Great Olympic Swindle: When the World Wanted its Games Back*, London: Simon and Schuster.

Jones, C. and McNamee, M. (2003) 'Moral development and sport: Character and cognitive developmentalism contrasted', in J. Boxill (ed.) *Sports Ethics: An Anthology*, Oxford: Blackwell.

Kamber, R. (1998) 'Weitz reconsidered: A clearer view of why theories of art fail', *British Journal of Aesthetics*, 38: 33–46.

Kuhn, T. S. (2000) 'Theory change as structure change: Comments on the Sneed formalism', in T. S. Kuhn *The Road Since Structure: Philosophical Essays 1970– 1993*, Chicago, IL: University of Chicago Press.

Leaman, O. (1995) 'Cheating and fair play in sport', in W. J. Morgan and K. V. Meier (eds) *Philosophic Inquiry in Sport*, second edn, Champaign, IL: Human Kinetics.

Loland, S. (1998) 'Fair play: Historical anachronism or topical ideal?', in M. J. McNamee and S. J. Parry (eds), *Ethics and Sport*, London: Routledge.

—— (2002) *Fair Play in Sport: A Moral Norm System*, London: Routledge.

Lorenz, K. (1966) *On Aggression*, London: Methuen.

Los Angeles Times (2002) 'US alleges Olympic skating bribery', Thursday 1 August: A1, A28.

Los Angeles Times, Sports (2002a) 'Morning briefing', Wednesday 25 December: D2.

Los Angeles Times, Sports (2002b) '10 Worst: a look at the 10 worst stories of 2002', Tuesday 31 December: D12.

Los Angeles Times, Sports (2003a) 'If NCAA is involved, better read the fine print', Sunday 5 January: D2.

Los Angeles Times, Sports (2003b) 'Positioning of officials to change immediately', Thursday 9 January: D5.

Los Angeles Times, Sports (2003c) 'Official taken off Superbowl crew', Friday 10 January: D8.

Los Angeles Times, Sports (2003d) 'O'Neal issues apology', Saturday 11 January: D1, D7.

Luntley, M. (1995) *Reason Truth and Self*, London: Routledge.

Lyotard, J-F. (1984) *The Postmodern Condition*, Manchester: Manchester University Press.

McDowell, J. (1998) *Mind Value, and Reality*, Cambridge, MA: Harvard University Press.

McFee, G. (1986) 'Goal of the month: Fact or fiction?', *Leisure Studies*, 5, 2: 159–74.

—— (1992) *Understanding Dance*, London: Routledge.

—— (1998a) 'Are there philosophical issues with respect of sport (other than ethical ones)?', in M. J. McNamee and S. J. Parry (eds) *Ethics and Sport*, London: Routledge.

—— (1998b) 'Truth, arts education and the "postmodern condition"', in D. Carr (ed.) *Education, Knowledge and Truth: Beyond the Postmodern Impasse*, London: Routledge.

—— (2000a) *Free Will*, Teddington: Acumen.

—— (2000b) 'Spoiling: An indirect reflection of sport's moral imperative?', in T. Tännsjö and C. Tamburrini (eds) *Values in Sport*, London: Routledge.

—— (2000c) 'Sport: A moral laboratory?', in M. McNamee *et al.* (eds) *Just Leisure: Policy, Ethics and Professionalism*, Eastbourne: Leisure Studies Association.

—— (2001) 'Wittgenstein, performing art and action', in M. Turvey and R. Allen (eds) *Wittgenstein, Theory and the Arts*, London: Routledge.

—— (2002) 'It's not a game: The place of philosophy in the study of sport', in J. Sugden and A. Tomlinson (eds) *Power Games: A Critical Sociology of Sport*, London: Routledge.

—— (forthcoming) 'Art, essence and Wittgenstein', in S. Davies (ed.) *Art and Essence*, Westport: Greenwood Publishing.

McIntosh, P. (1979) *Fair Play*, London: Heinemann.

MacIntyre, A. (1970) 'Is understanding religion compatible with believing?', in B. Wilson (ed.) *Rationality*, Oxford: Blackwell.

—— (1985) *After Virtue*, second edn, London: Duckworth.

McKibben, D. (2003) 'Rodman accused of domestic violence', *Los Angeles Times, Orange County*, Saturday 11 January: B3.

McNamara, M. (2002) 'The mob in skating? Godfather, where are you?', *Los Angeles Times, Southern California Living*, Friday 2 August: E1, E4.

McNamee, M. (1995) 'Theoretical limitations in codes of ethical conduct', in G. McFee, W. Murphy and G. Whannel (eds) *Leisure Cultures: Values, Genders, Lifestyles*, Eastbourne: Leisure Studies Association.

Mackay, D. (1996) 'Olympic cheats go unnamed', *The Observer*, Sunday 17 November: 2.

—— (2003) 'New false-start rule makes debut', *The Guardian Sport*, Saturday 1 February: 18.

Malcolm, N. (1963) *Knowledge and Certainty: Essays and Lectures*, Englewood Cliffs, NJ: Prentice-Hall.

—— (1995) *Wittgensteinian Themes: Essays 1978–1989,* Ithaca, NY: Cornell University Press.

Margolis, J. (1999) *What, After All, is a Work of Art*, University Park, PA: Pennsylvania University Press.

Meier, K. (1985) 'Restless sport', *Journal of the Philosophy of Sport*, XII: 64–77.

—— (1995) 'Triad trickery: playing with games and sports', in W. J. Morgan and K. V. Meier (eds) *Philosophic Inquiry in Sport*, second edn, Champaign, IL: Human Kinetics.

Mitchell, K. (2002) 'Cheats prosper', *The Observer, Sport*, Sunday 23 June: 7.

Moore, B. (2003) 'It's crunch time!', *The Observer Sports Monthly* (OSM), February: 44–9.

Morgan, W. J. (1994) *Leftist Theories of Sport: A Critique and Reconstruction*, Chicago, IL: University of Illinois Press.

Morgan, W. J. (1995) 'The logical incompatibility thesis and rules: a reconsideration of formalism as an account of games', in W. J. Morgan and K. V. Meier (eds) *Philosophic Inquiry in Sport*, second edn, Champaign, IL: Human Kinetics.

Mumford, K. and Wordsworth, M. A. (1974) *A Beginner's Guide to Basketball*, London: Pelham Books.

Nagel, E. and Newman, J. (1958) *Gödel's Proof*, New York: New York University Press.

Nagel, T. (1986) *The View from Nowhere*, Oxford: Oxford University Press.

—— (1995) *Other Minds: Critical Essays 1969–1994*, Oxford: Clarendon Press.

Nielsen, K. (1982) *An Introduction to the Philosophy of Religion*, London: Macmillan.

Norris, C. (1987) *Derrida*, London: Fontana.

Nussbaum, M. (1990) *Love's Knowledge: Essays on Philosophy and Literature*, Oxford: Oxford University Press.

—— (2001) *Upheavals of Thought: The Intelligence of Emotions*, Cambridge: Cambridge University Press.

OSM (2002) *The Observer Sports Monthly*, June.

O'Hear, A. (1991) 'Wittgenstein and the Transmission of Traditions', in A. Phillips Griffiths (ed.) *Wittgenstein: Centenary Essays*, Cambridge: Cambridge University Press.

Parry, J. [S. J.] (1988) 'Physical education, justification and the National Curriculum', *Physical Education Review*, 11: 2: 106–18.

—— (1998) 'Violence and aggression in contemporary sport', in M. J. McNamee and S. J. Parry (eds), *Ethics and Sport*, London: Routledge.

Pearson, K. (1973) 'Deception, sportsmanship and ethics', *Quest*, 19: 115–118: reprinted (1995) in W. J. Morgan and K. V. Meier (eds) *Philosophic Inquiry in Sport*, second edn, Champaign, IL: Human Kinetics.

Phillips, D. Z. (1970) *Faith and Philosophical Enquiry*, London: Routledge & Kegan Paul.

Phillips, D. Z. and Mounce, H. (1969) *Moral Practices*, London: Routledge & Kegan Paul.

Putnam, H. (1981) *Reason, Truth and History*, Cambridge: Cambridge University Press.

—— (1992) *Renewing Philosophy*, Cambridge, MA: Harvard University Press.

Ramsey, F. P. (1931) *The Foundations of Mathematics*, London: Routledge & Kegan Paul.

—— (1978) *Foundations*, London: Routledge & Kegan Paul.

Reddiford, G. (1985) 'Constitutions, institutions, and games', *Journal of the Philosophy of Sport*, 12: 41–51.

Rorty, R. (1979) *Philosophy and the Mirror of Nature*, Princeton, NJ: Princeton University Press.

—— (1989) *Contingency, Irony and Solidarity*, Cambridge: Cambridge University Press.

—— (1991) *Objectivity, Relativism and Truth (Philosophical Papers Vol. One)*, Cambridge: Cambridge University Press.

Russell, J. S. (1999) 'Are the rules all an umpire has to work with?', *Journal of the Philosophy of Sport*, XXVI: 27–49.

Scruton, R. (1980) *The Meaning of Conservatism*, London: Macmillan.

Searle, J. (1969) *Speech Acts: An Essay in the Philosophy of Language*, Cambridge: Cambridge University Press.

—— (2002) *Consciousness and Language*, Cambridge: Cambridge University Press.

Skillen, T. (1998) 'Sport is for losers', in M. J. McNamee and S. J. Parry *Ethics and Sport*, London: Routledge.

Sugden, J. (1996) *Boxing and Society: an International Analysis*, Manchester: Manchester University Press.

Sugden, J. and Bairner, A. (1993) *Sport, Sectarianism and Society in a Divided Ireland*, Leicester: Leicester University Press.

Suits, B. (1978) *The Grasshopper: Games, Life and Utopia*, Edinburgh: Scottish Academy Press.

—— (1995a) 'The elements of sport', in W. J. Morgan and K. V. Meier (eds) *Philosophic Inquiry in Sport*, second edn, Champaign, IL: Human Kinetics.

—— (1995b) 'Tricky triad: Games, play and sport', in W. J. Morgan and K. V. Meier (eds) *Philosophic Inquiry in Sport*, second edn, Champaign, IL: Human Kinetics.

Sullivan, R. [with S. Song] (2000) 'Are drugs winning the Games?', *Time*, 156, 11: 54–6.

Tamburrini, C. (2000) *The 'Hand of God': Essays in the Philosophy of Sport*, Göteborg, Sweden: Acta Universitatis Gothobergensis.

Tomlinson, A. (1999) 'Standing on ceremony: Representation, ideology and the Olympic Games', in A. Tomlinson *The Game's Up: Essays in the Cultural Analysis of Sport, Leisure and Popular Culture*, Aldershot: Arena/Ashgate.

Travis, C. (1984) 'Are belief ascriptions opaque?', *Proceedings of the Aristotelian Society*, LXXXV: 73–100.

—— (1985) 'On what is strictly speaking true', *The Canadian Journal of Philosophy*, 15: 187–229.

—— (1989) *The Uses of Sense*, Oxford: Clarendon Press.

—— (1991) 'Annals of analysis', *Mind*, 100: 237–64.

—— (1994) 'On constraints of generality', *Proceedings of the Aristotelian Society*, XCIV: 165–88.

—— (1996) 'Meaning's role in truth', *Mind*, 105: 451–66.

—— (1997a) 'Pragmatics', in Crispin Wright and Bob Hale (eds) *Blackwell Companion to the Philosophy of Language*, Oxford: Blackwell.

—— (1997b) 'Reply to Simmons', *Mind*, 106: 119–20.

—— (2000) *Unshadowed Thoughts*, Cambridge, MA: Harvard University Press.

Wallechinsky, D. (1988) *The Complete Book of the Olympics*, Harmondsworth: Allen Lane.

Wharton, D. (2002) 'Second-hand smoke', *Los Angeles Times, Sports*, Tuesday 10 September: D3.

Wilkes, G. (1994) *Basketball*, sixth edn, Madison, WI: Brown & Benchmark.

Williams, B. (2002) *Truth and Truthfulness*, Princeton, NJ: Princeton University Press.

Willis, P. (1973) 'Women in sport in ideology', in J. E. Hargreaves (ed.) *Sport, Culture and Ideology*, London: Routledge & Kegan Paul.

Wisdom, J. (1952) *Other Minds*, Oxford: Blackwell.

—— (1965) *Paradox and Discovery*, Oxford: Blackwell.

—— (1991) *Proof and Explanation (The Virginia Lectures)*, (ed. S. Barker) Washington, DC: University Press of America.

Wittgenstein, L. (1953) *Philosophical Investigations*, trans. G. E. M. Anscombe, Oxford: Blackwell.

Wittgenstein, L. (1967) *Zettel*, trans. G. E. M. Anscombe, Oxford: Basil Blackwell.

—— (1969) *On Certainty*, trans. D. Paul and G. E. M. Anscombe, Oxford: Blackwell.

—— (1978) *Remarks on the Foundations of Mathematics*, third edn, Oxford: Blackwell.

—— (1980) *Culture and Value*, trans. Peter Winch, second edn, 1998, Oxford: Basil Blackwell.

—— (1993) *Philosophical Occasions 1912–1951*, eds J. Klagge and A. Nordmann, Indianapolis: Hackett Publishing Company.

Wolfe, G. (1980) *The Book of the New Sun*, London: Sidgwick and Jackson.

Wright, C. (2001) *Rails of Infinity: Essays on Themes from Wittgenstein*, Cambridge, MA: Harvard University Press.

Index